The Just Shall Live by Faith

Revelations
That Will Set You Free

THE BIBLICAL ROADMAP FOR SPIRITUAL AND PSYCHOLOGICAL GROWTH

Dr. Troy Reiner

Reiner Publishing

Unless otherwise noted, Scripture quotations in this book are taken from the King James Version of the Bible.

Scripture references marked NLT are taken from the Holy Bible, New Living Translation, copyright© 1996 by Tyndale Charitable Trust. Used by permission of Tyndale House Publishers, Wheaton, Illinois 60189. All rights reserved.

Scripture references marked NIV are taken from the Holy Bible, New International Version, Copyright © 1973, 1978, 1984 by the International Bible Society. Used by permission of Zondervan Publishing House. The "NIV" and "New International Version" trademarks are registered in the United States Patent and Trademark Office by International Bible Society.

Scripture references marked WEY are taken from Weymouth: The Modern Speech New Testament by Richard E. Weymouth, 3rd Edition (1912), Revised & edited by E. Hampden-Cooke. Public Domain

Cover Photograph by David Philips

ISBN 978-0-9903856-3-9
Library of Congress Catalog Card Number: 2005905980

Table of Contents

Introduction

Ever since I first fully committed my life to Christ and made Him the Lord of my life on the little island of Shemya, near the end of the Aleutian Islands, I have had a deep desire to share what the Lord has taught me to help other hurting people. Many people today are caught up in the "rat race" of life in spite of the fact that they may have even been brought up in a church for the majority of their lives. I was, what I now call, a Codependent Independent Worldly Success. I was driven to succeed and believed that if I just tried hard enough I could do anything! I was on Shemya Island, which is located over one thousand miles from both Anchorage, Alaska and Japan, as a United States Air Force space track radar crew commander. In actuality, my assignment to this remote island was a God-ordained intervention in my life to assist me in taking the next step toward becoming a whole and mature Christian.

Although I had been brought up in a denominational church all of my life, I was little different than my non-Christian friends. Yes, I had read the Bible, taught all the grades in Sunday school, and, during the years I spent in college, I was even the principal of the Sunday school. I believed that God wanted me to be somebody, so I expected Him to help me in whatever I decided to do. I was a "human doing rather than a human being." After being commissioned as an officer in the U. S. Air Force, my first assignment was generating computer command sequences for space satellites. I began work on a master's degree in Cybernetic Systems, I earned my private pilot's license, received a black belt in Jujitsu, trained to become a swimming instructor, became the Sunday school superintendent of my church, took up technical rock climbing as a hobby, joined a mountain rescue team, and started climbing a major mountain someplace in the world each year. I was so busy trying to make something out of my life and overcome my fears of inadequacy that I did not have any time to think about why I was doing all these things. Shemya brought all that to a relative halt, even though I was still able to teach a course on general aviation, provide a private pilot ground school on the island and climb Mount McKinley during my leave.

As I tried to fill my "extra time" on the island of Shemya, I began reading some books provided by the Chaplain. I was surprised to find out that some people really had a very close, personal relationship with Jesus Christ and were so enthusiastic about it that all they wanted to do was to live for Him. After a while, I began to realize that, to me, God was my genie. Each year, in January, I would make my list of what I was going to accomplish that year and I expected God to bless it. I guess I expected that if I rubbed my Bible three times, God was supposed to appear and ask me what three wishes I wanted Him to grant for me. At the least, I expected Him to protect me from the dangers of the challenging activities I had chosen to do to make myself feel more adequate. Although I had been reasonably successful and had been promoted to captain, I knew there was something missing. At this point (I do not remember exactly how, but possibly through my reading) God asked me three troubling questions that I still use to help others in counseling today:

1. <u>What had I accomplished in my life up to that point that would really make a difference in the world 200 years from now?</u> Although by this time I had climbed the highest peaks on three continents and was involved in critical Air Force operations, I realized that in 200 years people would probably not even be able to find my gravestone. In fact, all that I did to improve Space Track Radar Operations

on Shemya that year would accomplish little, since the entire radar was scheduled for replacement the next year.

2. <u>Did I know exactly what was going to happen to me tomorrow?</u> Of course, none of us can truly predict the future without God. I had to admit that I did not know the future. This was especially true on Shemya because the island is located on an earthquake fault, our activities were constantly monitored by Russian trawlers, and at that time we were still engaged in the "cold war."

3. <u>What had God designed me to do and what specific mission had He sent me on when I was born?</u> Everything I had done up to this point in my life, I had chosen to do without any clear direction from God. My main understanding of God's guidance to this point in my life was that since God had created me, I was supposed to do something significant with my life. However, I did not know specifically what I was supposed to do.

The Lord then asked me, "If it was true that I could really do nothing of significance in my life without Him, I did not know the future and I did not even know what I was designed to do or what mission He had sent me on, how could I expect to direct my life?" The truth is that all of us "rats" are running around in circles not knowing where we are going! There was an Air Force joke going around at that time that truly typified my life. An aircraft was flying across the Atlantic Ocean when the pilot called back to the navigator requesting how they were doing. After a long pause and some calculations, the navigator came back over the intercom, "Sir, we are making outstanding time...but we are lost!" I was lapping some of the other rats running around in circles but none of us had any idea of where we were going, what we had been called to do or how everything fit into God's overall plan for the universe. I later found a Bible verse, Jeremiah 10:23, that said all this very clearly, "O LORD, I know that the way of man is not in himself: it is not in man that walketh to direct his steps."

It was this revelation on the island of Shemya, many years ago, that led me finally to turn my life completely over to Christ and to rely on His direction, instead of mine, for my life. Since that time He has taken me step-by-step through His process of healing that we call salvation and taught me many things from His Word that have transformed my life and brought me into the calling for which He originally designed me. In my barracks room on that little island only 1 ½ miles wide and 2 ½ miles long, I told my Lord and Savior that "if He would be real to me, I would do whatever He asked me to do," and my life has never been the same since that time! He has continued to help me grow spiritually toward His goal for every one of us—a life of spiritual and psychological maturity motivated by love.

This book is part of a complete system for implementing salvation-based therapy within the church. The remaining three books in the series—*Faith Therapy, Transformation!, and Principles for Life*—provide an in-depth understanding of the process of salvation by faith, tools for applying faith in counseling, a detailed plan for the conduct of counseling, biblical models for addressing the most complex and difficult problems, and a comprehensive method for building counseling plans from biblical principles.

I want specifically to thank all of my clients and students, my wife, Nancy, my mother, Hildegard, my daughter, Sarah, our assistant administrator, Loretta Goetting, and Karen Shrank for their contributions in preparing this manuscript for publication. My gratitude also goes to Athena Dean and all the other wonderful people at Pleasant Word Publishing for their patience and assistance in publishing this book.

All Bible references are from the Authorized Version (AV) of the King James Bible, The New International Version (NIV), The New Living Translation (NLT), or the Weymouth New Testament (WEY). These versions of the Bible are quoted as originally written and therefore spelling, grammar and capitalization may not agree with modern usage. For example, in my writing I have chosen to capitalize all references to God. This is not done in the King James Version of the Bible. Greek, Hebrew, most Bible translations and biblical dictionary references are obtained and quoted directly from The Online Bible Millennium Edition (2000) by Larry Pierce.

PART I

A Biblical Foundation

Chapter 1

Salvation
God's Solution for the Natural Man

When we are born each and every one of us has one goal—survival—and we will do whatever it takes to meet our own needs. First, we cry for our mothers, for food, and to have our diapers changed. Later, we learn to cope in more complex ways as we adapt to the environment in which we find ourselves. We are clearly interested in one thing—ourselves.

Unfortunately, many of us never really grow up. We just learn how to get our selfish needs met in more socially acceptable and complex ways. We learn how to run with the other "rats" and to play "king of the hill" so that we can be "successful." This selfishness is at the very root of our failure to make life work for us and is the core of our inability to become all that God intends us to be. The problem is that there is nothing that <u>we</u> can do about it. The Bible calls this the state of the "natural man." It is hopeless.

Although most of us do not realize it at first, we eventually come to recognize that we are doomed to a life of selfishness that does not really work. We are sinners. Some people are more talented and have learned to cope more effectively with life than others. It just takes them longer to hit the concrete wall. And there are some that, due to pride, will never admit life does not work for them until it is too late. But down deep each of us eventually recognizes that we cannot be self-sufficient in ourselves, overcome sin in our lives, or be our own God.

It is this revelation—that in our own effort and strength we cannot have an abundant, full, and healthy life—that is the beginning of the process of salvation by faith. If we could be sufficient in ourselves, we would not need God, and Christ did not have to die!

The Natural Man

Let us try to get a deeper understanding of the situation in which we find ourselves. The Bible describes the natural man this way:

1. <u>The natural man attempts to fulfill the desires of the flesh and is dominated by his flesh, lust, and evil spirits.</u>

   Eph 2:1 And you [hath he quickened], who were dead in trespasses and sins;

   2 Wherein in time past ye walked according to the course of this world, according to the prince of the power of the air, the spirit that now worketh in the children of disobedience:

   3 Among whom also we all had our conversation in times past in the lusts of our flesh, fulfilling the desires of the flesh and of the mind; and were by nature the children of wrath, even as others.

2. <u>Because the natural man has a carnal mind, he cannot please God or do what is right.</u>

   Ro 8:7 Because the carnal mind [is] enmity against God: for it is not subject to the law of God, neither indeed can be.

   8 So then they that are in the flesh cannot please God.

3. <u>The natural man can only operate by his natural or sense knowledge.</u> He receives data only through his five senses—seeing, hearing, tasting, smelling, and touching—and tries to reason things out.

   Eph 4:17 This I say therefore, and testify in the Lord, that ye henceforth walk not as other Gentiles walk, in the vanity of their mind,

   18 Having the understanding darkened, being alienated from the life of God through the ignorance that is in them, because of the blindness of their heart:

4. <u>The natural man cannot understand spiritual things.</u>

   1 Co 2:14 But the natural man receiveth not the things of the Spirit of God: for they are foolishness unto him: neither can he know [them], because they are spiritually discerned.

5. <u>He has no real hope.</u> All he can do is try to cope with life's challenges the best he can by relying on his own limited resources. Without faith, he has no legal standing with God and he has no basis for asking or relying on God to meet his needs.

   Eph 2:11 Wherefore remember, that ye [being] in time past Gentiles in the flesh, who are called Uncircumcision by that which is called the Circumcision in the flesh made by hands;

   12 That at that time ye were without Christ, being aliens from the commonwealth of Israel, and strangers from the covenants of promise, having no hope, and without God in the world:

As a natural man, we are dominated by our need to be loved, secure, worthwhile and significant. These are the needs of the self; and when we attempt to meet these needs in our own strength, we are acting selfishly. As long as we act selfishly to meet these needs, our decisions will be biased so that we can never become a just or whole person. It is impossible for us to extricate ourselves from this selfish state, because the harder we try to be unselfish in order to better ourselves, the more we are trying to meet these basic needs, making ourselves more selfish. This was the plight of the Pharisees of Jesus' day. Because they were trying so hard to be good by obeying the law out of a need to make themselves better, they actually became more corrupt inside while attempting to look righteous on the outside. We simply cannot become righteous in our own strength.

Because we live in a world of natural men, we are motivated to compete with others to meet these needs. We find ourselves inextricably enmeshed in the "rat race" of life attempting to meet our needs at the expense of others. We perceive that there are limited resources in the world to meet our needs, and, therefore, we must compete in order to get our needs met. This is called a zero-sum game. In a zero-sum game, if others get the resource, we do not get it, or if we get it, they do not get it. Consequently, all sorts of corruption has entered into the world. If we feel inferior to someone, we will be tempted to be critical to bring him or her down to our level. In order to feel significant, we will vigorously compete for promotion and do anything necessary to be "successful." In fact, we will see everyone else in our lives, either as a resource to meet our needs (a friend) or someone we are in competition with (an enemy).

The needs of the natural man can never be completely satisfied. Even if all our needs are satisfied for today, we will still have to meet these same needs again the next day. This results in lust or unlimited desire for the things of the world that we feel will meet our needs. As we attempt and succeed in meeting our needs for today, our appetite for more grows. Consequently, no matter how hard we try or how successful we might be, we will always have an increased need for more. If we fail to meet our needs, we will become more desperate to meet them and do whatever it takes, good or bad, to get them met. These desperate attempts violate others and do not meet our needs in the end. As a result, no matter what we do, we will never be completely satisfied.

Another byproduct of this competition in life is that we all eventually lose. Although we envy those who seem to have more talent than ourselves, the more talent a person has simply results in promotion to greater responsibility and a more intense level of competition. As long as we succeed, we will be promoted. We will no longer be promoted when we fail to do our current job adequately. For example, if I was a good high jumper, I would be advanced first to State, then Regional, and then the Olympic Games. If I was good enough to win the gold medal at the Olympics, I would be expected to do it again in four years. If I did not, and won only the silver medal, I would have failed. Eventually all of us fail, especially as we grow older and eventually have to retire.

Another temptation for the natural man is to fall into addictive behavior. Addictions result from attempting to meet deep needs through short-term fixes that result in long-term losses. For example, when a crack addict is feeling worthless and depressed, he uses crack. In the very short term, his need to feel better is wonderfully fulfilled. In the long-term, as his drug wears off, he feels even more depressed and worthless, so he is even more motivated to use the drug again. Process addictions can also result from lust where the workaholic, shop-aholic, over-eater, or sexual addict simply needs more and more to meet the unending demands of the lust of the flesh, lust of the eyes, or pride of life.

Codependency is a common trap for the natural man in our society. Since the natural man is not relying on God to meet his needs, he has a tendency to either try to be his own god or excessively rely on others to "meet all his needs according to their riches in glory." This excessive independence (relying on ourselves) or dependence (relying on others) results in attempting to manipulate others to meet his needs. Of course, the other person in the relationship is also attempting to manipulate him to meet his or her needs. Consequently, codependency results in dysfunctional relationships where the need for unconditional love is never met and which are punctuated by chaos and conflict.

The natural man is also prone to either attempt to control others or to be controlled by other people. The more insecure we feel in life, the more we desire to be in control of our circumstances and those around us. It seems easier to control others than to deal with ourselves. This is another trap. It never works. The more we attempt to control others, the more they rebel since we are violating their free will; and the more they rebel, the more we have to increase our attempts to control them. This inevitably leads to broken relationships and many times to violence.

Abuse is simply attempting to force others to meet our needs. When the natural man feels threatened or desperate, this is his final resort. If we cannot get our needs met in any other way, we will violate another's rights and boundaries to meet our own needs. In our modern society, we often attempt to channel abuse into more socialized forms such as gossip and verbal backstabbing.

In a world without God, the natural man has derived a system of evaluation in order to meet his need for self-worth. Although there are innumerable variations of this system that values intelligence, possessions, accomplishments, power, position, popularity, prestige, degrees, money and exterior morality, it can all be summed up in one general formula. To the world, self-worth is equal to the sum of our performance, our approval by others, and our conformity to the values of society. This results in an excessive drive for accomplishment, seeking the approval of others, and trying to conform to human standards. Since none of us can ever succeed in everything we do, always find the approval of others, or live up to what our society demands, we are placed on an emotional roller coaster dominated by our perceived failures and successes. (For a more in-depth understanding of these issues, see my book *Faith Therapy*.)

God's Plan of Salvation

Because we were hopeless, and there was no one else who could save us, God Himself devised a plan to save us through faith in Him.

Isa 59:11 We roar all like bears, and mourn sore like doves: we look for judgment, but there is none; for salvation, but it is far off from us.

15 Yea, truth faileth; and he that departeth from evil maketh himself a prey: and the LORD saw it, and it displeased him that there was no judgment.

16 And he saw that there was no man, and wondered that there was no intercessor: therefore his arm brought salvation unto him; and his righteousness, it sustained him.

20 And the Redeemer shall come to Zion, and unto them that turn from transgression in Jacob, saith the LORD.

Through the death and resurrection of Jesus Christ, God has provided all that we need to be saved and overcome the problems of the natural man. These change agents of salvation (which I will briefly discuss below) become the basic tools of transformation when we accept them as fact. I will explain each of them in more depth later in this book as we apply them to the subject of spiritual development.

The Forgiveness of Sins

Through the sacrifice of Jesus on the cross, God has put our sins and failures behind us and has taken away the wrath that we deserve for our sins. This is called propitiation. I like to explain it this way. We have been tried and convicted of our sins in the court of heaven based on God's complete, detailed knowledge of everything that we have done. We are declared guilty and sentenced to death for rebellion against God. But as the death angel is leading us away to execution, Jesus stands up in the court and offers to be crucified in our place, even though He has never sinned. We must choose to accept His offer or die for our own sins. For those of us who accept His offer, since he has already died for our sins, our court record of conviction is stamped paid in full! The fact that Christ paid the price for our sins is called redemption. Without forgiveness, because of our sins, we could never escape the guilt of our past, would be the servant of Satan and destined for destruction.

Justification

The judicial declaration that we are just or "just as if we had never sinned," is called justification. It is also called imputed righteousness. It makes it possible for us to have a new start in life, be reconciled with God, and have a personal, life-changing relationship with Him. Justification is freely given to us through grace, or God's unmerited favor, without works. It means that no matter what we do, good or bad, God will still love us unconditionally and work for our good. This, of course, does not mean that we will not receive consequences for our sins. Without justification, we could never be holy enough to have a personal relationship with a holy God. Without this relationship, we could never learn to love God and believe that He will meet all of our needs. We must trust God that he will meet all of our needs in order to overcome our selfishness and learn to love others.

The Spirit of God

The problem of the natural man is that he always wants to direct his own life, do what he wants to do, and tries to meet his needs his own way and in his own strength. In order to resolve this, God sent His Holy Spirit to draw us to want to do things His way and to live a holy life. By faith, we yield to God's Spirit so that we are motivated to do what is right. This is called regeneration. It is what happens in our hearts when we are born again. Through faith, we invite the Spirit of God into our hearts. The Holy Spirit then draws our will to want to serve God. This results in a change of heart so that we truly want to do what is right.

Jer 31:33 But this shall be the covenant that I will make with the house of Israel; After those days, saith the LORD, I will put my law in their inward parts, and write it in their hearts; and will be their God, and they shall be my people.

The Spirit of God also leads us into all truth and will direct our lives if we will yield to His influence. It is through walking according to the Spirit that we are able to overcome the influence of the flesh and act righteously.

Jo 16:13 Howbeit when he, the Spirit of truth, is come, he will guide you into all truth: for he shall not speak of himself; but whatsoever he shall hear, that shall he speak: and he will shew you things to come.

Ro 8: 3 For what the law could not do, in that it was weak through the flesh, God sending his own Son in the likeness of sinful flesh, and for sin, condemned sin in the flesh:

4 That the righteousness of the law might be fulfilled in us, who walk not after the flesh, but after the Spirit.

The Law

God gave the law through Moses to help us understand what is right and wrong and to teach us one critical fact: we cannot obey the law in our own strength. Because our natural man wants to direct his own life and take credit for his own psychological wholeness, God had to show us that, in our strength, we could never be good enough to earn heaven or do right things for the right reasons. The Apostle Paul makes this very clear in Romans 7:19 when he states concerning the law, "For the good that I would I do not: but the evil which I would not, that I do." The law provided external motivation (the schoolmaster) to hold us in check until Christ, through grace, sets us free and delivers us from sin.

Grace

Grace (God's unmerited favor for us without works) is the means by which we are delivered from the curse of the law (The fact that we cannot fulfill the law by our own efforts). God's grace means that, because of what Christ did for us, no matter how badly we fail, God will always love us and work for our good. This sets us free from trying, in our own efforts, to please God. Because of grace we learn to choose to do what is right because it is the right thing to do and out of gratitude for what He has done for us. It is the very basis of our freedom in Christ. Unfortunately, many Christians have not yet realized the freedom they have in Christ.

Jo 1:17 For the law was given by Moses, but grace and truth came by Jesus Christ.

Ro 13:8 Owe no man any thing, but to love one another: for he that loveth another hath fulfilled the law.

Adoption

If we were adopted as a child into a very rich, well-known, powerful and loving family, we would assume that all of our needs would be met. If our adopted family was very rich, we would lack nothing that money could buy. If it was a very loving family, our need for love would be fulfilled. If this family enjoyed a good reputation, our perceived worth would increase, at least in the eyes of others. If it was a family of great influence, and we were to help in managing its vast empire, we would be seen as more significant in life. In the same way, when God adopted us into His family this fact guaranteed that all of our needs for love, security, worth, and significance will be met. To the extent we realize our new position in Christ, to that degree we will actually experience the many promises that God has made to His family. This sets us free from searching through the garbage cans of life to ensure our own survival and allows us to focus our care on the needs of other people and on the Kingdom of God. We must believe that we actually are who God says we are.

Ga 4:5 To redeem them that were under the law, that we might receive the adoption of sons.

Eph 1:5 Having predestinated us unto the adoption of children.

Another way of discussing this new state of adoption is to say that we are now "in Christ" and that Christ now lives in us. Both are true. When we were adopted into the family of God, we became part of the "body of Christ." The Holy Spirit now dwells within us because we have accepted Christ.

Ro 8:9 But ye are not in the flesh, but in the Spirit, if so be that the Spirit of God dwell in you. Now if any man have not the Spirit of Christ, he is none of his.

Sanctification

Sanctification means two things. It means that God has selected us and set us aside for a particular purpose. It also refers to the entire process of becoming whole in body, soul and spirit through what Christ has done for us. It can even refer to the final step of this process, the redemption of our physical bodies. Instead of squandering our life on fruitless attempts to meet our own psychological and physical needs, God promises to meet our needs and gives our life meaning that far outstrips all that this physical world can offer. This is accomplished through the process of sanctification directed by the Spirit of God that dwells within us. He not only calls us to a specific purpose, but He motivates us to do it and assists us in carrying out all that He has called us to do.

1 Th 4:3 For this is the will of God, even your sanctification, that ye should abstain from fornication:

1 Co 1:30 But of him are ye in Christ Jesus, who of God is made unto us wisdom, and righteousness, and sanctification, and redemption:

The Wonderful State of the Spiritual Man

With these tools of transformation provided us, through the death and resurrection of Jesus Christ, the Bible tells us we have become a new creature. (2 Corinthians 5:17) We are forgiven so that we are not burdened down by our past sins. We are judiciously declared innocent so that we can boldly pursue a personal relationship with God Himself. We are convinced by the law that we cannot live the Christian life in our own strength, so that we will rely on Christ. We are given the unmerited favor of God and accepted just the way we are, so that we can be set free from the "rat race" of life. We are adopted into God's family of infinite resources so that we can accomplish His will for our lives. Finally, we are progressively sanctified so that we can become all that God has called us to be. What more could we ask for?

However, you might ask, if this is the case, then why do so many Christians still struggle with sin, seem to fall far short of what God wants for them, and seem to remain only a step above the predicaments of the natural man? The answer lies in the subject that I will address in the remainder of this book—successfully overcoming the obstacles and surmounting the steps to spiritual maturity. God has provided a clear roadmap for us to follow that leads to both psychological wholeness and spiritual maturity. All we have to do is yield to His direction, trust Him to meet our needs, and use the tools He has provided for us.

Chapter 2

Spiritual Growth through Revelation Knowledge

Our Need to Know God

In order to be truly successful in life we must know who God is and what He is like. Since He designed, constructed and is actively involved in our world, we must understand Him in order to know how to cope effectively with the challenges presented to us. This knowledge of God is the very basis of truth. As we come to understand the truth about God, we begin to understand the truth about the universe in which we live and about ourselves. How we perceive our universe and ourselves is the foundation of how we act and react to it. For example, if we see God as judgmental and ready to strike us with lightning for even the smallest mistake and ourselves as wretched members of a dysfunctional world without hope, we will act like animals fighting for survival. But if we see ourselves as redeemed children of a God Who will always love and forgive us, (even if we fail over and over again), Who will meet all of our needs and Who will do anything for us that we ask for our good, we will want to trust God and live for Him.

The Need for Revelation Knowledge

Almost everyone agrees that knowing a fact in our mind is not enough. We must believe that it is true. However, even if we believe that something is true in our minds, this is not usually enough to motivate us to change our behavior. It is when something becomes real to us that we change. This experience of knowing that something is real is called revelation. Revelation is "An uncovering, a bringing to light of that which had been previously wholly hidden or only obscurely seen. The Greek word *apokalupsis* is most often translated as "revelation." It means "laying bare, making naked, a disclosure of truth, instruction concerning things before unknown." (Quoted from The Online Bible Millennium Edition (2000) by Larry Pierce.)

It should be of no surprise that God, Who is a spirit, would work through revelation knowledge, which is the enlightenment of the spirit. God has many ways of doing this. Probably the gifts of the Spirit, visions and dreams come to mind first. But it is important to realize that we also receive revelation through reading the Word of God, preaching, teaching, reading, talking to others, and especially through our experiences.

Getting Knowledge from Our Head to Our Spirit

The most usual route for transforming thoughts into revelations is that of meditation on the Word of God. That is why it is so strongly emphasized in the Bible.

Ps 1:2 But his delight is in the law of the LORD; and in his law doth he meditate day and night.

3 And he shall be like a tree planted by the rivers of water, that bringeth forth his fruit in his season; his leaf also shall not wither; and whatsoever he doeth shall prosper.

Jos 1:8 This book of the law shall not depart out of thy mouth; but thou shalt meditate therein day and night, that thou mayest observe to do according to all that is written therein: for then thou shalt make thy way prosperous, and then thou shalt have good success.

9 Have not I commanded thee? Be strong and of a good courage; be not afraid, neither be thou dismayed: for the LORD thy God is with thee whithersoever thou goest.

If we learn and believe something to be true in our mind, it may not yet have become a revelation to us. The Bible makes this clear when it teaches us that faith without works is dead. (James 2:17) While it is true that our faith should result in works if it is genuine, it is also true that what we do affects what we think. The psychological term is dissonance. It suggests that we cannot do something that contradicts what we believe is true for very long. Either our thinking will change or our actions will change. Consequently, if we act on what we believe to be true in our minds, these actions make it more true for us and can assist us in moving what we think in our minds to our spirits. Note the encouragement in verse 9 above to act, immediately following the direction to meditate in Joshua Chapter 1. This all makes sense when we understand that faith is "the evidence of things not seen."

Heb 11:1 Now faith is the substance of things hoped for, the evidence of things not seen.

The strongest type of evidence in a court is that which has actually been experienced by a witness. We can believe something in our mind, we can feel something is true, we can want to do something but many times, it does not become revelation knowledge to us until we have experienced it. Then it becomes part of us. For example, you can tell me all day that you believe parachutes work. You can show me convincing evidence that the theory of parachute design is true. You can show me films of parachute jumps and introduce me to witnesses who have made successful jumps. But it is only when I have experienced a parachute jump myself (I have) that it becomes my experience and I have a revelation of what it is all about. Consequently, it is only as I experience God's actions in my life, feel His presence, hear His voice, or receive healing that my knowledge of Him becomes a life-changing part of me. A person with an experience is never at the mercy of someone with an argument.

I use a technique, which I have named, "If it is true…" I state a simple biblical truth about some issue in my life and then ask myself that if this is true, how would I act? For example, "If it is true that my worth is not dependent on my performance or what other people think of me but on God's unmerited favor…how would I act?" I then act according to the truth that I have just stated. My actions now confirm what I believe and strengthen my belief that it is so. This method helps move the biblical truth from my mind to my spirit. It makes it more real until it becomes part of me.

What the Bible Says About Revelation

1. <u>Direct revelations from God can increase our understanding of spiritual truth.</u>

    Ga 1:12 For I neither received it of man, neither was I taught it, but by the revelation of Jesus Christ.

2. <u>God can give us direct revelation through the gifts of the Spirit.</u>

    1 Co 14:6 Now, brethren, if I come unto you speaking with tongues, what shall I profit you, except I shall speak to you either by revelation, or by knowledge, or by prophesying, or by doctrine?

3. <u>A revelation from God can radically change the direction of our lives.</u>

    Ac 26:13 At midday, O king, I saw in the way a light from heaven, above the brightness of the sun, shining round about me and them which journeyed with me.

14 And when we were all fallen to the earth, I heard a voice speaking unto me, and saying in the Hebrew tongue, Saul, Saul, why persecutest thou me? it is hard for thee to kick against the pricks.

15 And I said, Who art thou, Lord? And he said, I am Jesus whom thou persecutest.

16 But rise, and stand upon thy feet: for I have appeared unto thee for this purpose, to make thee a minister and a witness both of these things which thou hast seen, and of those things in the which I will appear unto thee;

19 Whereupon, O king Agrippa, I was not disobedient unto the heavenly vision:

4. Revelation in the knowledge of God can transform our understanding, our calling, our concept of His care for us, and the mighty power available to us.

Eph 1:17 That the God of our Lord Jesus Christ, the Father of glory, may give unto you the spirit of wisdom and revelation in the knowledge of him:

18 The eyes of your understanding being enlightened; that ye may know what is the hope of his calling, and what the riches of the glory of his inheritance in the saints,

19 And what is the exceeding greatness of his power to us-ward who believe, according to the working of his mighty power,

The Revelation of God in the Old Testament

Although the Old Testament (or covenant) has been superceded by the New Testament (covenant), it is a type and shadow of the spiritual principles more fully revealed in the New Testament. (1 Corinthians 10:11) Throughout the Old Testament, as God related directly in the lives of men, they learned new revelations about God from their experiences. In many of these situations, they gave or were given a new name for God that expressed the new revelation that they had learned about God. It was these revelations that gave them an expanded vision of God and that transformed them. In addition, many times as they were transformed, God renamed them to clearly demonstrate that they were a new person due to their experience with Him. As examples, Abram was renamed Abraham, Sarai was renamed Sarah, and Jacob was renamed Israel.

Below is a list of the revelations of some of the names of God with their references in the Old Testament. A number of excellent books have been written on the history and meanings of these names, so I will only present a summary here of those that will prove significant in our study of spiritual growth later in this book. (See Stone, 1944, Sumurall, 1982, and Towns, 1991) I will also discuss the significance of each to spiritual growth.

1. **Jehovah Elohim.** In Genesis 1:1 we are introduced to the Triune God Who created everything in an orderly manner and Who provides all that we have. The ongoing struggle between evolutionists and creationists demonstrate how critical it is that we understand that all that is around us was made by God. If there is no God and everything has come about by chance, then we will attempt to be our own God, make our own morals and do whatever we wish. Only when we recognize that we are limited and cannot be self-sufficient, will we become interested in knowing the true God Who made everything.

    Ge 1:1 In the beginning God created the heaven and the earth.

2. **Yahweh Jehovah.** In Genesis 2:4-25, 13:4 we learn of a personal God Who displays Himself to His rational creatures, Who has always existed, is essential to life, has permanent existence, is eternal and unchangeable. He is the God of Revelation, Ever-becoming One, Who requires moral obligation and wants a personal relationship with us. Just because I believe that there is a God of creation does

not necessarily lead me to a personal relationship with Him. Some people want to believe that God is impersonal. They believe that God made the universe, turned it over to us and left us to fend for ourselves. If so, we are free to do as we see fit and direct our own lives. But if God is a personal God, desiring a relationship with us, then it only makes sense that we as His creatures have an obligation to know Him.

Ge 2:7 And the LORD God formed man of the dust of the ground, and breathed into his nostrils the breath of life; and man became a living soul.
8 And the LORD God planted a garden eastward in Eden; and there he put the man whom he had formed.

13:4 Unto the place of the altar, which he had made there at the first: and there Abram called on the name of the LORD.

3. **Jehovah Elyon.** In Genesis 14:18-20 and Psalm 7:17 we meet the Lord Most High, the God of ultimate authority and the possessor of heaven and earth Who judges between right and wrong. When we know God as the ultimate authority, we are no longer free to serve other gods or try to be our own authority. Either we come under His authority and serve Him or we are in rebellion against Him. If He judges right and wrong, then when we choose to do wrong, we are rebelling against the ultimate authority of the universe. If He owns everything, including us, then all that we have belongs to Him and He has a right to tell us how to live and what to do with what He has given us.

Ge 14:18 And Melchizedek king of Salem brought forth bread and wine: and he was the priest of the most high God.
19 And he blessed him, and said, Blessed be Abram of the most high God, possessor of heaven and earth:
20 And blessed be the most high God, which hath delivered thine enemies into thy hand. And he gave him tithes of all.

Ps 7:17 I will praise the LORD according to his righteousness: and will sing praise to the name of the LORD most high.

4. **Jehovah Adonai.** In Genesis 15:2, 8 and Genesis 18:3 God reveals Himself as the sovereign Lord and Master Who can do anything, Who is the master Who provides for His servants and requires the obedience of all. When we understand that God is our Master, we become His servants or slaves to do His bidding. It is also real that if we work for Him, He has an obligation to direct us, give us what we need for the work He directs us to do, and provide for all our personal needs. He also has a right to judge us according to our work and to expect us to be productive for Him. He must be the director and provider of our lives or He is not Lord at all.

Ge 15:2 And Abram said, Lord GOD, what wilt thou give me, seeing I go childless, and the steward of my house is this Eliezer of Damascus?

4 And, behold, the word of the LORD came unto him, saying, This shall not be thine heir; but he that shall come forth out of thine own bowels shall be thine heir.

5. **El Roi.** In Genesis 16:13 God revealed Himself to Hagar when she was in great distress. She called God, "The one who sees me" and she named the well where God provided for her as "the well of the living one who sees me." We must learn that God does love and care for us even in the worst of times and that He sees and cares about everything that happens to us. If God was blind or unconcerned, then we might have an excuse to rely on ourselves and do the best that we could to direct our lives.

But because God is always watching out for us and has our best interest in mind, we are obligated to trust and rely on His unlimited resources.

Ge 16:13 And she called the name of the LORD that spake unto her, Thou God seest me: for she said, Have I also here looked after him that seeth me?

14 Wherefore the well was called Beerlahairoi; behold, it is between Kadesh and Bered.

6. **Jehovah El Shaddai** in Genesis 17:1 is the Almighty God Who is the nourisher and supplier, the All-powerful One who is able to change nature. He nourishes us, supplies our needs, satisfies us, and is self-sufficient, the All-bountiful One, and shedder forth of blessings. He wants a personal relationship with each of us. God wants to make a covenant of blessing with us, but on the condition that we serve and obey Him. Covenants in the Bible are the strongest form of agreement. They are never to be violated and they never end. In a covenant, it was agreed that everything one has, was at the disposal of the other if it was needed. What a wonderful agreement! All we have (which is very little and which really belongs to God anyway) is His if He needs it, and all He has (absolutely everything) is ours if we need it! Covenants were also in force from generation to generation. The penalty for violating the covenant was death.

Ge 17:1 And when Abram was ninety years old and nine, the LORD appeared to Abram, and said unto him, I am the Almighty God; walk before me, and be thou perfect.

2 And I will make my covenant between me and thee, and will multiply thee exceedingly.

7. **El Olam** in Genesis 21:33 means "the Everlasting God." His covenant with us lasts forever, just as He exists and will exist forever. He wants to progressively reveal Himself to us forever. Through our personal covenant relationship with Him, as God and man work together for the benefit of both of them, we become everlasting friends.

Ge 21:31 Wherefore he called that place Beersheba; because there they sware both of them.

32 Thus they made a covenant at Beersheba: then Abimelech rose up, and Phichol the chief captain of his host, and they returned into the land of the Philistines.

33 And Abraham planted a grove in Beersheba, and called there on the name of the LORD, the everlasting God.

8. **Jehovah Jireh.** In Genesis 22: 8-14 God provided a ram, caught in a bush, as a substitute for the sacrifice of Isaac. He has also provided through the sacrifice of Christ all that we and all humanity need to be saved. We must realize that God is not only our friend with whom we have an everlasting covenant, but that in this lopsided agreement, God provided even His own Son to perfect us and make us whole. Just as Abraham's sacrifice was made to cover his sins, God Himself, in the form of Jesus, came to deliver us from our sins. Because we could not deliver ourselves, God provided all that was needed for every aspect of our deliverance. All we have to do is accept what He has already done for us through Jesus Christ. It is not by our works, but by His grace that we are saved.

Ge 22:13 And Abraham lifted up his eyes, and looked, and behold behind him a ram caught in a thicket by his horns: and Abraham went and took the ram, and offered him up for a burnt offering in the stead of his son.

14 And Abraham called the name of that place Jehovahjireh: as it is said to this day, In the mount of the LORD it shall be seen.

9. **Jehovah Rophe** in Exodus 15:26 means "God, our healer." Although this name has most often been associated with physical healing, it also implies complete health in every area of our lives. This means help in overcoming all of our problems, restoration, healing, and cure in all aspects of the physical, moral, and spiritual lives. God wants to sweeten the bitterness of human existence. Whether we need physical, moral or spiritual healing, He is our doctor. He has all the answers to life. We just need to follow what He orders, and our life will become sweet again.

   Ex 15:24 And the people murmured against Moses, saying, What shall we drink?

   25 And he cried unto the LORD; and the LORD shewed him a tree, which when he had cast into the waters, the waters were made sweet: there he made for them a statute and an ordinance, and there he proved them,

   26 And said, If thou wilt diligently hearken to the voice of the LORD thy God, and wilt do that which is right in his sight, and wilt give ear to his commandments, and keep all his statutes, I will put none of these diseases upon thee, which I have brought upon the Egyptians: for I am the LORD that healeth thee.

10. **Jehovah Nissi.** In Exodus 17:15 God is our banner and the focal point of our battle with the flesh. When He was lifted up (on the cross), He became our rallying point. We need God's presence and power to defeat the flesh and the other problems in our lives. We can have complete victory in our lives by relying on Jesus, instead of the flesh, to meet our needs. The Bible tells us that in our flesh dwelleth no good thing (Romans 7:18). One of the most important lessons a Christian has to learn is that he cannot win the spiritual battle on his own. To rely on the flesh to overcome the influence of the flesh clearly does not make sense. We must learn to rely on the Spirit for all of our victories. In the verses below, we should understand that Amalek is a type of the flesh.

    Ex 17:10 So Joshua did as Moses had said to him, and fought with Amalek: and Moses, Aaron, and Hur went up to the top of the hill.

    11 And it came to pass, when Moses held up his hand, that Israel prevailed: and when he let down his hand, Amalek prevailed.

    12 But Moses' hands were heavy; and they took a stone, and put it under him, and he sat thereon; and Aaron and Hur stayed up his hands, the one on the one side, and the other on the other side; and his hands were steady until the going down of the sun.

    15 And Moses built an altar, and called the name of it Jehovahnissi:

11. **Jehovah Eloheka** in Exodus 20:2 is the Lord Your God Who is the ruler and judge Who gives us His law for our good. He will judge men according to their works. We are to fear Him and do good. The fear of God is knowing that He will do what is best for us and will not fail to discipline us if we need it. We must learn what is right and wrong in a moral sense and then do it because we respect God as our faithful judge. This respect or fear of God provides the external motivation (the beginning of wisdom) to keep us in line until Christ is fully formed in us.

    Ex 20:1 And God spake all these words, saying,

    2 I am the LORD thy God, which have brought thee out of the land of Egypt, out of the house of bondage.

    3 Thou shalt have no other gods before me.

12. **Jehovah Mekaddishkhem.** In Exodus 31:13 and Leviticus 20:8 we find the God Who sanctifies and consecrates us to His service. We are called to be part of His family and to be holy in all we do since

our God is holy. We who God has set apart as sacred should walk worthy of God, making us fit for His holy presence. We are to separate ourselves from evil to do His will. We are to participate in the very nature of Jehovah through washing and purification. We must learn internal motivation and to do this we must take on the character of God, which is holiness. We must realize that a holy God is perfect in justice and love, and cannot do anything else but to love and care for us. It is He that sets us apart for Himself and transforms us to want to do His will, not because we have to, but because we want to. It is His Holy Spirit within us that transforms us from the inside out.

Ex 31:13 Speak thou also unto the children of Israel, saying, Verily my sabbaths ye shall keep: for it is a sign between me and you throughout your generations; that ye may know that I am the LORD that doth sanctify you.

Lev 20: 7 Sanctify yourselves therefore, and be ye holy: for I am the LORD your God.

8 And ye shall keep my statutes, and do them: I am the LORD which sanctify you.

13. **Jehovah Shalom.** The Lord our Peace in Judges 6:24 and Isaiah 9:6 shows us God's desire to lead us into complete peace. In the Hebrew language, peace includes completeness, soundness, welfare, prosperity, peace and friendship. It means to be whole or finished, and having perfect contentment and satisfaction. Our peace comes through fully yielding ourselves to the reign of God in our lives. This peace overcomes our fear and results in peaceful rest. Jesus is the Prince of Peace. Another measure of our trust in God is our peace.

Jud 6:22 And when Gideon perceived that he was an angel of the LORD, Gideon said, Alas, O Lord GOD! for because I have seen an angel of the LORD face to face.

23 And the LORD said unto him, Peace be unto thee; fear not: thou shalt not die.

24 Then Gideon built an altar there unto the LORD, and called it Jehovahshalom: unto this day it is yet in Ophrah of the Abiezrites.

14. **Jehovah Sabaoth.** In 1ˢᵗ Samuel 1:3 and Isaiah 6:3 God is called the Lord of Hosts (or armies). This is the God Who will win all our battles. The hosts referred to here are the armies of heaven, which initially are the angels, sent for our aid and protection. However, we are also destined to become part of that army at His second coming. As we work together for the furtherance of the Kingdom of God, we are knit together as one body, caring for one another. Since we are part of that one body, we can expect God to provide all we need as we work for Him and glorify His name.

Isa 6:1 In the year that king Uzziah died I saw also the Lord sitting upon a throne, high and lifted up, and his train filled the temple.

2 Above it stood the seraphims: each one had six wings; with twain he covered his face, and with twain he covered his feet, and with twain he did fly.

3 And one cried unto another, and said, Holy, holy, holy, is the LORD of hosts: the whole earth is full of his glory.

15. **Jehovah Raah** in Psalm 23:1 means "The Lord is My Shepherd." God is the gentle shepherd of His flock, those who are in relationship with Him. God loves us and gently takes care of us in every circumstance, leading us to good pastures, protecting us from those who would hurt us, and ensuring that only goodness and mercy shall follow us all the days of our lives. This kind of relationship implies trust and a quiet, loving relationship between God and His people. When we have this revelation of the care and protection of a shepherd for his sheep, we too can lie down in green pastures with full assurance that only good and mercy will come to us for the rest of our lives. It is no longer necessary to struggle and fret when we

have complete confidence in the one Who deeply cares for us, leads, provides and protects us in every circumstance.

Ps 23:1 The LORD is my shepherd; I shall not want.

2 He maketh me to lie down in green pastures: he leadeth me beside the still waters.

3 He restoreth my soul: he leadeth me in the paths of righteousness for his name's sake.

4 Yea, though I walk through the valley of the shadow of death, I will fear no evil: for thou art with me; thy rod and thy staff they comfort me.

5 Thou preparest a table before me in the presence of mine enemies: thou anointest my head with oil; my cup runneth over.

6 Surely goodness and mercy shall follow me all the days of my life: and I will dwell in the house of the LORD for ever.

16. **Jehovah Melek.** In Isaiah 6:5 God reveals Himself as King. We owe complete allegiance and obedience, honor, praise, and worship to our King. As His subjects, we may come into His presence and request all that we need. Everything we have is under His control. We need to understand that God is in complete charge of everything, that He cannot fail, and that He can never make a mistake. We are free to obey His every command with full assurance in every circumstance of achieving the ultimate victory. He cannot fail; therefore, as we rely on Him, we are more than conquerors in everything we do!

Isa 6:5 Then said I, Woe is me! for I am undone; because I am a man of unclean lips, and I dwell in the midst of a people of unclean lips: for mine eyes have seen the King, the LORD of hosts.

6 Then flew one of the seraphims unto me, having a live coal in his hand, which he had taken with the tongs from off the altar:

7 And he laid it upon my mouth, and said, Lo, this hath touched thy lips; and thine iniquity is taken away, and thy sin purged.

17. **El Gibbor** in Isaiah 9:6 means "Mighty God." It comes from the word for strong and valiant. God can do anything and will do it, not based on our works, but out of His love for us. Since God has provided all we need for our complete salvation through Jesus, we have only to trust and rely on His plan and mighty power. We are to be careful not to rely on ourselves for anything.

Isa 9:6 For unto us a child is born, unto us a son is given: and the government shall be upon his shoulder: and his name shall be called Wonderful, Counsellor, The mighty God, The everlasting Father, The Prince of Peace.

18. **Awb** in Jer 31:9 and **Pater** in Matthew 6:9 are translated as Father. We are to realize that God is our true Father, that He loves us and that we are part of His family, the Church. As such, we have all the privileges and obligations of the family of God, and we are expected to love and cherish our brothers and sisters. As a part of this new family, we have certain obligations as well as privileges. We have been chosen eventually to rule the universe. We are joint heirs with Christ and, therefore, we will own a large portion of the universe. As a member of God's family, God will abundantly provide all we need. However, we have an obligation to work for the furtherance of the Kingdom of God, to live a life worthy of the name of Christ, and do everything to honor His Holy name.

Jer 31:9 They shall come with weeping, and with supplications will I lead them: I will cause them to walk by the rivers of waters in a straight way, wherein they shall not stumble: for I am a father to Israel, and Ephraim is my firstborn.

Mt 6:9 After this manner therefore pray ye: Our Father which art in heaven, Hallowed be thy name.

19. **Jehovah Tsidkenu.** In Jeremiah 23:6 we find God described as the Lord Our Righteousness. It is not by our works that we are righteous, but by what Jesus has done on our behalf. It is God's grace that makes us righteous, not anything that we have done. Therefore, we are to love and extend that same acceptance, mercy and benevolence to all of our fellow men. Because God is love and His love is unconditional to all His creation, we are to have this same kind of benevolence even toward our enemies. As God has accepted us without any works on our part, we are to accept others without any works on their part and always have their best interest in mind; especially their salvation. Just as we are to love God with all of our heart, we are called to love our neighbors as ourselves. (Luke 10:27) Love is the highest level of Christian maturity, which, in fact, is becoming one with God Himself (Who is love).

Jer 23:5 Behold, the days come, saith the LORD, that I will raise unto David a righteous Branch, and a King shall reign and prosper, and shall execute judgment and justice in the earth.

6 In his days Judah shall be saved, and Israel shall dwell safely: and this is his name whereby he shall be called, THE LORD OUR RIGHTEOUSNESS.

20. **Jehovah Shammah** in Ezekiel 48:35 means "the Lord is There." In these verses, God gives us a vision of what is to come. God's final goal is to inhabit us completely and totally, with His love and peace. It is the presence of God in us that is our promise and pledge of the completion of our final rest and the Glory in God. The final eternal fulfillment of God in us is heaven where we will become one with Him and with all Christians forever.

Exe 48:31 And the gates of the city shall be after the names of the tribes of Israel: three gates northward; one gate of Reuben, one gate of Judah, one gate of Levi.

35 It was round about eighteen thousand measures: and the name of the city from that day shall be, The LORD is there.

The Revelation of God in the New Testament

When we compare these revelations of the names of God in the Old Testament to the New Testament, we find that God revealed Himself in an even greater way in the New Testament through sending Jesus as the full manifestation of Himself. The Bible tells us that God has spoken this new revelation to us through the experience of His Son. The majority of our knowledge concerning Jesus is revealed to us throughout the gospels.

Heb 1:1 God, who at sundry times and in divers manners spake in time past unto the fathers by the prophets,

2 Hath in these last days spoken unto us by his Son, whom he hath appointed heir of all things, by whom also he made the worlds;

Jo 14:9 Jesus saith unto him, Have I been so long time with you, and yet hast thou not known me, Philip? he that hath seen me hath seen the Father; and how sayest thou then, Shew us the Father?

As we have discussed earlier, the word revelation means "to enlighten or to make known something that was not known." Jesus came to show us God and to allow us to experience Him in the fullest sense known to man—in physical form.

> Jo 1:14 And the Word was made flesh, and dwelt among us, (and we beheld his glory, the glory as of the only begotten of the Father,) full of grace and truth.

Possibly the second most important direct revelation in the New Testament is the actions of the Holy Spirit, the third member of the Godhead, as revealed in the story of the New Testament church in the Book of Acts. We can learn many wonderful insights about the reality of God, such as how He chose to reveal Himself, operate through the manifestations of the Holy Spirit, and guide the early church.

The remainder of new revelations concerning God in the New Testament come to us through the inspired letters or epistles, primarily through Paul, Peter, James, and John. Through direct statements that they made concerning the nature of God and through the direction that they provided to the early churches, we can gain further insights into "the knowledge of God."

In this chapter, we have seen that spiritual growth is primarily based on how we know and perceive God in our spirit. We grow revelation by revelation as we get a fuller understanding of Who God really is and what He is like. God demonstrated this process of growth in the lives of Old Testament saints as He revealed Himself progressively through the compound names by which He and others referred to Him. In the New Testament, God has primarily revealed Himself through the manifestation of Jesus Christ, the Acts of the Holy Spirit, and the Epistles. In the next chapter, we will study the most important biblical models of spiritual growth.

Chapter 3

Biblical Models of Spiritual Growth

Throughout the Bible, there are a number of ongoing patterns and growth analogies used to describe our progress toward spiritual maturity. These models of spiritual growth tend to follow a reasonably consistent pattern. It is important for the reader to have a basic understanding of these models, since I will use this terminology and attempt to integrate these concepts into the overall pattern of growth presented later in this book. Because many books have previously been written on these subjects, in this section I will provide only a basic understanding of these biblical concepts. (For more on this subject, see Hagin, 1976)

The Natural, Carnal, and Spiritual Man

The Bible describes a war between the flesh and the spirit. The flesh (attempting to meet our physical and psychological needs in our own strength) attempts to dominate the soul (our mind, emotions and will). At the beginning of our salvation experience, a struggle begins between our flesh and our spirit for the control of the soul and our lives. To the degree that our spirit predominates, we become more spiritually mature or perfect.

Ro 8:5 For they that are after the flesh do mind the things of the flesh; but they that are after the Spirit the things of the Spirit.

9 But ye are not in the flesh, but in the Spirit, if so be that the Spirit of God dwell in you. Now if any man have not the Spirit of Christ, he is none of his.

13 For if ye live after the flesh, ye shall die: but if ye through the Spirit do mortify the deeds of the body, ye shall live.

The term **natural man**, as we have already discussed, refers to the state of the human person as he is when he is born. We have already discussed the hopeless state of the natural man because, without salvation, he is unable to overcome the selfishness and sin nature that lies within him.

1 Co 2:14 But the natural man receiveth not the things of the Spirit of God: for they are foolishness unto him: neither can he know them, because they are spiritually discerned.

Because God does not take away our ability to choose when we accept Christ, it is possible for the new Christian to continue to be dominated by his carnal or fleshly nature. A Christian who is still governed by the desires of his body and senses is called a carnal man or **carnal Christian**. In his life, he relies on his own natural efforts and directs his own life. Another way of stating this is that in the carnal Christian, the outward man dominates the inward or spirit man. As a result, the carnal man acts just like the natural man, struggling to meet his needs through the flesh and participating in all of the aspects and struggles of life. He will do whatever it takes to get the needs of his self met and therefore, falls frequently into sin or is addicted just like the natural man.

Ro 8:7 Because the carnal mind is enmity against God: for it is not subject to the law of God, neither indeed can be.

1 Co 3:1 And I, brethren, could not speak unto you as unto spiritual, but as unto carnal, even as unto babes in Christ.

3 For ye are yet carnal: for whereas there is among you envying, and strife, and divisions, are ye not carnal, and walk as men?

When a Christian chooses to yield himself to the direction of the Spirit of God, he becomes a **spiritual man** to the degree his soul is controlled and directed by the Spirit of God. In this case, the spirit man dominates the desires of the outward man. These issues will be discussed in more detail later in this book.

Babyhood, Childhood, Manhood

The Bible also discusses the steps to spiritual maturity in an analogy of physical growth. We progress from being newborn babies, to little children, to children, to young men, and finally to fathers. Babies in Christ are usually those who have just now been born again in the spirit. They have become a new spiritual person because the Spirit of God has come into them, but little else has changed. They still must have their mind renewed so that they can start acting like a different person.

Jo 3:3 Jesus answered and said unto him, Verily, verily, I say unto thee, Except a man be born again, he cannot see the kingdom of God.

1 Pe 1:23 Being born again, not of corruptible seed, but of incorruptible, by the word of God, which liveth and abideth for ever.

Ro 12:2 And be not conformed to this world: but be ye transformed by the renewing of your mind, that ye may prove what is that good, and acceptable, and perfect, will of God.

1. <u>Babies are those who are still worldly, hard to teach, still need to understand the basic principles of the Bible, and have still not reached a basic level of righteousness.</u> They are usually unable to understand the difference between good and evil.

   Heb 5:11 Of whom we have many things to say, and hard to be uttered, seeing ye are dull of hearing.

   12 For when for the time ye ought to be teachers, ye have need that one teach you again which [be] the first principles of the oracles of God; and are become such as have need of milk, and not of strong meat.

   13 For every one that useth milk [is] unskilful in the word of righteousness: for he is a babe.

   14 But strong meat belongeth to them that are of full age, [even] those who by reason of use have their senses exercised to discern both good and evil.

   They need to drink in the fundamentals of the Word of God and stop sinning and acting like the world.

   1 Pe 2:1 Wherefore laying aside all malice, and all guile, and hypocrisies, and envies, and all evil speakings,

   2 As newborn babes, desire the sincere milk of the word, that ye may grow thereby:

2. <u>Little children are those who know the fundamentals of the Scriptures, but are still struggling to understand that they have been forgiven and to overcome the sinful acts in their lives.</u> They know God the Father, but they are not yet changed significantly by that relationship.

   1 Jo 2:1 My little children, these things write I unto you, that ye sin not. And if any man sin, we have an advocate with the Father, Jesus Christ the righteous:

12 I write unto you, little children, because your sins are forgiven you for his name's sake.

4:4 You are of God, little children, and have overcome them: because greater is he that is in you, than he that is in the world.

3. <u>Children are still unstable in their beliefs and are easily shaken by what others tell them.</u>

   Eph 4:14 That we [henceforth] be no more children, tossed to and fro, and carried about with every wind of doctrine, by the sleight of men, [and] cunning craftiness, whereby they lie in wait to deceive;

   15 But speaking the truth in love, may grow up into him in all things, which is the head, [even] Christ:

   Children need to learn to be obedient to follow God in what they do. They are in the process of learning self-control.

   Eph 5:1 Be ye therefore followers of God, as dear children;

4. <u>Young men are those who know the Word of God, consistently overcome temptation, and have defeated the attack of Satan in their lives.</u> They want to do and are able to consistently do what is right.

   1 Jo 2:13b I write unto you, young men, because ye have overcome the wicked one.

   2:14b I have written unto you, young men, because ye are strong, and the word of God abideth in you, and ye have overcome the wicked one.

5. <u>Fathers or mature (perfect) men are those who know God experientially and have been conformed to the image of Jesus.</u>

   1 Jo 2:13a I write unto you, fathers, because ye have known him that is from the beginning.

   Eph 4:13 Till we all come in the unity of the faith, and of the knowledge of the Son of God, unto a perfect (mature) man, unto the measure of the stature of the fulness of Christ:

   They have become mature through their trials, are strong, and settled in their faith.

   1 Pe 5:10 But the God of all grace, who hath called us unto his eternal glory by Christ Jesus, after that ye have suffered a while, make you perfect, stablish, strengthen, settle [you].

   The things of the world mean little to them.

   1 Jo 2:15 Love not the world, neither the things [that are] in the world. If any man love the world, the love of the Father is not in him.

The Law

As we progress in our level of spirituality, we come under a progression of laws. Each has its place and purpose, but each one supercedes the previous one.

1. <u>The ceremonial law.</u> It provided regulations for approaching a Holy God. It was done away with through the complete sacrifice of Christ. This was made clear by the rending of the veil of the temple when Christ, the final sacrifice, died on the cross.

2. <u>The Ten Commandments or moral law.</u> It was given on Mount Sinai through Moses and provided the precepts for living a moral life. It was our "schoolmaster" to prevent sin until Christ came. This law provides external motivation to do right. It was fulfilled by Christ for us.

3. <u>The law of liberty.</u> Through God's grace, we were set free from the external control of the two previous laws to obey the law of liberty. This law requires us to obey the spirit rather than the letter of the law. It gives us a choice to obey it and provides internal motivation.

4. <u>The law of love.</u> This is the ultimate law of the Kingdom of God. If we love others as Christ loved us, we will never do them harm and will fulfill the intent of all of the previous laws.

Peter's Steps to Spiritual Maturity

One of the most detailed explanations of spiritual growth is found in 2nd Peter Chapter 1. These verses provide the most specific sequential understanding of how this plan of salvation, which includes both psychological wholeness and spiritual maturity, is accomplished by the Holy Spirit in our lives. God promises that He will meet all of our needs beyond any expectation that we can even imagine, as we pursue His gift of salvation by faith. He gives us His unmerited favor and power, without any works on our part (grace) as well as the peace that passes all understanding. Finally, He provides absolutely everything that we need for our current life on earth and for our transformation to become like Him, with all of His excellence and holiness.

> 2 Pe 1:2 Grace and peace be multiplied unto you <u>through the knowledge of God</u>, and of Jesus our Lord,
> 3 According as his divine power hath given unto us all things that pertain unto life and godliness, <u>through the knowledge of him</u> that hath called us to glory and virtue:

All this is to be accomplished through "the knowledge of Him." God's plan is to make us like Him, full of glory and virtue. The word in the Greek, translated here as knowledge, is *epignosis* which means "Precise and correct knowledge of things ethical and divine." It has an intensive meaning as compared with *gnosis*, which means "knowledge, cognition, the understanding of facts or truths, or else insight or discernment." It is a fuller, clearer, more thorough knowledge of divine things. Consequently, it is clear that these verses are referring to a deeper knowledge in the spirit or revelation concerning God.

> 2 Pe 1:4 Whereby are given unto us exceeding great and precious promises: that by these ye might be partakers of the divine nature, having escaped the corruption that is in the world through lust.

The method that God uses in transforming us is to increase our faith and knowledge of God so that we can be delivered from the selfish lust of this world that leads to corruption and take on the divine nature of God, which is love. As we get to know God experientially, each new revelation leads to greater faith and further spiritual and psychological growth in our lives.

> 2 Pe 1:5 And beside this, giving all diligence, add to your faith virtue; and to virtue, knowledge;
> 6 And to knowledge temperance; and to temperance patience; and to patience godliness;
> 7 And to godliness, brotherly kindness; and to brotherly kindness charity.

We have a part in this process—that of giving all diligence to make it happen. We must cooperate with the Holy Spirit as He leads us through each of the steps of spiritual and psychological maturity that are listed below.

1. FAITH: <u>We must be saved.</u> In 2nd Peter 1:5, we find that our salvation begins with faith. In order to be willing to commit our lives to God, we must believe and trust that He will meet our needs and give us eternal life.

2. VIRTUE: <u>We must end our selfishness and self-centeredness and make Jesus Lord.</u> The word virtue here is the Greek *arete*, which is interpreted as virtue, goodness, or worthiness. It means "a virtuous course of thought, feeling, or action and suggests any moral excellence such as modesty or purity." It is our faith that leads us to virtue since it is faith that delivers us from selfishness. We will never be free of our self-centeredness until Jesus is Lord and is directing our lives.

3. KNOWLEDGE: <u>We have to know what is right and wrong and come to the realization that in our own strength we cannot do right and fulfill the law.</u> The fear of God provides external motivation, but not the will power to do what is right. The word interpreted as knowledge is *gnosis*, which, when applied to religion, means "advanced knowledge especially of things lawful and unlawful for Christians (moral wisdom)." After we have become unselfish and unbiased through faith, then it is finally possible to know God's will for our lives. Nevertheless, it is still not possible, through our own effort, to obey it.

4. TEMPERANCE: <u>We must learn internal control through grace.</u> Once we have overcome our selfishness and know what is right and wrong, we must learn to be self-motivated to do what is right. The word *egkrateia* is translated as temperance or self-control. It means "the ability to master one's desires and passions, especially sensual appetites." Once we achieve enough self-control to choose the control of the spirit instead of the flesh, then we must learn to consistently do it.

5. PATIENCE: <u>We must become strong and persevere in doing right through a knowledge of who we are in Christ.</u> The word here is *hupomone* and is translated as patience, endurance, or perseverance. It means "patient continuance, steadfastness, and constancy." It is characteristic of a man who is not swerved from his deliberate purpose and his loyalty to faith and piety by even the greatest trials and sufferings. We may be able to do God's will at certain times and in ideal circumstances for a short period, but now we must learn to do it under extreme circumstances for an extended period of time.

6. GODLINESS: <u>We must die to ourselves and the flesh so that the character of Christ may live through us.</u> Once we are consistently obedient, we are finally in a position to do God's will, maintain constant fellowship with Him, and get to know and worship Him as He really is. The word interpreted as godliness or holiness is *eusebeia* and means "reverence, respect, or piety towards God." This is what leads to our desire to be like God, walk according to His Spirit, develop godly character and live in the "peace that passes all understanding." In order for this to occur, we must purify our lives.

7. BROTHERLY KINDNESS: <u>We must learn to accept other Christians, faults and all, and learn true compassion and fondness for them.</u> Once we have experienced the unconditional acceptance of God and are working hand in hand with God's people for the good of the Kingdom of God, we must accept each other like God accepts us. We must become fond of God's other children, despite their faults. The word interpreted as brotherly kindness or love is *philadelphia*, which means "the love with which Christians cherish or appreciate each other as brethren."

8. CHARITY: <u>We must finally realize that God is love so that we will be free to love everyone else just as they are.</u> The word interpreted love or charity is *agape* and denotes "universal unconditional affection, good will or benevolence." When we have experienced the unconditional love of God, in spite of all of our failures and faults, we can offer this same unconditional love, which is the very character of God, to others.

2 Pe 1:8 For <u>if these things be in you, and abound,</u> they make [you that ye shall] neither [be] barren nor unfruitful <u>in the knowledge of our Lord Jesus Christ.</u>

9 But he that lacketh these things is blind, and cannot see afar off, and hath forgotten that he was purged from his old sins.

10 Wherefore the rather, brethren, give diligence to make your calling and election sure: for <u>if ye do these things,</u> ye shall never fall:

11 For so an entrance shall be ministered unto you abundantly into the everlasting kingdom of our Lord and Saviour Jesus Christ.

These verses again make it clear that it is through the revelation knowledge of Christ that we are changed and become fruitful. These things must be in us and must abound! We have to experience and actually do these steps in order to mature in Christ. Although it is not directly stated, these verses imply that it is possible to achieve each of these steps in varying amounts. It is only when we come into full maturity in each of these steps that they ensure that we will never fall. Without developing faith along these lines, we have no guarantee of continuing victory over sin or fulfilling our election or calling.

What more could we ever ask for or desire? All that we need for life and becoming like God has been provided through Jesus and is available to us as we grow in our knowledge of God. This gift of salvation leads to such complete psychological and spiritual maturity that we can have such constant victory over our selfish desires that we will never fall! As we grow in Christ, we can become so fruitful in our lives that we can completely fulfill our calling and election, and finally, have an abundant and glory-filled entrance into heaven itself! Could there be anything more important than this?

God has already done His part through Jesus Christ and has provided the "great and precious promises" for our future as well as a plan for our spiritual development. In the chapters that follow, we must understand what it means to "give all diligence" to see these promises become a reality in our lives, as we grow in the "knowledge of God" one step at a time. On the following pages, I have provided a diagram illustrating these steps, a correlation of the spiritual growth models discussed in this chapter, and a correlation of Peter's steps with the names of God discussed in the previous chapter.

STEPS OF FAITH TOWARD CHRISTIAN MATURITY

CHARITY
LOVE FOR EVERYONE
Knowing that God <u>is</u> love
Being motivated by love

BROTHERLY KINDNESS
LOVING CHRISTIANS
Accepting Christians as they are
Learning true compassion

GODLINESS
ACQUIRING THE CHARACTER OF GOD
Walking according to the Spirit
Dying to self

PATIENCE
UNSWERVING DEDICATION TO DO RIGHT
Knowing that God will always meet all my needs
Knowing who I am in Christ

TEMPERANCE
CHOOSING TO DO RIGHT BECAUSE I WANT TO
Understanding God's unmerited favor without works
Developing internal motivation through grace

KNOWLEDGE
UNDERSTANDING WHAT IS TRULY RIGHT AND WRONG
Learning that in my own strength, I cannot obey the law
Being externally motivated by the Law

VIRTUE
YIELDING DIRECTION OF MY LIFE TO THE HOLY SPIRIT
Learning that I do not have enough information to direct my life
Making Jesus Lord of my life

FAITH
HAVING FAITH IN GOD FOR ETERNAL LIFE
Being "born again" of the Holy Spirit so that I want to do what is right
Repentance, forgiveness of sins, and accepting salvation

CORRELATION OF SPIRITUAL GROWTH MODELS

Peter's Steps	Growth Analogies			
	Faith	Spirit Man	Growth	Law
UNSAVED Knowing God as Judge	In myself	Natural	Dead	Ceremonial law
FAITH Knowing Jesus as Savior	For heaven	Carnal	Babe	
VIRTUE Knowing Jesus as Lord	For direction		Little child	
KNOWLEDGE Knowing God as Master	In God's Word	Servant	Child	Moral law
SELF-CONTROL Knowing God as Friend	Unmerited favor		Teenager	Law of liberty
PERSEVERANCE Knowing God as Father	Who I am	Son	Young man	
GODLINESS Knowing God as Holy Spirit	Live through me	Spiritual	Man	
BROTHERLY LOVE Knowing Jesus as Brother	To care for me		Father	
AGAPE LOVE Knowing God as Love	Never fail me			Law of love

CORRELATION OF THE NAMES OF GOD AND PETER'S STEPS

Peter's step	Name	Meaning	Revelation
FAITH (Savior)	Jehovah Elohim	The Lord My Creator	God made everything and provides for us.
	Jehovah Jireh	God Our Provider	God wants to provide for our salvation/wholeness.
	Jehovah Rophe	God Our Healer	God wants to heal us body, soul, and spirit.
	El Olam	Everlasting God	God wants to have an everlasting covenant with us.
VIRTUE (Lord)	Jehovah Raab	The Lord is My Shepherd	God wants to be our loving Shepherd as we yield to Him.
	Jehovah Adonai	Sovereign God	God wants to be ruler of our lives for our good.
	Jehovah El Shaddai	Almighty God/Nourisher	God wants a personal, nourishing relationship with us.
	Yahweh Jehovah	The Lord Our (personal) God	God wants to be our personal God.
KNOWLEDGE (Master)	Jehovah Melek	The Lord My King	As God's subject, we owe Him complete allegiance.
	Jehovah Eloheka	The Lord Your God	God is our judge Who gives us the law for our good.
	Jehovah Elyon	The Lord God Most High	God is our ultimate authority and has a right to judge us.
SELF-CONTROL (Friend)	Jehovah Mekaddishkhem	The Lord Our Sanctification	God has called us and makes us holy in order to obey Him.
	Jehovah Shalom	The Lord Our Peace	God, through His grace, accepts us/provides for our total prosperity.
PERSEVERANCE (Father)	Awb or Pater	Father God	As part of the family of God, we are to faithfully serve Him.
	Jehovah Sabaoth	The Lord of Hosts	God will help all of His children consistently win all their battles.
GODLINESS (Holy Spirit)	Jehovah Nissi	God Our Banner	God wants us to rely on Him for our victory over the flesh.
	El Gibbor	Mighty God	When God lives through us, we can do anything.
	Jehovah Tsidkenu	The Lord Our Righteousness	As we rely on what Jesus did, we are made righteous.
BROTHERLY LOVE (Brother)	El Roi	The One Who Sees Me	God wants us to watch out for our brothers to help them as He does.
AGAPE LOVE (Love)	Jehovah Shammah	The Lord is There	God wants us to be there for others and love them as He does.

PART II

Faith—Knowing Jesus as My Savior

Chapter 4

Jesus as Savior
God Will Meet All My Needs

2 Pe 1:5 And beside this, giving all diligence, add to your faith virtue; and to virtue, knowledge;

It all starts with faith

Everything in Christianity operates by faith. In verse five, we find that the sequence of the steps to spiritual and psychological maturity begins with faith; which in the Greek means "belief with the predominate idea of trust (or confidence) whether in God or in Christ, springing from faith in the character of the one who can be relied on." At the most fundamental level, we must believe that God will meet our needs or we will not turn our lives over to Him and accept Jesus as our Savior. Unfortunately, some who have a difficult time trusting God, may accept Jesus as Savior when times are difficult, but never make Him in charge of their lives as Lord (the next step). Because many Christians are primarily motivated to receive Christ in order to meet their own needs, they tend to treat God as their "genie" (as I did). Therefore, I call this the "genie stage."

Repentance

Before we can be saved, we must repent and decide to trust God to meet our needs. The word in the Greek is *metanoe*, which means "to change one's mind for the better or to heartily make amends with abhorrence of one's past sins." A second word sometimes translated as repent is *Metamellomai*, which means "to care about something afterward or to regret." To regret is passive and does not necessarily imply action as in the case where Judas repented (regretted) what he had done. This is not true repentance! Repentance actually occurs at each step of our spiritual growth since change always requires that we begin to act in a different way than we did before.

1. Repentance is turning from our own way of doing things.

   Jer 8:6 I hearkened and heard, but they spake not aright: no man repented him of his wickedness, saying, What have I done? every one turned to his course, as the horse rusheth into the battle.

2. Repentance is the first step in asking for the remission of sins.

   Isa 55:7 Let the wicked forsake his way, and the unrighteous man his thoughts: and let him return unto the LORD, and he will have mercy upon him; and to our God, for he will abundantly pardon.

3. <u>If we truly repent, it will become clear to others through our actions.</u>

Mt 3:7 But when he saw many of the Pharisees and Sadducees come to his baptism, he said unto them, O generation of vipers, who hath warned you to flee from the wrath to come?

8 Bring forth therefore fruits meet for repentance:

4. <u>It is the goodness of God that leads us to repentance.</u>

Ro 2:4 Or despisest thou the riches of his goodness and forbearance and longsuffering; not knowing that the goodness of God leadeth thee to repentance?

5. <u>No amount of evidence can make people repent if they do not want to do so.</u>

Lu 16:31 And he said unto him, If they hear not Moses and the prophets, neither will they be persuaded, though one rose from the dead.

6. <u>Repentance comes before we can believe and embrace the gospel.</u>

Mr 1:15 And saying, The time is fulfilled, and the kingdom of God is at hand: repent ye, and believe the gospel.

7. <u>God highly values repentance.</u>

Lu 15:7 I say unto you, that likewise joy shall be in heaven over one sinner that repenteth, more than over ninety and nine just persons, which need no repentance.

10 Likewise, I say unto you, there is joy in the presence of the angels of God over one sinner that repenteth.

8. <u>God is extremely patient waiting for people to repent because He wants everyone to be saved.</u>

2 Pe 3:9 The Lord is not slack concerning his promise, as some men count slackness; but is longsuffering to us-ward, not willing that any should perish, but that all should come to repentance.

9. <u>All that do not repent will perish.</u>

Lu 13:3 I tell you, Nay: but, except ye repent, ye shall all likewise perish.

Until we are willing to repent we cannot be saved, but simple repentance is not sufficient to bring salvation by itself.

Salvation

The root Greek word *sozo*, which is interpreted to be saved, actually means much more than being delivered from hell and destined for heaven. It means "to save, make whole, heal, and be whole." It indicates both that we have accepted Christ and that we have begun the process of salvation, which eventually leads to complete wholeness here on earth and eternal life after we die.

The Bible tells us that the salvation or wholeness that God provides through Christ is complete: spirit, soul and body. When we believe and accept Christ, our spirit is regenerated or saved, and we are born of the Spirit. We receive a new nature, are forgiven, and Christ's Spirit comes to dwell within us so that we can have fellowship with Him. In this lifetime, as we get to know God better, grow in faith, yield to the Holy Spirit and renew our mind, our soul becomes progressively whole. Finally, our bodies will be renewed in the resurrection.

1. <u>The requirements for salvation are most clearly described in Romans 10: 9.</u>

    Ro 10:9 That if thou shalt confess with thy mouth the Lord Jesus, and shalt believe in thine heart that God hath raised him from the dead, thou shalt be saved.

According to this verse, we must:

   a. <u>Believe with the heart:</u> In the Bible, the Greek word here for heart is *kardia*. It means "the center of all physical and spiritual life." Verses can be found where it refers to the mind, emotions, will, or spirit, or any combination of these. To be saved, we must believe in our hearts that God raised Jesus from the dead. We must have faith that Jesus was "to be the firstborn of many brethren" (Romans 8:29), and that God will also resurrect us, meet our needs, and give us eternal life. The Greek word for believe here is *pisteuo* which is defined as, "to think to be true, to be persuaded of, to credit, place confidence in, to trust in Jesus or God as able to aid either in obtaining or in doing something: saving faith, to entrust a thing to one or to be entrusted with a thing." It is the same root word as the word translated as faith. To believe is the verb and faith is the noun. Therefore, believing is a lot more than mental assent of the mind to agree about something. At issue here is that we must actually place our confidence in, rely on and trust God to aid, obtain, or do what we need, and to have enough confidence to commit our needs to Him.

   b. <u>Confess with our mouth what we believe.</u> The Greek word for confess is *homologeo* which means "To say the same thing as another, i.e. to agree with, assent, to promise, not to deny, to declare openly, speak out freely, to profess one's self the worshipper of one, to praise, and celebrate." The meaning here is to openly and outwardly speak as well as act in accordance with what we believe—that God has and will meet our needs through Jesus' death and resurrection and will take us to heaven when we die. In James Chapter 2, it is clear that faith without works or action is dead, and that salvation will not work if we fail to act according to our trust in God.

   c. <u>Confess Jesus as Lord.</u> The Greek word for Lord here is *kurios* which means "he to whom a person or thing belongs, about which he has power of deciding; master, lord, the possessor and disposer of a thing, the owner; one who has control of the person, the master." The issue here is submission and control. This verse states that, at least, in order to accept Christ we must be willing to declare that He is the Lord of our lives. Unfortunately, for many of us this declaration is not always followed by a complete yielding of all aspects of our lives to God's control. This complete yielding of the direction of our lives will be discussed in the next step.

The Bible goes on, in verse ten, to clarify what has already been stated in verse nine: it is faith that produces righteousness, it is <u>acting on that faith</u> which brings <u>real change</u> and it is real change that <u>delivers us</u> from our <u>sin</u> or <u>dysfunction.</u>

    Ro 10:10 For with the heart man believeth unto righteousness; and with the mouth confession is made unto salvation.

2. <u>Salvation or wholeness comes only through believing in Jesus and acting according to our faith.</u>

    Ac 4:12 Neither is there salvation in any other: for there is none other name under heaven given among men, whereby we must be saved.

3. <u>The Gospel or good news about Jesus is the life-changing force that results in complete wholeness for everyone who believes it.</u>

    Ro 1:16 For I am not ashamed of the gospel of Christ: for it is the power of God unto salvation to every one that believeth; to the Jew first, and also to the Greek.

4. <u>It is God's will that everyone be saved.</u>

    1 Ti 2:4 Who will have all men to be saved, and to come unto the knowledge of the truth.

My Experience

In these steps, Peter has described what he experienced in his own spiritual road to maturity (see Chapter 7). Through the lives of numerous other Christians, we find additional corroboration that these steps provide a reasonably consistent pattern of spiritual growth. (See the models for achieving each step in the remainder of this book.) In my own Christian experience, I have also found this to be true.

I was born into a family that for several generations had attended what I would call today, an ecclesiastical church. My mother's side of the family included a number of pastors. I was baptized as an infant and, as is the tradition in this type of church, I studied church doctrine, and was confirmed when I was a teenager. At that time, I definitely believed in a resurrected Christ, openly confessed that I was a Christian and declared that He was in charge of my life. From what we have already discussed, I met the definition of accepting Christ as my Savior. I was fully convinced that if I died I would have gone to heaven. In reality, I was little different from my non-Christian friends. Although I went to church weekly and even became the principal of the Sunday school while attending college, I somehow never realized that there was any other way to live except to rely primarily on myself to direct the daily details of life and to make and achieve the goals that I set for myself. At this point in my life, I was similar to many others in my denominational church; we were fully convinced that Jesus was our Savior and we had a strong hope of making heaven our home, but, experientially, Christ was not Lord of our lives. God was our solution for eternal life, but we relied primarily on ourselves to meet the needs of this life here on earth.

Do not misunderstand what I am saying. As a child, I did pray for my needs. I especially remember praying every day that a bicycle that I had ordered from a mail order catalogue would come. I was disappointed when it took over a month to arrive. Of course, I never thought to ask God if having that particular bicycle was in His plan for my life. Because my relationship with Christ was little more than an intellectual one, I decided what I wanted to do and hoped that God would help me accomplish it. I wrote essays on why God had to exist and even witnessed to a friend of mine. When I was in trouble, I cried out to God for help. I felt guilty when I did things that were wrong and asked God to forgive me. I felt that I was completely committed to God, was willing to die for Him, and that I had a thorough understanding of the Bible.

I do not remember ever hearing from God at this point in my life. In fact, I remember my logic when considering a critical decision that led to one of the most traumatic times in my life. I had always wanted to be a hero. I understand now this was probably related to my struggle to meet my need for self-worth. As a consequence, in high school, I enrolled and enthusiastically participated in the California Cadet Corps, similar to high school ROTC. After graduation, I applied for a nomination to attend the West Point Military Academy and was turned down twice. At the same time, I was accepted into the AFROTC program at San Diego State College and even received a four-year scholarship. When, after three years of college, I was offered an appointment to West Point, I had a critical decision to make. My AFROTC instructor recommended against it, but I reasoned that if God made me, then He wanted me to be the best I could be. To me, that meant graduating from West Point; even though I would have to start over as a freshman. To abbreviate a much longer story, I resigned from West Point after attending about eight months. I had a hard time putting up with that type of pressured lifestyle and knuckling under to upper classmen younger than myself. Many years later, during Theophostic Ministry (Smith, 1996), I asked the Lord why things had not gone well for me at West Point. He simply said, "I never designed you to do that. That was your idea!"

The problem was that I had never progressed beyond this first step of accepting Jesus as Savior. I was directing my own life. My method of guidance—if you can call it that—was the open door policy. I decided what I wanted to do and tried to make it happen. In fact, at this time in my life it was probably more like, "if the door is closed, kick it down." God was supposed to bless whatever I wanted to do and bail me out if I got in trouble doing it. In fact, I was still my own God running my own life, and He was supposed to be my genie. Although I believe that at this time if I had died I would have gone to heaven, God would not play my game. Even though I was able to re-enter the AFROTC program, graduate, and become a commissioned officer in the United States Air Force, God was already laying plans to bring my self-directed lifestyle to an end. In His mercy, He would not let me continue to be a carnal babe in Christ. He wanted me to grow up!

Chapter 5

Forsaking All
(The Call of the Disciples)

Perhaps the best model we have in the Scriptures concerning evangelism and a call to salvation is that of Jesus' call of his disciples. In the gospels, we are given this story from several different perspectives. Although this method is somewhat different than that currently used in most evangelical churches (preaching the gospel followed by an altar call and a "sinners" prayer), it does provide considerable insight into the process of initial salvation.

1. <u>God draws us to Him through the testimony of others or the preaching of His Word.</u> God used John the Baptist to preach and testify about Christ. He told the people that Jesus would be the anointed one of God. Every Jew knew that Messiah would deliver Israel and bring in a time of great blessing.

   Jo 1:26 John answered them, saying, I baptize with water: but there standeth one among you, whom ye know not;

   27 He it is, who coming after me is preferred before me, whose shoe's latchet I am not worthy to unloose.

2. <u>The process of accepting Jesus as Savior begins with developing trust or faith in Jesus.</u> In this case, they were introduced to Jesus Himself.

   Jo 1:37 And the two disciples heard him speak, and they followed Jesus.

   38 Then Jesus turned, and saw them following, and saith unto them, What seek ye? They said unto him, Rabbi, (which is to say, being interpreted, Master,) where dwellest thou?

3. <u>In order to want to be saved, we must realize that we are lost and cannot meet our own needs.</u> The number ten usually stands for human infirmity and failure.

   Jo 1:39 He saith unto them, Come and see. They came and saw where he dwelt, and abode with him that day: for it was about the tenth hour.

4. <u>In order to be saved, we must overcome our doubt.</u> God sometimes uses supernatural gifts to convince us. Although Nathanael was initially skeptical, he was won over when Jesus exercised the gift of knowledge telling him about his thoughts under the fig tree. It convinced him, because he had a good heart.

   Jo 1:47 Jesus saw Nathanael coming to him, and saith of him, Behold an Israelite indeed, in whom is no guile!

48 Nathanael saith unto him, Whence knowest thou me? Jesus answered and said unto him, Before that Philip called thee, when thou wast under the fig tree, I saw thee.

49 Nathanael answered and saith unto him, Rabbi, thou art the Son of God; thou art the King of Israel.

5.   <u>We must be willing to act according to our faith.</u> Jesus asked Simon Peter to allow Him to preach from his boat. Many times after an altar call, a pastor will ask the persons who raised their hands to come forward in order to pray. This is an act of faith. Nets are usually a type of our methods and ships stand for our capabilities. God will ask us first to do something small with our faith. Jesus asked Simon to thrust out a little from the land.

Lu 5:3 And he entered into one of the ships, which was Simon's, and prayed him that he would thrust out a little from the land. And he sat down, and taught the people out of the ship.

6.   <u>God wants to bless us and will eventually ask us to do something more substantial with our faith.</u> Here Simon was asked to "launch out into the deep and let down his nets."

Lu 5:4 Now when he had left speaking, he said unto Simon, Launch out into the deep, and let down your nets for a draught.

7.   <u>God sometimes asks us to do something that does not make natural sense.</u> Fisherman on the sea of Gennesaret (or Galilee) do not normally fish during the day because the water is so clear that the fish will see and avoid the nets.

Lu 5:5 And Simon answering said unto him, Master, we have toiled all the night, and have taken nothing: nevertheless at thy word I will let down the net.

8.   <u>We must learn that our methods and capabilities are not sufficient for all the blessings that God wants to give us.</u> The nets broke and the ships began to sink.

Lu 5:6 And when they had this done, they inclosed a great multitude of fishes: and their net (methods) brake.

7 And they beckoned unto their partners, which were in the other ship, that they should come and help them. And they came, and filled both the ships (capabilities), so that they began to sink.

9.   <u>We must be convicted by our sins.</u> New Christians are many times astonished by all that God will do for them. God is trying to prove to them that He can meet all of their needs, but sometimes they only come to God for what they can get from Him. Peter was convicted by his sin and was humbled that Jesus would do something like this for him, a sinful man.

Lu 5:8 When Simon Peter saw it, he fell down at Jesus' knees, saying, Depart from me; for I am a sinful man, O Lord.

9 For he was astonished, and all that were with him, at the draught of the fishes which they had taken:

10.   <u>God will challenge us to leave everything, work for His Kingdom, and follow Him.</u> It is fear that our needs will not be met if we follow Christ that hinders us from fully committing our lives to Him. Jesus told them not to fear.

Lu 5:10 And so was also James, and John, the sons of Zebedee, which were partners with Simon. And Jesus said unto Simon, Fear not; from henceforth thou shalt catch men.

11 And when they had brought their ships to land, they forsook all, and followed him.

11. We must be willing to repent in order to be saved. Repentance means to turn one's life around. In this case, Simon Peter, Andrew, James and John made the final decision to change what they were doing and follow Jesus. Although it is not clear if this is an abbreviated version of the same stories that I have previously discussed or another step in their call to discipleship, it is clear that this was a major milestone in their lives. At this time, to leave one's father was to make a major change in one's future life. Christ must become more important than anything else in life.

Mt 4:21 And going on from thence, he saw other two brethren, James the son of Zebedee, and John his brother, in a ship with Zebedee their father, mending their nets; and he called them.

22 And they immediately left the ship and their father, and followed him.

12. When God calls us, He also provides the power to serve Him.

Mt 10:1 And when he had called unto him his twelve disciples, he gave them power against unclean spirits, to cast them out, and to heal all manner of sickness and all manner of disease.

13. He expects us, as His disciples, to rely primarily on Him and not on our own resources.

Mt 10: 7 And as ye go, preach, saying, The kingdom of heaven is at hand.

8 Heal the sick, cleanse the lepers, raise the dead, cast out devils: freely ye have received, freely give.

9 Provide neither gold, nor silver, nor brass in your purses,

10 Nor scrip for [your] journey, neither two coats, neither shoes, nor yet staves: for the workman is worthy of his meat.

11 And into whatsoever city or town ye shall enter, enquire who in it is worthy; and there abide till ye go thence.

The Steps to Salvation

1. God, through the Holy Spirit, draws all men to be saved, come to a knowledge of the truth, and become whole.

2. God demonstrated His love for us through the sacrifice of Jesus Christ on the cross and assures us that He will meet all of our needs according to His riches in glory.

3. God calls us, through His love and goodness, to repent from our dysfunctional attempts to be our own God and run our own lives. Unless we repent, we cannot be saved.

4. God asks us to sacrifice all that we have for the good of the Kingdom of God, to follow Him, and to become His disciples.

5. In order to be saved, we must believe that Jesus is the Son of God and that He rose from the dead. We must also openly confess allegiance to Him, and declare that He is to be the Lord of our lives. Romans 10:9-10

6. When we accept Christ, we are born again, receive the Holy Spirit into our heart, and become new spiritual persons. His Holy Spirit changes us from the inside out, to want to do what is right and to be transformed into the image of Jesus Christ.

7. We can tell that we are saved by our desire to do right, our reliance on God, and the good things that we do. However, we are not saved by these works, but by grace through faith.

8. As our faith grows, we are transformed, revelation by revelation, into the image of Jesus Christ, from selfishness to agape love, and from dysfunction into complete wholeness: mind, emotions, will, and spirit.

PART III

Virtue—Knowing Jesus as My Lord

Chapter 6

Jesus as Lord
I Cannot Direct My Own Life

Even though we might say we believe in Christ, openly confess Him, and say that He is Lord of our lives, this does not necessarily mean that we have actually yielded the direction of our lives to God. The Bible suggests that a person can do many things that look spiritual to convince others that they are Christians when, in reality, they are not saved and do not know Him.

Mt 7:21 Not every one that saith unto me, Lord, Lord, shall enter into the kingdom of heaven; but he that doeth the will of my Father which is in heaven.

22 Many will say to me in that day, Lord, Lord, have we not prophesied in thy name? and in thy name have cast out devils? and in thy name done many wonderful works?

23 And then will I profess unto them, I never knew you: depart from me, ye that work iniquity.

If we refuse to cooperate with God's day-by-day direction of our lives, God's plan for making us completely whole (salvation) can be thwarted or at least made significantly more difficult. The child, who will not obey his parents, makes the wonderful life they intend for him impossible. Either God is our boss, or we are our boss. God will not be our genie and just bless whatever we selfishly want to do! To the extent we seek His direction for our lives, to that extent salvation or the process of moving toward wholeness will be worked out in our lives. From my own experience, I have found that the desire to direct my own life is one of the greatest hindrances to "working out my own salvation." (Philippians 2:12b)

When we try to direct our own steps, we are walking around like a man in a fog without a compass. We may try hard, but we have no idea where we are going and, specifically, what we are called to do. The result, at best, is "carnal Christianity," where although we are trusting God to keep us out of hell, we are still continuing to try to meet our own needs on this earth with our own strength and resources. Until we start trusting God to meet all our needs, we will never be able to overcome our selfishness and grow to the next step of Christian maturity.

As we have previously discussed briefly, the word interpreted as virtue in 2nd Peter 1:5, is the Greek word *arete*." It means a "virtuous course of thought, feeling, or action and suggests any moral excellence such as modesty or purity." In essence, virtue is wanting to do what is right and being willing to do what is right in our innermost being. All of us begin life self-centered, self-focused, and if given a choice, we desire to be fully in control of our lives in order to be self-sufficient in everything. This was the original temptation in the garden—to be the all self-sufficient one or to be our own god. Since everyone is motivated to meet their own needs, if we are not delivered, we are doomed to the "rat race" of life, since each new day brings new needs. When we accept Christ, the Holy Spirit comes into us and we find we have the desire to do what is right. As we have discussed before, because we are needy, we are still biased and desire to meet our own needs above those of others. Because our needs reside in our member called the self, if we are intent on meeting our own needs, we are by definition, selfish. If we should try hard not to be selfish, so that we could be a better person, this very attempt would be selfish because we want to be a better person in order to meet our need to be worthwhile. This trap is only overcome when we fully realize and trust God to meet all our needs. (For more on this subject see my book *Faith Therapy*.)

In order to be delivered from this trap of selfishness, we need to realize that our selfish ways do not work and that we cannot meet our needs through our own efforts, desires, or strategies. In fact, because of the curse that came upon the earth after Adam and Eve fell into sin, the world has become such a difficult place to live in, that no person will ever again be able to live the kind of abundant life that God desires for us without His help.

Ge 3: 16 Unto the woman he said, I will greatly multiply thy sorrow and thy conception; in sorrow thou shalt bring forth children; and thy desire shall be to thy husband, and he shall rule over thee.

17 And unto Adam he said, Because thou hast hearkened unto the voice of thy wife, and hast eaten of the tree, of which I commanded thee, saying, Thou shalt not eat of it: cursed is the ground for thy sake; in sorrow shalt thou eat of it all the days of thy life;

18 Thorns also and thistles shall it bring forth to thee; and thou shalt eat the herb of the field;

19 In the sweat of thy face shalt thou eat bread, till thou return unto the ground; for out of it wast thou taken: for dust thou art, and unto dust shalt thou return.

When we realize that we cannot achieve God's abundant life ourselves in our own efforts or direct our own lives, we are finally ready to try His ways, which are better than ours.

Isa 55:8 For my thoughts are not your thoughts, neither are your ways my ways, saith the LORD.

9 For as the heavens are higher than the earth, so are my ways higher than your ways, and my thoughts than your thoughts.

When we experientially understand and get the revelation that we cannot do it, we finally yield our lives to His direction and become willing to obey what He tells us to do. When this occurs, we have the basic foundation for virtue, which can only be achieved through a life directed by God Himself, relying on God to meet our needs, and a desire to do His will.

However, allowing God to direct our lives is only the beginning in the process of making Him Lord. When this foundation of yielding to God to direct our lives is firmly laid, we can proceed on to develop a personal relationship with Christ, learn to hear His voice, experience His manifested presence in our lives, receive the baptism of the Holy Spirit, and find God's specific call for our lives. Let me make it clear that not everyone has to wait 25 years before progressing beyond accepting Jesus as Savior, as I did.

Lordship

One of the very basic principles of Christianity is that if Jesus is not Lord of our lives, He is not Lord at all. God can help us only to the extent that we actually make Him our Lord and yield to His will for us. If we refuse to do this and continue to direct our own lives and rely on ourselves, we will be little better off than non-believers. Christians who insist on directing their own lives many times expect God to bless what they have decided to do as I did. Because He cares for us and wants us to grow, either we yield to Him or He will watch us flounder until we decide to make Him Lord.

1. Salvation requires declaring that Jesus is Lord. As we have seen, a declaration that He is Lord does not necessarily mean that we have fully yielded all aspects of our lives to God.

   Ro 10:9 That if thou shalt confess with thy mouth the Lord Jesus, and shalt believe in thine heart that God hath raised him from the dead, thou shalt be saved.

   13 For whosoever shall call upon the name of the Lord shall be saved.

2. <u>We must yield our will and our lives unto God.</u>

   Ro 6:16 Know ye not, that to whom ye yield yourselves servants to obey, his servants ye are to whom ye obey; whether of sin unto death, or of obedience unto righteousness?

   2 Co 8:5 And this they did, not as we hoped, but first gave their own selves to the Lord, and unto us by the will of God.

3. <u>Even after we have accepted Christ as our Savior, God will resist our efforts if we continue to want to direct our own life and do evil.</u>

   1 Pe 3:12 For the eyes of the Lord are over the righteous, and his ears are open unto their prayers: but the face of the Lord is against them that do evil.

4. <u>Either God is in charge of our lives or we are.</u>

   Lu 16:13 No servant can serve two masters: for either he will hate the one, and love the other; or else he will hold to the one, and despise the other. Ye cannot serve God and mammon.

5. <u>We do not have enough information to direct our lives.</u>

   Pr 27:1 Boast not thyself of to morrow; for thou knowest not what a day may bring forth.

   Jer 10:23 O LORD, I know that the way of man is not in himself: it is not in man that walketh to direct his steps.

6. <u>If we want God to direct our lives, we must trust Him and quit relying on what we think is best.</u>

   Pr 3:5 Trust in the LORD with all thine heart; and lean not unto thine own understanding.

   6 In all thy ways acknowledge him, and he shall direct thy paths.

7. <u>We will not trust or yield to God until we believe He has our best interest in mind.</u> This is a rudimentary definition of love. If we feel loved, we will love God and want to follow His directions and commandments.

   1 Jo 4:19 We love him, because he first loved us.

8. <u>If we feel unloved by our parents, we will usually have a difficult time yielding our will to God.</u> Our first concept of God comes from our parents. We must realize that <u>God is not like our parents.</u>

   Nu 23:19 God is not a man, that he should lie; neither the son of man, that he should repent: hath he said, and shall he not do it? or hath he spoken, and shall he not make it good?

9. <u>We will not have rest and peace until, through faith, we cease trying to control our own lives.</u>

   Heb 4:11 Let us labour therefore to enter into that rest, lest any man fall after the same example of unbelief.

10. <u>Ultimately, everyone will yield to God.</u>

> Isa 45:23 I have sworn by myself, the word is gone out of my mouth in righteousness, and shall not return, That unto me every knee shall bow, every tongue shall swear.

Developing a Personal Relationship with Christ

When we finally make Jesus Lord of our lives on an experiential level, we are in a position to develop a personal relationship with Him. This is because we are willing to listen to His direction for our lives. When we realize that the totality of our righteousness or wholeness is dependent on our faith "from first to last" (Romans 1:17 NIV), we naturally want to increase our faith. Jesus' disciples made the same request in Luke 17:5 and received an interesting reply. Jesus did not tell them to study the Word of God more or to pray more. He told them that if they just had enough faith to overcome their unbelief they could do great things. He explained that faith had to do with a trusting relationship, where the servant humbly did what he was requested to do and met the needs of his master before his needs were met. The reward of faith comes after we act on our faith. It is through a humble, obedient, and loving relationship with our master that our faith or trust in Him grows. In fact, if we are simply obedient, we should consider ourselves to have only fulfilled the minimum requirement of servanthood. In a more modern rendition, "When we work a job (have faith), we usually do not expect to get paid (receive more faith or blessing) until we have completed it (acted on our faith)." We have to trust our boss to provide our wages after we have accomplished the work. Faith that is acted upon results in more faith. In addition, if we only do what we are told instead of truly having the best interests of the business in mind, we are only an average worker. When we realize that faith or trust comes primarily from a loving relationship, then we can understand that an intimate relationship with God is the key to having faith in Him and His Word, and is required for spiritual growth.

> Lu 17:5 And the apostles said unto the Lord, Increase our faith.
>
> 6 And the Lord said, If ye had faith as a grain of mustard seed, ye might say unto this sycamine tree, Be thou plucked up by the root, and be thou planted in the sea; and it should obey you.
>
> 7 But which of you, having a servant plowing or feeding cattle, will say unto him by and by, when he is come from the field, Go and sit down to meat?
>
> 8 And will not rather say unto him, Make ready wherewith I may sup, and gird thyself, and serve me, till I have eaten and drunken; and afterward thou shalt eat and drink?
>
> 9 Doth he thank that servant because he did the things that were commanded him? I trow not.
>
> 10 So likewise ye, when ye shall have done all those things which are commanded you, say, We are unprofitable servants: we have done that which was our duty to do.

A. W. Tozer, in *The Pursuit of God* (1993) states, "For it is not mere words that nourish the soul, but God Himself, and unless and until the hearers find God in personal experience they are not the better for having heard the truth. The Bible is not an end in itself, but a means to bring men to an intimate and satisfying knowledge of God, that they may enter into him, they may delight in his Presence, may taste and know the inner sweetness of the very God himself in the core and center of their hearts."

1. <u>Relationships offer the greatest arena for the development of faith.</u> As we get to know God and work with Him for the good of the Kingdom of God, we learn by experience that He and His Word can be trusted completely. In turn, He will provide all that we need for ourselves and for the ministries that He has called us to accomplish. Abraham, the father of faith, developed faith in God through experience over a considerable period and became God's friend. This faith and friendship made him righteous.

   > Jas 2:23 And the scripture was fulfilled which saith, Abraham believed God, and it was imputed unto him for righteousness: and he was called the Friend of God.

2. <u>God wants us to seek Him with all of our hearts.</u> This is because the amount of trust or faith we will have in Him is directly related to the depth of our relationship with Him. The more we know and understand Him in depth, the more we will trust Him. The more we trust Him, the more we will eventually obey and serve Him. In addition, the more we obey Him, the more He will manifest Himself to us (which will result in a closer relationship with Him), which will again lead to a greater faith in Him.

De 4:29 But if from thence thou shalt seek the LORD thy God, thou shalt find him, if thou seek him with all thy heart and with all thy soul.

Jer 29:13 And ye shall seek me, and find me, when ye shall search for me with all your heart.

3. <u>Without seeking a powerful personal relationship with God, we will rely on ourselves to do whatever we think is best to meet our own needs.</u> This inevitably results in evil.

2 Chr 12:14 And he did evil, because he prepared not his heart to seek the LORD.

4. <u>God wants to have a friendship with us, but loving relationships take time, communication, obedience, and sacrifice.</u> Most of us have not been willing to pay the price. But for those willing to develop a strong, loving relationship with God, it becomes the key to their ongoing spiritual development.

Ex 33:11 And the LORD spake unto Moses face to face, as a man speaketh unto his friend. And he turned again into the camp: but his servant Joshua, the son of Nun, a young man, departed not out of the tabernacle.

Jo 15:15 Henceforth I call you not servants; for the servant knoweth not what his lord doeth: but I have called you friends; for all things that I have heard of my Father I have made known unto you.

5. <u>When we have a close relationship with God, we are changed by it.</u> When we develop close relationships with other people, we become more like them.

2 Co 3:18 But we all, with open face beholding as in a glass the glory of the Lord, are changed into the same image from glory to glory, even as by the Spirit of the Lord.

6. Prayer is essential to a relationship with God. To develop human relationships, we must communicate with the other person in that relationship. Whatever works in human relationships will also help in developing a relationship with God.

1 Th 5:17 Pray without ceasing.

Php 4:6 Be careful for nothing; but in every thing by prayer and supplication with thanksgiving let your requests be made known unto God.

7. <u>We must cultivate the ability to hear from God in order to have a relationship with Him.</u> God speaks to us through the Scriptures, through intuition, and through spiritual manifestations. Humility, repentance, and honesty are keys to hearing from God.

Jo 10:27 My sheep hear my voice, and I know them, and they follow me:

8. We must be willing to obey God in order to develop a loving relationship and experience His manifested presence.

Jo 14:21 He that hath my commandments, and keepeth them, he it is that loveth me: and he that loveth me shall be loved of my Father, and I will love him, and will manifest myself to him.

9. Fasting helps us mortify the flesh and makes us more sensitive to the Spirit of God.

Ezr 8:23 So we fasted and besought our God for this: and he was intreated of us.

Da 9:3 And I set my face unto the Lord God, to seek by prayer and supplications, with fasting, and sackcloth, and ashes:

10. Worship brings us into the presence of God.

Jo 4:23 But the hour cometh, and now is, when the true worshippers shall worship the Father in spirit and in truth: for the Father seeketh such to worship him.

24 God is a Spirit: and they that worship him must worship him in spirit and in truth.

Learning to Hear His Voice

It has been my experience that God seldom talks to those who are not willing to listen. He speaks to those who are willing to follow, have a personal relationship with Him and obey Him. Our connection or ability to hear God speaking to us is based on our faith in Him. This is clear in the story of Job when, through major losses in his life, his faith was shaken and he complained that God would not speak to him. After his faith was rebuilt, he was again able to hear and know God face-to-face. In my own experience, it was only after I made Him Lord, that I was able to hear His voice clearly and experience His presence.

In the popular book and workbook *Experiencing God: Knowing and Doing the Will of God* (1990), Blackaby states that if a person is unable to hear from God his Christian experience is in trouble at the most fundamental level. If a Christian has not yet learned to hear from God, it is impossible for them to be led by God or to walk according to the Spirit. If they cannot be led by God's Spirit, they will be controlled by their circumstances and will be little better off in making the critical decisions of life than an unbeliever.

1. The first step in hearing from God is being willing to trust and listen to Him.

Ge 3:8 And they heard the voice of the LORD God walking in the garden in the cool of the day: and Adam and his wife hid themselves from the presence of the LORD God amongst the trees of the garden.

Pr 3:5 Trust in the LORD with all thine heart; and lean not unto thine own understanding.

6 In all thy ways acknowledge him, and he shall direct thy paths.

2. Sometimes God speaks and directs us through visions.

Ac 11:5 I was in the city of Joppa praying: and in a trance I saw a vision, A certain vessel descend, as it had been a great sheet, let down from heaven by four corners; and it came even to me:

3. Sometimes He speaks to us through prophets.

Jer 38:20 But Jeremiah said, They shall not deliver thee. Obey, I beseech thee, the voice of the LORD, which I speak unto thee: so it shall be well unto thee, and thy soul shall live.

4. <u>Sometimes He speaks to us through an audible voice.</u>

    1 Sa 3:4 That the LORD called Samuel: and he answered, Here am I.

    10 And the LORD came, and stood, and called as at other times, Samuel, Samuel. Then Samuel answered, Speak; for thy servant heareth.

5. <u>Sometimes He helps and directs us through the ministries of the church.</u>

    Eph 4:11 And he gave some, apostles; and some, prophets; and some, evangelists; and some, pastors and teachers;

    12 For the perfecting of the saints, for the work of the ministry, for the edifying of the body of Christ:

6. <u>Sometimes God speaks to us through circumstances.</u> Unfortunately, for many Christians, this is their sole method of hearing from God.

    Ac 19:9 But when divers were hardened, and believed not, but spake evil of that way before the multitude, he departed from them, and separated the disciples, disputing daily in the school of one Tyrannus.

7. <u>God usually speaks to us through the small voice of our spirit's intuition; not through cataclysmic events, visions, or an audible voice.</u>

    1 Ki 19:11 And he said, Go forth, and stand upon the mount before the LORD. And, behold, the LORD passed by, and a great and strong wind rent the mountains, and brake in pieces the rocks before the LORD; but the LORD was not in the wind: and after the wind an earthquake; but the LORD was not in the earthquake:

    12 And after the earthquake a fire; but the LORD was not in the fire: and after the fire a still small voice.

    Isa 30:21 And thine ears shall hear a word behind thee, saying, This is the way, walk ye in it, when ye turn to the right hand, and when ye turn to the left.

8. <u>God speaks most clearly through His infallible, inspired Word, the Bible.</u>

    2 Ti 3:16 All scripture is given by inspiration of God, and is profitable for doctrine, for reproof, for correction, for instruction in righteousness:

9. <u>We learn to discern the difference between the voice of our soul and our spirit, through the Word of God.</u>

    Heb 4:12 For the word of God is quick, and powerful, and sharper than any twoedged sword, piercing even to the dividing asunder of soul and spirit, and of the joints and marrow, and is a discerner of the thoughts and intents of the heart.

10. <u>We learn to hear His voice through our relationship with Him just as a child or animal learns to know the voice of its mother or shepherd.</u>

    Jo 10:3 To him the porter openeth; and the sheep hear his voice: and he calleth his own sheep by name, and leadeth them out.

11. <u>We can ask God to direct our lives and to tell us His will.</u>

    Ac 16:6 Now when they had gone throughout Phrygia and the region of Galatia, and were forbidden of the Holy Ghost to preach the word in Asia,

    7 After they were come to Mysia, they assayed to go into Bithynia: but the Spirit suffered them not.

12. <u>It is the peace of God that is to rule in our hearts and to confirm God's direction for our lives.</u>

    Co 3:15 And let the peace of God rule in your hearts, to the which also ye are called in one body; and be ye thankful.

Experiencing the Manifested Presence of God

As we have already seen, experiencing the manifested presence of God requires that we have a personal loving relationship with Him and that we are willing to obey His direction for our lives. The Tabernacle, which was a type and shadow of things to come, provides a detailed pattern for coming into the manifested presence of God and developing a loving relationship with Him. The typology of each aspect of the Tabernacle provides us with specific requirements for approaching God. (For a more in-depth description see Slemming, 1974).

1. <u>The Gate—We must enter the gate by trusting Jesus alone.</u>

    Jo 10:9 I am the door: by me if any man enter in, he shall be saved, and shall go in and out, and find pasture.

2. <u>The Courts—We are to enter with thanksgiving and praise.</u>

    Ps 100: 4 Enter into his gates with thanksgiving, and into his courts with praise: be thankful unto him, and bless his name.

3. <u>The Altar of Sacrifice—We must repent, admit that we are sinners and accept the sacrifice of Jesus for our sins.</u>

    Heb 9:26 For then must he often have suffered since the foundation of the world: but now once in the end of the world hath he appeared to put away sin by the sacrifice of himself.

4. <u>The Laver—We must examine ourselves and be washed clean by the Word of God from the daily defilement of our actions.</u>

    Eph 5:26 That he might sanctify and cleanse it with the washing of water by the word,

5. <u>The Holy Place—We must not rely on our own works but on those of Jesus Christ for salvation.</u> Only those who are saved and therefore have become priests of God are qualified to enter into the Holy Place dressed in the priest's garments. Garments normally stand for character, indicating that we are not to attempt to enter the presence of God, relying on our own works, which are unacceptable to God, but instead by the righteousness of Christ as our justification.

Ex 28:43 And they (the priest's garments) shall be upon Aaron, and upon his sons, when they come in unto the tabernacle of the congregation, or when they come near unto the altar to minister in the holy place; that they bear not iniquity, and die: it shall be a statute for ever unto him and his seed after him.

6. <u>The Lampstand—We are to take our place in the church, as the light of the world, and openly confess and exhibit our faith through our Christ-like walk.</u> In order to let our light shine, we must die to the flesh daily. Christ is the shaft of the candlestick and we, the members of the church, are the branches or lamps that need to be trimmed of the flesh daily.

Jo 8:12 Then spake Jesus again unto them, saying, I am the light of the world: he that followeth me shall not walk in darkness, but shall have the light of life.

Mt 5:14 Ye are the light of the world. A city that is set on an hill cannot be hid.

7. <u>The Table of Shew Bread—We are to partake of the Word of God, daily examining ourselves so that through faith we are cleansed and worthy of being part of His body.</u> Today this is symbolized by the Lord's supper. If we are in Christ, we can trust God to meet our every need (the bread of life) just as God meets all of the needs of Christ.

Jo 6:51 I am the living bread which came down from heaven: if any man eat of this bread, he shall live for ever: and the bread that I will give is my flesh, which I will give for the life of the world.

1 Co 11:26 For as often as ye eat this bread, and drink this cup, ye do shew the Lord's death till he come.

28 But let a man examine himself, and so let him eat of that bread, and drink of that cup.

29 For he that eateth and drinketh unworthily, eateth and drinketh damnation to himself, not discerning the Lord's body.

8. <u>The Altar of Incense—We are to bring our prayers of intercession for the saints unto God.</u>

Re 8:4 And the smoke of the incense, which came with the prayers of the saints, ascended up before God out of the angel's hand.

9. <u>The Curtain or Veil—We are to die to our self-life, so that we can receive the life of God.</u> The veil was torn in two when Christ died, so that we can now enter the Holy of Holies.

Mr 15:38 And the veil of the temple was rent in twain from the top to the bottom.

Heb 10:20 By a new and living way, which he hath consecrated for us, through the veil, that is to say, his flesh;

10. <u>The Holy of Holies—We are to enter boldly with spiritual worship, trusting in the blood of Christ, knowing and expecting that He will meet with and manifest Himself to us.</u> The Holy of Holies is our spirit, the center of our heart, in which the Spirit of God dwells.

Heb 4:16 Let us therefore come boldly unto the throne of grace, that we may obtain mercy, and find grace to help in time of need.

11. The mercy seat—We must trust in what Christ has done for us, to find mercy and cleansing for all our sins and failures, so that we are acceptable to God. We must cease from our own labors and efforts. The mercy seat covers the law (which was in the Ark) that we could not keep.

    1 Jo 4:10 Herein is love, not that we loved God, but that he loved us, and sent his Son [to be] the propitiation (mercy seat) for our sins.

    Le 16:13 And he shall put the incense upon the fire before the LORD, that the cloud of the incense may cover the mercy seat that is upon the testimony, that he die not:

12. Ark of the Covenant—We must strive to fill our ark (our heart) with the contents of the Ark of the Covenant. We must have:

    a. The manna or the Word of God.

    b. The moral law of God (which we can now keep as we walk according to the power of the Spirit because Jesus fulfilled the law for us.)

    c. Aaron's rod that budded. This is the authority that Jesus has given to us. The almonds stand for the fruit of the Spirit.

    Heb 9:4 Which had the golden censer, and the ark of the covenant overlaid round about with gold, wherein was the golden pot that had manna, and Aaron's rod that budded, and the tables of the covenant;

13. The Shekinah Glory—Here we meet God face-to-face in the most intimate of relationships, as we worship His Holiness and experience His manifested presence.

    Nu 7:89 And when Moses was gone into the tabernacle of the congregation to speak with him, then he heard the voice of one speaking unto him from off the mercy seat that was upon the ark of testimony, from between the two cherubims: and he spake unto him.

Receiving the Baptism of the Holy Spirit

For some, the critical step of actually making Jesus the experiential Lord of their lives happens at the moment of initial salvation. However, for many other it does not occur until sometime after they are saved. This is also true concerning the baptism of the Holy Spirit. When we trust God to receive the baptism of His Spirit, we fully yield our spirit to the control of the Spirit of God.

The attempt to combine these first two steps into one has caused confusion in the body of Christ. This is especially true when the subject of the baptism of the Holy Spirit is discussed. In many churches, you will hear the pastor state that "when you receive Christ into your heart you receive the Holy Spirit, and that is all of the Holy Spirit you will ever receive." This is true. However, simply having the Holy Spirit in us and experiencing the full manifestation of Holy Spirit in our lives are two different things. Spirits enter us and influence us only to the extent that we desire and yield to them. When we accept Christ, we desire His influence in our lives so He enters us. Nevertheless, He will only be able to change us and manifest Himself in us to the extent that we yield to that influence.

This is clear from the experience of the disciples. When Christ was still on this earth, after His resurrection, He breathed on them and gave them the gift of the Holy Spirit.

Jo 20:22 And when he had said this, he breathed on them, and saith unto them, receive ye the Holy Ghost:

But it was not until Pentecost that it "came upon them" or was fully manifested in their lives.

Ac 2:1 And when the day of Pentecost was fully come, they were all with one accord in one place.

2 And suddenly there came a sound from heaven as of a rushing mighty wind, and it filled all the house where they were sitting.

3 And there appeared unto them cloven tongues like as of fire, and it sat upon each of them.

4 And they were all filled with the Holy Ghost, and began to speak with other tongues, as the Spirit gave them utterance.

Later in the book of Acts, when Philip preached in Samaria and they "received the word of God," the Bible is clear that many were saved and even baptized in water (a clear sign of salvation in the early church). However, it was not until Peter and John traveled all the way from Jerusalem, prayed for them, and laid their hands on them that they received the manifestation of the Holy Ghost.

Ac 8:12 But when they believed Philip preaching the things concerning the kingdom of God, and the name of Jesus Christ, they were baptized, both men and women.

14 Now when the apostles which were at Jerusalem heard that Samaria had received the word of God, they sent unto them Peter and John:

15 Who, when they were come down, prayed for them, that they might receive the Holy Ghost:

16 (For as yet he was fallen upon none of them: only they were baptized in the name of the Lord Jesus.)

17 Then laid they their hands on them, and they received the Holy Ghost.

When a person is saved and baptized, he receives the Spirit of God. According to Romans 8:9, "Now if any man have not the Spirit of Christ, he is none of his." Since the people of Samaria were already saved, it is clear that receiving the Holy Ghost must refer at least to a second experience or further manifestation of the Holy Spirit.

Another example of two separate experiences occurred when Paul passed through Ephesus and met some disciples. Note that they were disciples, that they had repented, and that they did believe. But it was still necessary for Paul to lay his hands on them in order to receive the full manifestation of the Holy Ghost. They spoke in tongues as on the day of Pentecost.

Ac 19:1 And it came to pass, that, while Apollos was at Corinth, Paul having passed through the upper coasts came to Ephesus: and finding certain disciples,

2 He said unto them, Have ye received the Holy Ghost since ye believed? And they said unto him, We have not so much as heard whether there be any Holy Ghost.

3 And he said unto them, Unto what then were ye baptized? And they said, Unto John's baptism.

4 Then said Paul, John verily baptized with the baptism of repentance, saying unto the people, that they should believe on him which should come after him, that is, on Christ Jesus.

5 When they heard this, they were baptized in the name of the Lord Jesus.

6 And when Paul had laid his hands upon them, the Holy Ghost came on them; and they spake with tongues, and prophesied.

Just as we have had three examples that clearly demonstrate the separate experiences of receiving the Holy Spirit and the manifestation of the Holy Spirit, we also have an example of both receiving Christ and the manifestation of the Holy Spirit at the same time. In Acts Chapter 10, we find that the entire group of the friends and relatives of the Gentile centurion Cornelius received Christ and the baptism of the Holy Spirit at the same time. This is clear from the fact that they heard them speak in tongues (as at Pentecost) and that this experience is referred to as the gift of the Holy Ghost.

Ac 10: 44 While Peter yet spake these words, the Holy Ghost fell on all them which heard the word.

45 And they of the circumcision which believed were astonished, as many as came with Peter, because that on the Gentiles also was poured out the gift of the Holy Ghost.

46 For they heard them speak with tongues, and magnify God. Then answered Peter,

47 Can any man forbid water, that these should not be baptized, which have received the Holy Ghost as well as we?

48 And he commanded them to be baptized in the name of the Lord. Then prayed they him to tarry certain days.

I believe that in receiving the baptism of the Holy Spirit, we are allowing God, through faith, to immerse our spirit in the Spirit of God; this is somewhat similar to the baptism of water. Water baptism is dying to our old life of sin and the baptism of the Holy Spirit is dying to our right to control our own lives. Because this entails yielding our entire being to the direction and control of God's Spirit, it is part of this second step. As we have already seen, this step concerns yielding ourselves more fully to the influence of God in our lives. Both John the Baptist and Jesus predicted that there would be a further manifestation of the Spirit, which they described as being baptized with the Holy Ghost.

Mr 1:8 I (John) indeed have baptized you with water: but he (Jesus) shall baptize you with the Holy Ghost.

Ac 1:4 And, being assembled together with them, (Jesus) commanded them that they should not depart from Jerusalem, but wait for the promise of the Father, which, saith he, ye have heard of me.

5 For John truly baptized with water; but ye shall be baptized with the Holy Ghost not many days hence.

8 But ye shall receive power, after that the Holy Ghost is come upon you: and ye shall be witnesses unto me both in Jerusalem, and in all Judaea, and in Samaria, and unto the uttermost part of the earth.

It is clear from these verses that the baptism of the Holy Spirit would result in a deeper personal relationship with God and a more powerful anointing to do God's work.

Although in some Christian denominations there is still controversy over the baptism of the Holy Spirit, this spiritual experience can provide a very significant spiritual catalyst in the life of a believer, just as it did on the day of Pentecost in Acts Chapter 2. Unfortunately, we as people generally defend what we have been taught instead of more openly examining the Scriptures to find out what they really say. As discussed in my book *Transformation!*, two and one half of the tribes of Israel (Reuben, Gad, and the half tribe of Manasseh) asked to be allowed to dwell on the other side of the Jordan River outside of the land of Canaan. God granted their request as long as they were willing to help their brothers first conquer the land of Canaan. I believe that the supernatural parting of the Jordan River stands for the baptism of the Holy Spirit just as the supernatural parting of the Red Sea stands for water baptism. If this is so, then God has clearly indicated that each Christian should be given free choice to dwell on whichever side of this controversy they might choose.

Receiving God's Specific Call for Our Lives

We cannot be a candidate for God's service until we are willing to submit to His direction for our own lives. The Bible makes it clear that we cannot serve two masters. God requires us to value Him and His kingdom above our own families or the struggles that we might have serving Him.

Mt 10:37 He that loveth father or mother more than me is not worthy of me: and he that loveth son or daughter more than me is not worthy of me.

38 And he that taketh not his cross, and followeth after me, is not worthy of me.

When we have accepted Jesus as the Lord of our lives, we have certain obligations that go along with that commitment. We are to find and attend a church. God wants us to participate and financially support it with our tithes and offerings. As part of the body of Christ we are to do whatever we can to assist in whatever work He has chosen us to do. We are to submit to that pastor and the vision that God has given him for that church as long as he submits to the direction of God Himself. We are to do our best to live the Christian life, feed our spirit through the Word of God, witness for Him and obey His directions. This period of time, which has been referred to as our "general call" as a Christian, is a time of testing for future ministry. We must prove that we can be loyal to the body of Christ, faithfully carry out His directions and humbly serve God on a consistent basis.

After a time of testing God will reveal to us a more focused and specific call for our lives. This is the plan for which He has created and designed us even before we were born. Many times, we can get a general idea of our specific call by the talents and gifts that God has given us, but we must still await His specific call. This call can come through any of the many means through which God guides us, but it is critical that we clearly know what God has called us to do and that we absolutely know that it is God Who has called us. Otherwise, if after we have embarked on preparing or actually carrying out our call and meet opposition, we may begin to question if we are actually called. It is important to realize that not everyone is called to be a pastor or missionary. A large number are called to be part of the body of Christ that sends out and supports pastors and missionaries. Only a much smaller number are called to go out into full-time ministry. For example, there were many prophets and teachers at the church at Antioch (Acts 13:1), but only Paul and Barnabas (and later Silas) were sent out.

Whatever our call, God expects us to prepare ourselves prior to the time He actually places us into the ministry. Adequately preparing ourselves, after we know God's will for us, is very important as indicated in Luke Chapter 12. Those who have been given the talents to carry out a specific call for God are then expected to prepare and use them effectively for the Kingdom of God.

Lu 12:47 And that servant, which knew his lord's will, and prepared not himself, neither did according to his will, shall be beaten with many stripes.

48 But he that knew not, and did commit things worthy of stripes, shall be beaten with few stripes. For unto whomsoever much is given, of him shall be much required: and to whom men have committed much, of him they will ask the more.

In the parable of the talents, it is clear that not all of us have the same number of talents. God has given us the right talents for our calling. His expectation of us is in proportion to the talents He has given us. We do not choose how many talents we have, but we can choose how well we use those that have been given to us. In the verses below both the five talent man who made five talents and the two talent man who made two talents received the same commendation. Had the one talent man used his one talent to make another, he also would have received the same commendation. Because the one talent man was afraid and did not have the faith to trust his lord enough to even try to use his talent, it was taken away from him. Our calling from God is something that grows as we are faithful and as we use the talents He has given us.

Mt 25:20 And so he that had received five talents came and brought other five talents, saying, Lord, thou deliveredst unto me five talents: behold, I have gained beside them five talents more.

21 His lord said unto him, Well done, thou good and faithful servant: thou hast been faithful over a few things, I will make thee ruler over many things: enter thou into the joy of thy lord.

22 He also that had received two talents came and said, Lord, thou deliveredst unto me two talents: behold, I have gained two other talents beside them.

23 His lord said unto him, Well done, good and faithful servant; thou hast been faithful over a few things, I will make thee ruler over many things: enter thou into the joy of thy lord.

24 Then he which had received the one talent came and said, Lord, I knew thee that thou art an hard man, reaping where thou hast not sown, and gathering where thou hast not strawed:

25 And I was afraid, and went and hid thy talent in the earth: lo, there thou hast that is thine.

26 His lord answered and said unto him, Thou wicked and slothful servant, thou knewest that I reap where I sowed not, and gather where I have not strawed:

27 Thou oughtest therefore to have put my money to the exchangers, and then at my coming I should have received mine own with usury.

My Experience

The period of my life, directly after I made Jesus Lord of my life on Shemya Island, (described in the introduction of this book) was one of exceptionally rapid spiritual growth. Because I wanted more of Christ in my life, I focused on the things of God. I did everything I could to develop a closer personal relationship with Christ. I desired to see God fully manifested in my life and in the lives of others.

I began having fellowship with other Christians and read everything I could find about the Christian life. When I was reassigned to another base, I would begin searching for a church "where God was alive and well" regardless of the denomination. I just wanted more of Him. I eventually attended churches that were very different from the ones I had grown up attending. This was especially true of those that call themselves Pentecostal or charismatic. I had never been in a church where the gifts of the Spirit were in operation, and I was initially somewhat uncomfortable with this new way of doing things.

One particular church stood out because of the intense love I felt when I attended services there. On one particular Sunday night, I decided to attend that "charismatic" church again after spending several weeks at my denominational church. I have to admit that I was still undecided about the baptism of the Holy Spirit and speaking in tongues because some Christians preached against it. The baptism of the Holy Spirit was the topic of the pastor's sermon that night. When he concluded, he gave an altar call for those wishing to receive the baptism of the Holy Spirit to come forward. Of course, I did not respond or go to the front of the church; but I did feel the Holy Spirit tugging at my heart. By that time, the entire front of the church was filled with those wishing to receive the baptism of the Holy Spirit. I remembered in *The Cross and the Switchblade* (1963) that David Wilkerson put out a fleece to God in order to be sure he should go to New York City to work with the gangs. I told God that if He wanted me to go up to the front; I would need a special invitation just for me!

As I was still speaking those words to myself, the youth pastor stood up, looked in my direction and stated, "there are some more of you that are supposed to be up here." Since I had promised God I would try to do what He told me to do, I went forward. Finally, I had to kneel where the pastors sat since there was no more room at the regular altar. I remember both pastors coming by to pray for me, but without any noticeable result. I do not remember hearing any instruction on how to receive the baptism of the Holy Spirit that night so I just kept on praying to receive it. In my spirit, God said two things to me. First, if I really wanted it, I would have to be willing to give up my reputation and quit being concerned about what other people thought about me. Second, if I really believed that God would give it to me, I would have to be the one to open my mouth and start speaking, believing that what I said would be in "other tongues."

When I yielded to God and stepped out in faith, the power of the Holy Spirit fully manifested itself in me. Suddenly, I knew that I knew that God was real. I spoke in other tongues for over thirty minutes. After that time, when I read the Bible, everything made more sense to me. I was so filled with joy that all I wanted to do was to praise God. When I noticed people as I walked along, I felt intense love for each and every one of them. At this time, I was attending Purdue University part time. As I drove to the college, I would be praising God, and as I walked around the campus, I was filled with tremendous love for everyone I encountered. The baptism of the Holy Spirit was the most powerful and intense experience of the manifestation of God that I have ever received, and it significantly changed my life.

God had more work to do. Do you remember the question that God asked me about giving up my repu-tation? God still had some surgery to do to help me detach from the accomplishments of my life that meant so much to me. Even though I had told the Lord that He was in charge of my life, I still had some of those desires remaining in me to become somebody great. I had volunteered to become a "Combat Controller" for the Air Force. Combat Controllers are elite Air Force air traffic controllers that sometimes parachute in to set up drop and landing zones. I had to convince the flight surgeon that the plate and five screws used to repair my ankle (which I had broken rock climbing at Cathedral Peak in Yosemite National Park) had adequately healed in order to allow me to qualify for parachute training. In God's mercy, due to the needs of the Air Force, I was assigned to be trained as an Air Traffic Control Officer instead of a Combat Controller. Even this was no easy task. After completing Air Traffic Control School, I was assigned for on-the-job train-ing at an officer-training base near the town where I received the baptism of the Holy Spirit. Still somewhat influenced by my own drivenness, I had convinced my trainers to give me days off from my training so that I could attend Purdue University several days each week to work on a Ph. D. in Industrial Engineering.

Everything seemed to be fine until I reached the final phase of training for the approach control position. The approach control position receives aircraft from Air Traffic Control Centers and sequences the airplanes into the landing pattern. For some reason (that I still do not understand to this day), I was having trouble learning how to sequence airplanes on the radarscope and carry out all of my other duties. The instructors determined that I needed more practice so they assigned me to consecutive day shifts. Normally, crews rotated every two days and students were assigned a single trainer. Because I was only on day shifts, I received a new trainer every two days and each had a different way of doing things. So instead of improving, I became more confused and my stress and anxiety grew to the point that there was open discussion about washing me out of the program. If this happened, it would definitely not be good for my career in the Air Force. The inten-sity increased until almost everyone was convinced that I could not do the job. Due to the extreme stress, I was barely functioning well enough to go home after work, practice Air Traffic Control (on a mockup scope I had made at home), and convince myself go back to work the next morning! I had definitely come to an end of myself and was rapidly reaching the conclusion that "I just could not do it."

After I arrived home following another excruciating day of feeling like an absolute failure, I found a comic book in my mailbox. It was from a Christian girl who stayed at my Grandmother's rooming house and who had written to encourage me after I had received the baptism of the Holy Spirit. Although she knew noth-ing of what was currently happening in my life, she believed that God had told her to send me that comic book. It was the comic version of *Prison to Praise* by Merlin Carothers (1970). In it, the author states that we should praise God in everything that is happening in our lives because by faith we know God will work it all for our good (according to Romans 8:28). I told God that if He wanted me to leave the Air Force and do something different, my life belonged to Him. Therefore, I chose to praise and thank Him in my current situation, asking only that it result in His perfect will for me. I would trust and rely on Him no matter what happened. I got down on my knees and raised my hands in praise and worship to my God. The outcome was now up to Him.

Something changed. (Possibly my anxiety level decreased.) By the end of that week, I was fully qualified in the approach control position. In addition, an inspection team was due and my instructors realized that they had failed to send in the paper work saying I was overdue in my training. Rather than be written up by the inspectors, they subtracted from my training time all the time I had spent at Purdue University. This new calculation showed that I had competed training well ahead of schedule. When I left that unit, I received a perfect evaluation for my performance! God humbled me, and when I yielded to His will and relied on Him, He fully restored me. I now knew through experience that in my own strength I was inadequate to live life without relying on God. This experience further increased my desire to fully yield all of my life to His will.

At my next assignment, I was determined to be faithful to my church, read everything I could find about Christianity, and attend almost every Bible study I could find. God began to reveal to me the call He had on my life. At several Bible studies, different individuals prophesied over me that I would preach the gospel. I also had a deep desire to help others and felt directed to begin working on a Master's degree in psychology. One night I had a dream. In this dream, I was standing on one side of a river with vertical banks about twelve feet high. There was a bridge across that river, and on the other side was a long altar. At that altar were a number of people praying and a pastor ministering to them. In the dream, the pastor said to me, "Come over and help me," and I walked across the bridge. When I woke up, intuitively I knew that this dream was from God. I had received my specific call! At that time, I did not realize the significance of the twelve-foot banks on the river. It was exactly 12 years later that I entered the full time ministry; first as a pastor, and later as an associate pastor and counselor.

In this chapter, we have learned that in order for us to fully make Jesus Lord of our lives we must know experientially that we cannot direct our own lives or live the Christian life in our own strength. It is this revelation that motivates us to put our complete trust in God. When we actually rely on Him and prove ourselves faithful, we are finally in a position from which God can use us for the specific mission for which He designed and called us. I believe that God loves us so much that until we learn that we are inadequate in ourselves, He will allow us to continue to struggle until we are willing to fully yield our lives to Him.

Chapter 7

Yielding to the Will of God
(Peter the Rock)

The writers of the Scriptures were inspired by God in all that they wrote. However, inspiration is expressed through the character and the life of the writer. Consequently, by examining Peter's own life and experience, we will be better able to understand the meaning of the verses that he wrote and the steps to spiritual development that he suggested. As we have previously seen, Peter was among the first disciples called by Jesus. Let us reexamine the process that led Peter finally to yield His entire life to the service of God.

1. <u>The Holy Spirit began drawing Peter toward repentance and salvation through the actions of Jesus.</u> In the verses below, as we have already discussed, Jesus first asked Peter for something small; just allow Him to stand in his boat to preach. As Jesus preached from Peter's boat, Peter had the opportunity to hear the Word of God. As he listened Peter's faith grew. (Rom 10:17). Faith in Jesus is the first requirement for salvation.

   Lu 5:3 And he entered into one of the ships, which was Simon's, and prayed him that he would thrust out a little from the land. And he sat down, and taught the people out of the ship.

2. <u>Jesus challenged Peter to act on his faith by launching out into the deep.</u> Even though fishing during the day in the clear waters of the Sea of Galilee contradicted all that Peter had learned as a fisherman, Jesus had asked him to take his boat out into the deep water and throw over the nets. Peter had to decide if he really trusted Jesus. If he did what Jesus asked him to do, he would be making an open declaration that he believed in Jesus. When he acted on his faith, he was abundantly rewarded with what, most likely, was the greatest catch of fish ever taken in the Sea of Galilee.

   Lu 5:4 Now when he had left speaking, he said unto Simon, Launch out into the deep, and let down your nets for a draught.

   5 And Simon answering said unto him, Master, we have toiled all the night, and have taken nothing: nevertheless at thy word I will let down the net.

   6 And when they had this done, they enclosed a great multitude of fishes: and their net brake.

   7 And they beckoned unto their partners, which were in the other ship, that they should come and help them. And they came, and filled both the ships, so that they began to sink.

3. <u>When Peter saw what Jesus could do, he repented of his previous sinful life and called Jesus Lord.</u> The actions of Peter, James, and John in leaving their boats and that entire catch of fish to follow Jesus clearly demonstrates to us that they now trusted Jesus to meet all their needs and trusted Him to be the Lord of their lives.

   Lu 5:8 When Simon Peter saw it, he fell down at Jesus' knees, saying, Depart from me; for I am a sinful man, O Lord.

9 For he was astonished, and all that were with him, at the draught of the fishes which they had taken:

10 And so was also James, and John, the sons of Zebedee, which were partners with Simon. And Jesus said unto Simon, Fear not; from henceforth thou shalt catch men.

11 And when they had brought their ships to land, they forsook all, and followed him.

4. <u>Peter continued to demonstrate his faith in Christ and was rewarded with additional authority as his relationship with Jesus grew.</u>

Mt 16:16 And Simon Peter answered and said, Thou art the Christ, the Son of the living God.

17 And Jesus answered and said unto him, Blessed art thou, Simon Barjona: for flesh and blood hath not revealed [it] unto thee, but my Father which is in heaven.

18 And I say also unto thee, That thou art Peter, and upon this rock I will build my church; and the gates of hell shall not prevail against it.

19 And I will give unto thee the keys of the kingdom of heaven: and whatsoever thou shalt bind on earth shall be bound in heaven: and whatsoever thou shalt loose on earth shall be loosed in heaven.

5. <u>As a new Christian, Peter's faith was still weak.</u> Although he was willing to act on his faith, he was not yet strong enough to continue to believe when the wind and waves came. He did learn, however, that even when he failed, Jesus would be there to save him.

Mt 14:28 And Peter answered him and said, Lord, if it be thou, bid me come unto thee on the water.

29 And he said, Come. And when Peter was come down out of the ship, he walked on the water, to go to Jesus.

30 But when he saw the wind boisterous, he was afraid; and beginning to sink, he cried, saying, Lord, save me.

31 And immediately Jesus stretched forth his hand, and caught him, and said unto him, O thou of little faith, wherefore didst thou doubt?

6. <u>Although Peter had declared Jesus Lord, he was still attempting to be in charge, run his own life and look out for himself; rather than yielding completely to God's plan for him.</u> A large number of examples make this very clear. Peter tried to tell Jesus that he should not go to the cross and was rebuked. On the Mount of Transfiguration, Peter wanted to build three tents for Jesus, Moses, and Elijah, although Jesus had never suggested this. At the Last Supper, he tried to dissuade Jesus from washing his feet, because he thought it was not something someone as important as Jesus should do. Finally, when Jesus was arrested, Peter did not ask Jesus what to do, but drew his sword and cut off the High Priest's servant's ear.

Mt 16:22 Then Peter took him, and began to rebuke him, saying, Be it far from thee, Lord: this shall not be unto thee.

23 But he turned, and said unto Peter, Get thee behind me, Satan: thou art an offence unto me: for thou savourest not the things that be of God, but those that be of men.

Mt 17:1 And after six days Jesus taketh Peter, James, and John his brother, and bringeth them up into an high mountain apart,

4 Then answered Peter, and said unto Jesus, Lord, it is good for us to be here: if thou wilt, let us make here three tabernacles; one for thee, and one for Moses, and one for Elias.

Jo 13:6 Then cometh he to Simon Peter: and Peter saith unto him, Lord, dost thou wash my feet?

8 Peter saith unto him, Thou shalt never wash my feet. Jesus answered him, If I wash thee not, thou hast no part with me.

9 Simon Peter saith unto him, Lord, not my feet only, but also [my] hands and [my] head.

18:10 Then Simon Peter having a sword drew it, and smote the high priest's servant, and cut off his right ear. The servant's name was Malchus.

11 Then said Jesus unto Peter, Put up thy sword into the sheath: the cup which my Father hath given me, shall I not drink it?

7.   Peter was overconfident in his own ability and lacked spiritual desire. After declaring that he would never deny Jesus, even if he had to die with Him, Peter was unable to pray for even one hour, and fell asleep. As we have seen, although Peter was definitely saved and had declared Jesus Lord of his life, his actions suggested that many times he still controlled his own life, rather than asking for and relying on Jesus for direction. Before he would truly let go of directing his life, he needed a new revelation: that he could not successfully direct his own life relying on his own strength. It is simply not possible to truly live the Christian life in our own strength! For some reason most of us have to find this out the hard way, experientially.

Mt 26:33 Peter answered and said unto him, Though all men shall be offended because of thee, yet will I never be offended.

34 Jesus said unto him, Verily I say unto thee, That this night, before the cock crow, thou shalt deny me thrice.

35 Peter said unto him, Though I should die with thee, yet will I not deny thee. Likewise also said all the disciples.

40 And he cometh unto the disciples, and findeth them asleep, and saith unto Peter, What, could ye not watch with me one hour?

8.   Although Jesus had clearly warned him, and had even prayed that his faith would not fail, Jesus' arrest set the stage for Peter's denial. When confronted, Peter denied that he even knew Jesus three times and "went out and wept bitterly." He had failed three times to be the Christian he had declared himself to be. Through this experience, he finally realized that he could not rely on himself to live the Christian life successfully.

Mt 26:69 Now Peter sat without in the palace: and a damsel came unto him, saying, Thou also wast with Jesus of Galilee.

70 But he denied before them all, saying, I know not what thou sayest.

71 And when he was gone out into the porch, another maid saw him, and said unto them that were there, This fellow was also with Jesus of Nazareth.

72 And again he denied with an oath, I do not know the man.

73 And after a while came unto him they that stood by, and said to Peter, Surely thou also art one of them; for thy speech bewrayeth thee.

74 Then began he to curse and to swear, saying, I know not the man. And immediately the cock crew.

75 And Peter remembered the word of Jesus, which said unto him, Before the cock crow, thou shalt deny me thrice. And he went out, and wept bitterly.

9. <u>When we fail we will either turn to Jesus, repent, and ask for His help, or we will rely even more on our own devices.</u> At this point, Peter had three choices. 1. He could tell no one that he had denied Jesus and act like everything was okay. 2. He could give up on the Christian life and go back to fishing. 3. He could go to Jesus, admit that he could not do it, ask for forgiveness, quit relying on himself and experientially put his full trust in Jesus. Like many Christians who are faced with failure in their Christian life, Peter chose the second. He even convinced a majority of the other disciples to abandon "fishing for men" and go back to "fishing for fish." They were trying to meet their needs again through their own efforts. When they failed, Jesus demonstrated again that He could do for Peter what Peter could not do for himself. Now Peter was finally ready to face his own inadequacy and failure, and put his full trust in Jesus.

Jo 21:2 There were together Simon Peter, and Thomas called Didymus, and Nathanael of Cana in Galilee, and the [sons] of Zebedee, and two other of his disciples.

3 Simon Peter saith unto them, I go a fishing. They say unto him, We also go with thee. They went forth, and entered into a ship immediately; and that night they caught nothing.

6 And he said unto them, Cast the net on the right side of the ship, and ye shall find. They cast therefore, and now they were not able to draw it for the multitude of fishes.

7 Therefore that disciple whom Jesus loved saith unto Peter, It is the Lord. Now when Simon Peter heard that it was the Lord, he girt [his] fisher's coat [unto him], (for he was naked,) and did cast himself into the sea.

11 Simon Peter went up, and drew the net to land full of great fishes, an hundred and fifty and three: and for all there were so many, yet was not the net broken.

10. <u>When we realize we have no other hope and we have been completely humbled, we are finally ready for a life-changing confrontation with Jesus.</u> I believe that in our lives, each one of us eventually has to face the reality of our own inadequacy. Those with more talent and ability just take longer and progress further in life before facing their "concrete wall." In truth, Jesus has been waiting for each of us to come to this point, because it is here that we will finally yield our lives fully to Him. This revelation of our own inadequacy is what He needs in order to continue the process of transforming our lives. In the verses below, we find Peter so void of his self-confidence, that he is even unwilling to state that he loves Jesus unconditionally. To understand correctly this exchange of words, we need to understand the two Greek words translated as love in these verses. Agape is unconditional love and commitment and Phileo is to be fond of someone. What is significant here is that Peter is so humbled by his failure, that he refuses to make a full unconditional commitment to Jesus and admits that all he can only guarantee that he is still fond of Jesus. The fact that Jesus repeats the question three times clearly suggests that He is addressing Peter's denial. Jesus concludes by calling Peter to the specific ministry planned for him in the early church and predicting that Peter will be restored to such a degree by relying on Christ, that he will eventually die on a cross for Jesus rather than deny Him again. When we recognize our weakness, we are finally qualified for ministry.

Jo 21:15 So when they had dined, Jesus saith to Simon Peter, Simon, [son] of Jonas, lovest (agape) thou me more than these? He saith unto him, Yea, Lord; thou knowest that I love (phileo) thee. He saith unto him, Feed my lambs.

16 He saith to him again the second time, Simon, [son] of Jonas, lovest (agape) thou me? He saith unto him, Yea, Lord; thou knowest that I love (phileo) thee. He saith unto him, Feed my sheep.

17 He saith unto him the third time, Simon, [son] of Jonas, lovest (phileo) thou me? Peter was grieved because he said unto him the third time, Lovest (phileo) thou me? And he said unto him, Lord, thou knowest all things; thou knowest that I love (phileo) thee. Jesus saith unto him, Feed my sheep.

18 Verily, verily, I say unto thee, When thou wast young, thou girdedst thyself, and walkedst whither thou wouldest: but when thou shalt be old, thou shalt stretch forth thy hands, and another shall gird thee, and carry thee whither thou wouldest not.

19 This spake he, signifying by what death he should glorify God. And when he had spoken this, he saith unto him, Follow me.

11. <u>After we have truly made Jesus Lord, we must quietly wait for His direction and be careful not to try to do things for Him by our own efforts.</u> After his call to ministry, Peter and the remainder of the 120 disciples met together in the upper room as preparation for what Christ had promised. As they reached out in faith to God, yielding themselves fully to the will of God, they were immersed in the manifested power of the baptism of the Holy Spirit.

Ac 2:1 And when the day of Pentecost was fully come, they were all with one accord in one place.

2 And suddenly there came a sound from heaven as of a rushing mighty wind, and it filled all the house where they were sitting.

3 And there appeared unto them cloven tongues like as of fire, and it sat upon each of them.

4 And they were all filled with the Holy Ghost, and began to speak with other tongues, as the Spirit gave them utterance.

12. <u>In God's timing, as we rely on and are empowered by Him, we can do much more than we could even imagine doing in our own strength.</u> With the empowerment of the Holy Spirit, Peter now had the courage to declare boldly the Word of God. When we realize that we, in ourselves, are inadequate to do God's will, and we finally decide to rely on Him, we suddenly find that in His strength we can do anything He calls us to do.

Ac 2:14 But Peter, standing up with the eleven, lifted up his voice, and said unto them, Ye men of Judaea, and all [ye] that dwell at Jerusalem, be this known unto you, and hearken to my words:

22 Ye men of Israel, hear these words; Jesus of Nazareth, a man approved of God among you by miracles and wonders and signs, which God did by him in the midst of you, as ye yourselves also know:

23 Him, being delivered by the determinate counsel and foreknowledge of God, ye have taken, and by wicked hands have crucified and slain:

24 Whom God hath raised up, having loosed the pains of death: because it was not possible that he should be holden of it.

37 Now when they heard [this], they were pricked in their heart, and said unto Peter and to the rest of the apostles, Men [and] brethren, what shall we do?

38 Then Peter said unto them, Repent, and be baptized every one of you in the name of Jesus Christ for the remission of sins, and ye shall receive the gift of the Holy Ghost.

4:9 If we this day be examined of the good deed done to the impotent man, by what means he is made whole;

10 Be it known unto you all, and to all the people of Israel, that by the name of Jesus Christ of Nazareth, whom ye crucified, whom God raised from the dead, even by him doth this man stand here before you whole.

13. <u>In God's power, even miracles are possible.</u> Note that Peter refused to take any credit, realizing that it was his faith in God, not in himself, that had worked this miracle. God will not bless what we do if we try to take the credit for it, instead of giving all the glory to Him.

Ac 3:1 Now Peter and John went up together into the temple at the hour of prayer, [being] the ninth [hour].

3 Who seeing Peter and John about to go into the temple asked an alms.

4 And Peter, fastening his eyes upon him with John, said, Look on us.

6 Then Peter said, Silver and gold have I none; but such as I have give I thee: In the name of Jesus Christ of Nazareth rise up and walk.

11 And as the lame man which was healed held Peter and John, all the people ran together unto them in the porch that is called Solomon's, greatly wondering.

12 And when Peter saw [it], he answered unto the people, Ye men of Israel, why marvel ye at this? or why look ye so earnestly on us, as though by our own power or holiness we had made this man to walk?

14. <u>Once we have truly made Jesus Lord of our lives and rely only on Him, even other people will be amazed at the transformation that will occur in us.</u> Peter's transformation and new boldness was so dramatic that even the Pharisees recognized the change in him.

Ac 4:8 Then Peter, filled with the Holy Ghost, said unto them, Ye rulers of the people, and elders of Israel,

9 If we this day be examined of the good deed done to the impotent man, by what means he is made whole;

10 Be it known unto you all, and to all the people of Israel, that by the name of Jesus Christ of Nazareth, whom ye crucified, whom God raised from the dead, even by him doth this man stand here before you whole.

13 Now when they saw the boldness of Peter and John, and perceived that they were unlearned and ignorant men, they marvelled; and they took knowledge of them, that they had been with Jesus.

19 But Peter and John answered and said unto them, Whether it be right in the sight of God to hearken unto you more than unto God, judge ye..

15. <u>Great things will happen, without any planning on our part, when we rely on God's power, as we walk according to the direction of the Holy Spirit.</u> By relying on Christ, Peter performed special miracles and even raised the dead.

Ac 5:15 Insomuch that they brought forth the sick into the streets, and laid [them] on beds and couches, that at the least the shadow of Peter passing by might overshadow some of them.

9:40 But Peter put them all forth, and kneeled down, and prayed; and turning [him] to the body said, Tabitha, arise. And she opened her eyes: and when she saw Peter, she sat up.

41 And he gave her [his] hand, and lifted her up, and when he had called the saints and widows, presented her alive.

Making Jesus Lord

1. After we have accepted Jesus as our Savior, we must experientially make Him Lord, turning our lives over to the direction of the Holy Spirit. Until we do this, we will continue to try to direct our own lives and meet our own needs.

2. As long as we continue to try to direct our own lives and rely primarily on ourselves, we will limit the power of God in our lives, remain carnal Christians, and receive the negative consequences of our selfish choices.

3. Although we might deny it, most of us trust and rely on ourselves more than we do on God. Most of us will experience some type of failure in our lives. At this point, we will either continue in pride doing what we are doing with a hardened heart, or repent, humble ourselves, and truly turn our lives over to God.

4. In order to experience a fuller manifestation of the Spirit of God, we can accept the baptism of the Holy Spirit through faith.

5. Once we have made Jesus Lord, we must develop a deep, personal relationship with Him and learn to distinguish between His voice, the voice of Satan, and our own thoughts.

6. We must continue to faithfully serve God's general call on our life, seek to know His specific call, prepare ourselves, and carry it out.

7. When we finally trust in and allow God to direct our lives, He will use us beyond anything we have ever imagined and bring peace to our lives.

PART IV

Knowledge—Knowing God as My Master

Chapter 8

External Motivation
I Cannot Obey the Law

2 Pe 1:5 And beside this, giving all diligence, add to your faith virtue; and to virtue knowledge;

After achieving faith and virtue, the next step is knowledge. The word translated from the Greek is not the same as we have discussed earlier as spiritual understanding or revelation. It is the word *gnosis* which means "a general intelligence, or understanding, the general knowledge of Christian religion; the deeper more perfect and enlarged knowledge of this religion, such as belongs to the more advanced, especially of things lawful and unlawful for Christians."

Once we have finally realized that we are inadequate to direct our lives and rely on our own strength, we have a deepening desire to trust God and to do His will. As we study the Word of God in depth, we find that God has clearly given us direction concerning His will about what He views as right and wrong. This is called the law.

As we have discussed earlier, there are two types of the law: 1. The ceremonial law which teaches us about God's holiness and how to approach a holy God. These are the laws of Leviticus that are normally referred to as the Jewish laws, which are concerned with the sacrifices, about what could be eaten, and how to cleanse oneself from defilement. These laws teach us that we must be holy and undefiled through the sacrifice of Jesus, in order to have a personal relationship with God. 2. The moral law is the Ten Commandments, which was given by God to Moses and the Israelites on Mount Sinai. It was given to provide them and us with directions on how to live morally in relationships with God and others. God has made it clear throughout the Bible that the law itself is good and that the requirements of the law will never pass away. Because Jesus completely fulfilled the law, those that are in Christ (Christians) are no longer subject to the legalistic requirements of the law. Instead, we are set free to obey the spirit of the law through loving God and others.

Ro 7:12 Wherefore the law is holy, and the commandment holy, and just, and good.

De 10:13 To keep the commandments of the LORD, and his statutes, which I command thee this day for thy good?

Mt 5:18 For verily I say unto you, Till heaven and earth pass, one jot or one tittle shall in no wise pass from the law, till all be fulfilled.

Ga 5:14 For all the law is fulfilled in one word, even in this; Thou shalt love thy neighbour as thyself.

The Purpose of the Law

God has given us the law for a number of important reasons:

1. <u>The ceremonial law was given to us to reveal the holiness of God and to teach us that we must be perfectly holy in order to approach God.</u>

    Le 11:44 For I am the LORD your God: ye shall therefore sanctify yourselves, and ye shall be holy; for I am holy: neither shall ye defile yourselves with any manner of creeping thing that creepeth upon the earth.

    45 For I am the LORD that bringeth you up out of the land of Egypt, to be your God: ye shall therefore be holy, for I am holy.

2. <u>The moral law was given to us to teach what is right and wrong and to clarify our understanding of sin and its consequences.</u> Without a clear boundary line of what is right and wrong (the law), we might convince ourselves that the evil we are doing is not sinful. Because we now have a clearly defined law with a prescribed penalty (death), we can no longer say that we did not understand that what we did was wrong or that we did not know the penalty for what we did.

    Ro 5:13 For until the law sin was in the world: but sin is not imputed when there is no law.

    7:7 What shall we say then? Is the law sin? God forbid. Nay, I had not known sin, but by the law: for I had not known lust, except the law had said, Thou shalt not covet.

    13 Was then that which is good made death unto me? God forbid. But sin, that it might appear sin, working death in me by that which is good; that sin by the commandment might become exceeding sinful.

3. <u>The moral law made it clear that we are sinners.</u>

    Ro 3:19 Now we know that what things soever the law saith, it saith to them who are under the law: that every mouth may be stopped, and all the world may become guilty before God.

    20 Therefore by the deeds of the law there shall no flesh be justified in his sight: for by the law is the knowledge of sin.

4. <u>The moral law led us to a fear or reverence of God, knowing that He hates sin, sees it as rebellion against His kingdom and will punish it.</u> It is the <u>beginning</u> of wisdom and knowledge. However, we must realize that the fear or reverence of God is not the final goal of what God wishes to accomplish in us.

    2 Chr 19:7 Wherefore now let the fear of the LORD be upon you; take heed and do it: for there is no iniquity with the LORD our God, nor respect of persons, nor taking of gifts.

    Pr 16:6 By mercy and truth iniquity is purged: and by the fear of the LORD men depart from evil.

    Ps 111:10 The fear of the LORD is the beginning of wisdom: a good understanding have all they that do his commandments: his praise endureth for ever.

5. <u>The moral law was given to keep our carnality in check until Christ is formed in us.</u> The Bible calls the law our schoolmaster. In biblical times, the schoolmaster was a trusted slave that looked after a son between the ages of six and sixteen to ensure he did what was right and did not embarrass the family. After we accept Christ, we must have time to grow spiritually until we are able to overcome sin in our lives through faith. Until this happens, sin must be curbed in us by the external motivation of the law and the fear of God. Without it, we could possibly end up like Noah's generation (Genesis 6:5) or the time period in the book of Judges when there was no king and "everyone did what was right in their own eyes." (Judges 17:6, 21:25)

Ga 3:19 Wherefore then serveth the law? It was added because of transgressions, till the seed should come to whom the promise was made; and it was ordained by angels in the hand of a mediator.

23 But before faith came, we were kept under the law, shut up unto the faith which should afterwards be revealed.

24 Wherefore the law was our schoolmaster to bring us unto Christ, that we might be justified by faith.

6. <u>The moral law was given to show us that we cannot keep the law.</u> The curse of the law is that when we are told not to do something we either rebel or try to keep it through our own efforts. Both of these fail, and we find that no matter how hard we try we cannot keep the law perfectly.

Ro 7:18 For I know that in me (that is, in my flesh,) dwelleth no good thing: for to will is present with me; but how to perform that which is good I find not.

19 For the good that I would I do not: but the evil which I would not, that I do.

7. <u>The moral law was given to prepare us for something even better—the freedom of internal motivation by grace through the Spirit.</u>

2 Co 3:7 But if the ministration of death, written and engraven in stones, was glorious, so that the children of Israel could not stedfastly behold the face of Moses for the glory of his countenance; which glory was to be done away:

8 How shall not the ministration of the spirit be rather glorious?

8. <u>It leads to God's goal of having us fulfill the moral law through relying on God by walking according to the Spirit motivated by love.</u>

Ro 8:3 For what the law could not do, in that it was weak through the flesh, God sending his own Son in the likeness of sinful flesh, and for sin, condemned sin in the flesh:

4 That the righteousness of the law might be fulfilled in us, who walk not after the flesh, but after the Spirit.

The Problem of External Control

Although external control serves a temporary purpose, it is not God's ultimate plan for us. This is because the external control of the law fails in a number of important areas:

1. <u>We rebel against it.</u> When we are told not to do something, we automatically are tempted to do it. This internal rebellion results in attempts to find a way to get around the law rather than to obey it. This is because external control violates our free will. The Pharisees devised numerous ways to circumvent the law while externally appearing to obey it. In the end, external control will eventually result in open rebellion.

Ro 7:22 For I delight in the law of God after the inward man:

23 But I see another law in my members, warring against the law of my mind, and bringing me into captivity to the law of sin which is in my members.

2. <u>It cannot make us want to obey the law.</u> It is the Spirit of God within us that makes us want to obey God.

Ro 8:3 For what the law could not do, in that it was weak through the flesh, God sending his own Son in the likeness of sinful flesh, and for sin, condemned sin in the flesh:

4 That the righteousness of the law might be fulfilled in us, who walk not after the flesh, but after the Spirit.

3. <u>It cannot transform us internally or make us into better people.</u> We cannot change ourselves through the flesh, but only through the power of God's Spirit.

Ga 3:2 This only would I learn of you, Received ye the Spirit by the works of the law, or by the hearing of faith?

3 Are ye so foolish? having begun in the Spirit, are ye now made perfect by the flesh?

4. <u>It leads to evaluating ourselves by our performance and the approval of others.</u> This results in the extreme emotional swings of pride and shame. Our performance in obeying the law is easily attached to our self-evaluation. When we do good things, we feel happy, but when we fail, we experience shame. Since we cannot obey the law fully, we find ourselves on an emotional roller coaster dependent on our and other's evaluation of our performance.

Jas 2:10 For whosoever shall keep the whole law, and yet offend in one point, he is guilty of all.

Ro 8:5 For when we were in the flesh, the motions of sins, which were by the law, did work in our members to bring forth fruit unto death.

5. <u>External obedience is based on fear and results in a loss of feelings toward the one feared.</u> Because external motivation is based on obligation, not love, it leads to a loss of good feeling for the one in authority. Life becomes little more than living in a prison camp and thinking of ways to make an escape. God's ultimate goal for His people is motivation by love.

Jo 14:15 If ye love me, keep my commandments.

The Analogy of Parenting

In order to understand this stage of spiritual development to a greater degree, we can compare it to the raising of children. Until small children reach a reasonable level of maturity, external control in some form must be relied upon to keep them from bringing chaos to the family. If the children believe that their parents do not love them or have their best interest in mind, they will rebel against what their parents tell them to do and will do everything in their power to do what they want to do. They will only obey to the extent they see something as beneficial to themselves or to the extent that the consequences of disobeying exceed the benefits. They will only regret getting caught, not doing something bad. If they believe their parents love them, they will feel shame when they disobey and may try to hide their mistakes from their parents—frequently by lying. This many times brings distance to the child-parent relationship.

Of course, all parents want their children to obey out of love because they want to; not because they have to obey. The teenage years can become a difficult time in the growth process because teenagers can be more deceitful, manipulative, and do what they want to do, while obeying only the letter of the law. If the parents continue to use excessive external control during this time, their children will never internalize their parent's rules and will not learn self-discipline. When the children finally leave home and the external control of the family no longer exists, they will usually find life extremely challenging since they have never learned how to do what is right because they want to do it. Without self-control, they may even find themselves trying to circumvent the laws of society and suffer severe consequences.

Clearly, parents want their children to develop self-control and do what is right because they want to do it, not because they have to do it. To do this, parents must set their children progressively more free as they learn to take the responsibility for their own actions. They learn self-discipline as they are allowed to make their own decisions and receive the consequences of those decisions. This is the only way to develop internal control. In the same way, God does not want us obeying Him because we have to do it. Consequently, He sets us free as we grow spiritually to make our own decisions and learn from our own consequences, so that we too will learn self-discipline.

Many Christians have not progressed beyond this stage of the law. Because there is such a dramatic difference between Christians who are still externally motivated under the law and those who want to serve Christ, different terms have been developed in research for each of these. Those whose religion is motivated externally are called extrinsic compared to those who are motivated from within who are called intrinsic. Extrinsic Christians go to church and serve God out of obligation, attend church when they have to, and give and do as little as necessary. Intrinsic Christians want to attend, give, and serve God because they are internally motivated to want to do so out of appreciation and love. God wants each of us to grow up to want to serve Him out of love and appreciation—not because we have to do what is right.

My Experience

After fully committing my life to Christ and receiving the baptism of the Holy Spirit, I began reading, studying, and preparing myself for ministry. Since I was still serving in the United States Air Force, I was reassigned approximately every four years. When I arrived at my next assignment, I would search out a church and Bible studies where "God was alive and well." Most of these churches had some blend of legalism and liberty, even though they all confessed salvation by faith through grace and not by works. At one particular church, several of us were visiting a new convert. She was somewhat disillusioned because immediately after accepting Christ, the friend who had led her to the Lord then told her all the things she could not do since she was now a Christian. At another church, everyone in leadership was required to get rid of their television sets. Another time, we were told that no one should wear a cross because "you would not wear a shotgun to remember a friend that was killed by one."

Although I struggled and fell back into legalism from time to time, trying various methods to make myself do "what was right," I found that, like Paul, the good I would, I seldom did for very long in my own strength. Although I had fully given my life to God, no matter how hard I tried, I just could not seem to find the right "key" for living the Christian life. I tried, and when I eventually failed, I felt ashamed and felt that I had failed God. When I was able to do something for God, I felt good about myself, but that never lasted for long. I could always do better, couldn't I? I lived on an emotional roller coaster that depended on my perception as to how well I was pleasing God. Like many young men, I struggled with lust for the things of this world and when I was caught up in them, I experienced deep shame and vowed repeatedly to try to do better the next time. I remember a friend of mine in the church who married to control his sexual lust, but even getting married did not free him from his struggle to do what was right. Even after I was married and reached the level of church leadership, I still had times of struggle. It just did not seem that there was any way to live the Christian life and successfully obey the law! Of course, this was the very thing that God wanted me to learn!

Today, it seems almost too simple. What I needed to understand and accept was that I truly could not live the Christian life and succeed in obeying the law. The law was the stumbling block that led to the failure of the Jewish nation and that leads to our failure to live the Christian life as well. God never expected us to do it in our own strength. That is why He sent His son to fulfill the law for us. Only He could do it, and He had already provided the answer that I needed—His grace. Until I understood this, I was doomed to a life of frustration and failure.

Chapter 9

Trying to Obey the Law
(The Model of the Pharisees)

The Pharisees at the time of Christ were a group of people that dedicated themselves totally to obeying the law. Just as those today who try to find security in obedience to a set of laws, the Pharisees were so zealous in their attempts to insure that the law was wholly obeyed they attempted to "make a fence around the law." This was to ensure that they and others would not accidentally violate it. In doing so, they exaggerated the law to the point that it could not possibly be kept. Yet they provided loop holes in it for themselves so that they could be justified. The Mishna, or "second law" and the Talmud (explanatory notes on the Mishna) were their attempt to explain and build this fence. The Pharisees took legalism to such an extreme that today they might be diagnosed with Obsessive-Compulsive Personality Disorder.

These carried prohibitions farther than the written Law or oral law of Moses, in order to protect the Jewish people from temptations to sin or pollution. For example, the injunction, "Thou shalt not seethe a kid in his mother's milk," (Ex 23:19, 34:26, De 14:21); was interpreted by the oral law to mean that the flesh of quadrupeds might not be cooked, or in any way mixed with milk for food; so that even now amongst the orthodox Jews, milk may not be eaten for some hours after meat. But this was extended by the wise men to the flesh of birds; and now, owing to this "fence to the Law, " the admixture of poultry with any milk, or its preparations, is rigorously forbidden. When once a decree of this kind has been passed, it could not be reversed; and it was subsequently said that not even Elijah himself could take away anything from the 18 points which had been determined on by the school of Shammai and the school of Hillel. (Smith's Bible Dictionary, 1970)

As we will see, Jesus Himself was challenged and He condemned the Pharisees at every point. Unfortunately, today even many Christian churches have fallen back into legalism and have built their own hedge around the law by dress codes and traditions. Many others emphasize superficial actions and traditions over the things of the Spirit. This model demonstrates to us the dangers of the legalistic life.

1. <u>Legalism cannot save us.</u> No matter how much we may try to obey the law, we cannot ever do it perfectly. We must repent of trying to work our way to heaven and trust in Christ to be saved. John the Baptist made this clear when preaching to the Pharisees.

   Mt 3:7 But when he saw many of the Pharisees and Sadducees come to his baptism, he said unto them, O generation of vipers, who hath warned you to flee from the wrath to come?

2. <u>Self-effort can never make us good enough.</u> When someone tells us not to do something, we either naturally rebel or attempt to do it in our own strength. Real righteousness only comes by faith, as we are free to want to do what is right out of our heart and rely on Christ to transform us. To God the "righteousness of the Pharisees" was "filthy rags" because it was motivated by their selfish attempts to be worthwhile, significant, and secure.

Mt 5:20 For I say unto you, That except your righteousness shall exceed the righteousness of the scribes and Pharisees, ye shall in no case enter into the kingdom of heaven.

3. <u>Self-effort leads to pride, judging others, a lack of compassion, and thinking that we are better than others.</u> The Pharisees looked down on everyone who was not a Pharisee.

    Mt 9:11 And when the Pharisees saw it, they said unto his disciples, Why eateth your Master with publicans and sinners?

    Lu 18:10 Two men went up into the temple to pray; the one a Pharisee, and the other a publican.

    11 The Pharisee stood and prayed thus with himself, God, I thank thee, that I am not as other men are, extortioners, unjust, adulterers, or even as this publican.

    12 I fast twice in the week, I give tithes of all that I possess.

    13 And the publican, standing afar off, would not lift up so much as his eyes unto heaven, but smote upon his breast, saying, God be merciful to me a sinner.

    14 I tell you, this man went down to his house justified rather than the other: for every one that exalteth himself shall be abased; and he that humbleth himself shall be exalted.

    Jo 8:3 And the scribes and Pharisees brought unto him a woman taken in adultery; and when they had set her in the midst,

    4 They say unto him, Master, this woman was taken in adultery, in the very act.

    5 Now Moses in the law commanded us, that such should be stoned: but what sayest thou?

4. <u>Legalists are blinded to their own motivation and place the harshest criticism on what others do.</u> Because they were jealous of Jesus' power and miracles, they said He was doing it by the power of Satan. In actuality, legalism opens us to the influence of Satan.

    Mt 9:34 But the Pharisees said, He casteth out devils through the prince of the devils.

5. <u>They get so caught up in trying to obey the law, that they somehow miss the very intent of the law.</u> The Sabbath Day was created to prevent us from being so obsessed with work that we do not take time for rest. The Pharisees were complaining that the disciples were plucking and eating grain. I doubt that the disciples were working so hard harvesting a few handfuls of grain that it interfered with their observance of the Sabbath day of rest.

    Mt 12:1 At that time Jesus went on the sabbath day through the corn; and his disciples were an hungred, and began to pluck the ears of corn, and to eat.

    2 But when the Pharisees saw it, they said unto him, Behold, thy disciples do that which is not lawful to do upon the sabbath day.

    3 But he said unto them, Have ye not read what David did, when he was an hungred, and they that were with him;

    4 How he entered into the house of God, and did eat the shewbread, which was not lawful for him to eat, neither for them which were with him, but only for the priests?

    5 Or have ye not read in the law, how that on the sabbath days the priests in the temple profane the sabbath, and are blameless?

6. <u>Legalists attempt to make themselves feel secure by making their world black and white.</u> They are unable to accept any challenge to their point of view, and will attack anyone who challenges them. To truly listen and consider another's point of view would present the possibility that they might be wrong. If it was possible that they were wrong, then their attempt to make themselves completely secure in a black and white world would fail. Another sign of legalism is a belief that they and only they have all the answers to life. We should note that they simply ignored twenty-four of their own laws including the injunction, "Thou shalt not kill," in order to crucify Jesus.

   Mt 12:14 Then the Pharisees went out, and held a council against him, how they might destroy him.

7. <u>They have a hard time believing that anything is of God unless it fits into their legalistic concept of God.</u> They usually see God as one who demands strict performance of the law and who will severely punish every infraction. Even though Jesus had performed many miracles, they asked Him for another sign that He was from God. No matter how many signs He performed, they would never believe Him because His love for people did not fit their concept of God.

   Mt 12:38 Then certain of the scribes and of the Pharisees answered, saying, Master, we would see a sign from thee.

8. <u>Legalists value their own ideas and traditions over the laws of God.</u> The Pharisees honored their own traditions even when they directly contradicted biblical laws.

   Mt 15:1 Then came to Jesus scribes and Pharisees, which were of Jerusalem, saying,

   2 Why do thy disciples transgress the tradition of the elders? for they wash not their hands when they eat bread.

   3 But he answered and said unto them, Why do ye also transgress the commandment of God by your tradition?

   4 For God commanded, saying, Honour thy father and mother: and, He that curseth father or mother, let him die the death.

   5 But ye say, Whosoever shall say to his father or his mother, It is a gift, by whatsoever thou mightest be profited by me;

   6 And honour not his father or his mother, he shall be free. Thus have ye made the commandment of God of none effect by your tradition.

   7 Ye hypocrites, well did Esaias prophesy of you, saying,

   8 This people draweth nigh unto me with their mouth, and honoureth me with their lips; but their heart is far from me.

   9 But in vain they do worship me, teaching for doctrines the commandments of men.

9. <u>God is more interested in what comes out of our hearts, than strict adherence to external traditions and rules.</u> He saw the Pharisees as the blind leading the blind.

   Mt 15:10 And he called the multitude, and said unto them, Hear, and understand:

   11 Not that which goeth into the mouth defileth a man; but that which cometh out of the mouth, this defileth a man.

   12 Then came his disciples, and said unto him, Knowest thou that the Pharisees were offended, after they heard this saying?

13 But he answered and said, Every plant, which my heavenly Father hath not planted, shall be rooted up.

14 Let them alone: they be blind leaders of the blind. And if the blind lead the blind, both shall fall into the ditch.

10. <u>Jesus warned His disciples not to accept any legalistic teaching similar to that taught by the Pharisees.</u>

Mt 16:6 Then Jesus said unto them, Take heed and beware of the leaven of the Pharisees and of the Sadducees.

11 How is it that ye do not understand that I spake it not to you concerning bread, that ye should beware of the leaven of the Pharisees and of the Sadducees?

12 Then understood they how that he bade them not beware of the leaven of bread, but of the doctrine of the Pharisees and of the Sadducees.

11. <u>Legalists attempt to interpret the law to fit what they want to do.</u> Here they were trying to get Jesus to agree that divorce was okay.

Mt 19:3 The Pharisees also came unto him, tempting him, and saying unto him, Is it lawful for a man to put away his wife for every cause?

4 And he answered and said unto them, Have ye not read, that he which made them at the beginning made them male and female,

5 And said, For this cause shall a man leave father and mother, and shall cleave to his wife: and they twain shall be one flesh?

6 Wherefore they are no more twain, but one flesh. What therefore God hath joined together, let not man put asunder.

7 They say unto him, Why did Moses then command to give a writing of divorcement, and to put her away?

8 He saith unto them, Moses because of the hardness of your hearts suffered you to put away your wives: but from the beginning it was not so.

9 And I say unto you, Whosoever shall put away his wife, except it be for fornication, and shall marry another, committeth adultery: and whoso marrieth her which is put away doth commit adultery.

12. <u>Even when strongly warned, they will not usually repent but will simply attack the messenger.</u> This is what happened in Jesus' parable, and this is exactly what they tried to do to Jesus immediately after he told the parable.

Mt 21:33 Hear another parable: There was a certain householder, which planted a vineyard, and hedged it round about, and digged a winepress in it, and built a tower, and let it out to husbandmen, and went into a far country:

34 And when the time of the fruit drew near, he sent his servants to the husbandmen, that they might receive the fruits of it.

35 And the husbandmen took his servants, and beat one, and killed another, and stoned another.

36 Again, he sent other servants more than the first: and they did unto them likewise.

37 But last of all he sent unto them his son, saying, They will reverence my son.

38 But when the husbandmen saw the son, they said among themselves, This is the heir; come, let us kill him, and let us seize on his inheritance.

39 And they caught him, and cast him out of the vineyard, and slew him.

40 When the lord therefore of the vineyard cometh, what will he do unto those husbandmen?

41 They say unto him, He will miserably destroy those wicked men, and will let out his vineyard unto other husbandmen, which shall render him the fruits in their seasons.

42 Jesus saith unto them, Did ye never read in the scriptures, The stone which the builders rejected, the same is become the head of the corner: this is the Lord's doing, and it is marvellous in our eyes?

43 Therefore say I unto you, The kingdom of God shall be taken from you, and given to a nation bringing forth the fruits thereof.

44 And whosoever shall fall on this stone shall be broken: but on whomsoever it shall fall, it will grind him to powder.

45 And when the chief priests and Pharisees had heard his parables, they perceived that he spake of them.

46 But when they sought to lay hands on him, they feared the multitude, because they took him for a prophet.

13. <u>Legalism results in hypocrisy, resists all true religion, and makes us even more selfish and evil.</u> Legalists are often so focused on the laws, that they omit what really counts: judgment, mercy, and faith. They even prevent those who would seek God from truly finding Him.

Mt 23:13 But woe unto you, scribes and Pharisees, hypocrites! for ye shut up the kingdom of heaven against men: for ye neither go in yourselves, neither suffer ye them that are entering to go in.

14 Woe unto you, scribes and Pharisees, hypocrites! for ye devour widows' houses, and for a pretence make long prayer: therefore ye shall receive the greater damnation.

15 Woe unto you, scribes and Pharisees, hypocrites! for ye compass sea and land to make one proselyte, and when he is made, ye make him twofold more the child of hell than yourselves.

23 Woe unto you, scribes and Pharisees, hypocrites! for ye pay tithe of mint and anise and cummin, and have omitted the weightier matters of the law, judgment, mercy, and faith: these ought ye to have done, and not to leave the other undone.

14. <u>Legalists will even knowingly twist the truth in order to do what they want to do.</u> Prior to Jesus' death the Pharisees had acted as if they could not understand what Jesus meant when He prophesied that if they destroyed the temple, He would rebuild it in three days. However, immediately after his crucifixion they clearly demonstrated that they had understood what He had meant. When Jesus did rise from the dead and the soldiers told them that it had happened, they simply bribed the soldiers rather than consider what had happened and repent.

Mt 27:62 Now the next day, that followed the day of the preparation, the chief priests and Pharisees came together unto Pilate,

63 Saying, Sir, we remember that that deceiver said, while he was yet alive, After three days I will rise again.

64 Command therefore that the sepulchre be made sure until the third day, lest his disciples come by night, and steal him away, and say unto the people, He is risen from the dead: so the last error shall be worse than the first.

15. <u>If we will be truly open to hear what God is saying to us, even a strong legalist like a Pharisee can be converted and saved.</u> Nicodemus not only came to hear Jesus, but also demonstrated his faith by defending Him and helping to bury Him. Even a Pharisee, if he will repent, can be born again.

Jo 3:1 There was a man of the Pharisees, named Nicodemus, a ruler of the Jews:

2 The same came to Jesus by night, and said unto him, Rabbi, we know that thou art a teacher come from God: for no man can do these miracles that thou doest, except God be with him.

3 Jesus answered and said unto him, Verily, verily, I say unto thee, Except a man be born again, he cannot see the kingdom of God.

7:47 Then answered them the Pharisees, Are ye also deceived?

48 Have any of the rulers or of the Pharisees believed on him?

50 Nicodemus saith unto them, (he that came to Jesus by night, being one of them,)

51 Doth our law judge any man, before it hear him, and know what he doeth?

52 They answered and said unto him, Art thou also of Galilee? Search, and look: for out of Galilee ariseth no prophet.

19:39 And there came also Nicodemus, which at the first came to Jesus by night, and brought a mixture of myrrh and aloes, about an hundred pound weight.

40 Then took they the body of Jesus, and wound it in linen clothes with the spices, as the manner of the Jews is to bury.

41 Now in the place where he was crucified there was a garden; and in the garden a new sepulchre, wherein was never man yet laid.

42 There laid they Jesus therefore because of the Jews' preparation day; for the sepulchre was nigh at hand.

16. <u>Even after they are saved, the legalism of the Pharisee is hard to overcome. Many Christians today typify the Pharisees of the Bible.</u>

Ac 15:5 But there rose up certain of the sect of the Pharisees which believed, saying, That it was needful to circumcise them, and to command them to keep the law of Moses.

17. <u>If they are not saved, they can become great persecutors of the church.</u> The Apostle Paul is a good example of this.

Ac 26:5 Which knew me from the beginning, if they would testify, that after the most straitest sect of our religion I lived a Pharisee.

9 I verily thought with myself, that I ought to do many things contrary to the name of Jesus of Nazareth.

10 Which thing I also did in Jerusalem: and many of the saints did I shut up in prison, having received authority from the chief priests; and when they were put to death, I gave my voice against them.

11 And I punished them oft in every synagogue, and compelled them to blaspheme; and being exceedingly mad against them, I persecuted them even unto strange cities.

12 Whereupon as I went to Damascus with authority and commission from the chief priests,

17. <u>However, even the most adamant Pharisee and legalist can be saved and become a great minister of the gospel of grace.</u> Strong legalists, after they have a revelation of grace, usually have an even greater appreciation for the freedom that Christ bought for us on the cross.

Ac 26:13 At midday, O king, I saw in the way a light from heaven, above the brightness of the sun, shining round about me and them which journeyed with me.

14 And when we were all fallen to the earth, I heard a voice speaking unto me, and saying in the Hebrew tongue, Saul, Saul, why persecutest thou me? it is hard for thee to kick against the pricks.

15 And I said, Who art thou, Lord? And he said, I am Jesus whom thou persecutest.

16 But rise, and stand upon thy feet: for I have appeared unto thee for this purpose, to make thee a minister and a witness both of these things which thou hast seen, and of those things in the which I will appear unto thee;

Overcoming Legalism

1. Legalists attempt to make themselves feel secure by creating a black and white world based on law.

2. When they are told not to do something they naturally rebel or try to do it by their own efforts.

3. They can never be saved or made secure by their own efforts, because they are not perfect or powerful enough to wholly obey the law.

4. Because legalists trust in and rely on themselves they become prideful, judgmental, lack compassion, and think they are better than others.

5. Legalists pick and choose which laws they wish to obey, interpret the law to suit their own needs, and demand that others obey them perfectly.

6. They value their man-made traditions over the law of God and will attack anyone who does not agree with or challenges their ideas.

7. God is more interested in what comes out of their hearts, especially mercy and loving others, than the strict adherence to a set of human traditions that are supposed to help them obey the law.

8. Even the most adamant and strict legalist can be saved and become a servant of God if they are willing to accept the grace of God and repent.

Chapter 10

Christian Legalism
(James, The Brother Of Jesus)

There are large numbers of people in our world who struggle with legalism. For many it is an attempt to try to make themselves secure in an insecure world. Some may even suffer from Obsessive Compulsive Disorder or Obsessive Compulsive Personality Disorder. Others are legalists because they adhere to legalistic religions such as Islam, Judaism, or one of the cults such as the Jehovah's Witnesses or the Mormons. However, we must admit that legalism is still a prevalent problem within the Christian church today. Few Christians seem to move directly from their salvation experience into a full revelation of the grace of God. Unfortunately, even many churches and church leaders today have not moved beyond Christian legalism into grace and the law of liberty.

During the life of Jesus, the Pharisees were a prime example of the pride, hypocrisy, and selfish motivation that comes from attempting to obey the law in their own strength. Jesus confronted them repeatedly, and it was these legalists who eventually engineered His death on the cross. Even in the early church, this entire issue of obeying the law came up again and again as the Apostle Paul struggled with the legalists within the church at Jerusalem contending for the grace of God. Paul himself was a Pharisee and an extreme legalist prior to his salvation experience on the road to Damascus.

In order to examine the issues underlying Christian legalism, we must understand the viewpoint of James, the brother of Jesus, who headed the church in Jerusalem and was the main defender of legalism in the early church. Although many diverse dissertations have been written concerning exactly who James was, most agree that he may have been one of the original disciples and that he was related to Jesus. According to Smith's Bible Dictionary, James was…"The son of Alphaeus, or Cleopas, "the brother" or near kinsman or cousin of our Lord (Galatians 1:18,19) called James "the Less, " or "the Little, " probably because he was of low stature. He is mentioned along with the other apostles (Matthew 10:3, Mark 3:18, Luke 6:15). He had a separate interview with our Lord after his resurrection (1 Corinthians 15:7) and is mentioned as one of the apostles of the circumcision (Acts 1:13). He appears to have occupied the position of head of the church at Jerusalem, where he presided at the council held to consider the case of the Gentiles. (Acts 12:17,15:13-29, 21:18-24) This James was the author of the epistle that bears his name. (Smith, 1970)

1. <u>Christian legalists can come from very good homes with the very best teaching.</u> It appears that James was possibly a brother or a cousin to Jesus. Controversy exists because we are not sure if the Mary cited in this text was Mary the mother of Jesus or another close relative named Mary.

   Mt 13:55 Is not this the carpenter's son? is not his mother called Mary? and his brethren, James, and Joses, and Simon, and Judas?

2. <u>Legalists tend to see life from a human, physical point of view, rather than a spiritual one.</u> They are more concerned with actions than motivation and the intents of the heart. Jesus' brother and mother were afraid He would wear Himself out doing the things of God and they wanted to insure

His physical comfort. Jesus' reply was that the things of God were far more important and that true brotherhood was the spiritual fellowship of those that believed.

Mr 3:32 And the multitude sat about him, and they said unto him, Behold, thy mother and thy brethren without seek for thee.

33 And he answered them, saying, Who is my mother, or my brethren?

34 And he looked round about on them which sat about him, and said, Behold my mother and my brethren!

3. They try to accomplish the work of God by their own efforts and expect others to do the same. These attempts fail because the Spirit of God must provide the direction and the energy to accomplish what God has called them to do.

    Jo 7:3 His brethren therefore said unto him, Depart hence, and go into Judaea, that thy disciples also may see the works that thou doest.

    4 For there is no man that doeth any thing in secret, and he himself seeketh to be known openly. If thou do these things, shew thyself to the world.

    5 For neither did his brethren believe in him.

4. Legalist many times rise to places of prominence in the church. God may even use them to do great things. When Jesus arose from the dead, it is particularly mentioned that He appeared to James even before the rest of the apostles—possibly indicating that he had a particular call on his life. After Peter was miraculously delivered from prison, he specifically instructed that James be informed. Since James, the brother of John, had just been killed, this verse clearly suggests the prominence that James, the brother of Jesus, had already attained in the church. After the Apostle Paul's conversion, he specifically conferred with James and mentions he was one of the "pillars" of the church in Jerusalem.

    1 Co 15:7 After that, he was seen of James; then of all the apostles.

    Ac 12:17 But he, beckoning unto them with the hand to hold their peace, declared unto them how the Lord had brought him out of the prison. And he said, Go shew these things unto James, and to the brethren. And he departed, and went into another place.

    Ga 2:9 And when James, Cephas, and John, who seemed to be pillars, perceived the grace that was given unto me, they gave to me and Barnabas the right hands of fellowship; that we should go unto the heathen, and they unto the circumcision.

5. They will attempt to bring legalistic ways of thinking directly into the church doctrine. Because of the conflicts caused by some saved Pharisees who said that the Gentiles had to obey the law, the apostle Paul brought the issue before the church in Jerusalem.

    Ac 15:5 But there rose up certain of the sect of the Pharisees which believed, saying, That it was needful to circumcise them, and to command them to keep the law of Moses.

6. They must realize that we are saved by faith and not by works. In fact, there is nothing that they can do to save themselves or transform their lives. Our salvation is completely based on what Jesus has done for us.

Ac 15:7 And when there had been much disputing, Peter rose up, and said unto them, Men and brethren, ye know how that a good while ago God made choice among us, that the Gentiles by my mouth should hear the word of the gospel, and believe.

8 And God, which knoweth the hearts, bare them witness, giving them the Holy Ghost, even as he did unto us;

11 But we believe that through the grace of the Lord Jesus Christ we shall be saved, even as they.

7. <u>Unfortunately, legalists in high positions can sometimes influence the church to compromise, implying that we must do certain things or follow certain traditions in addition to our faith in order to be saved or to accommodate legalistic people.</u> Although Peter had clearly stated the will of God, James convinced them to accommodate the legalistic Pharisees that were among them by requiring that the Gentiles abstain from things sacrificed to idols, fornication, strangled animals, and blood. These were all Old Testament laws and traditions, which had nothing to do with salvation by faith. Exterior traditions can never make us holy.

Ac 15:13 And after they had held their peace, James answered, saying, Men and brethren, hearken unto me:

19 Wherefore my sentence is, that we trouble not them, which from among the Gentiles are turned to God:

20 But that we write unto them, that they abstain from pollutions of idols, and from fornication, and from things strangled, and from blood.

21 For Moses of old time hath in every city them that preach him, being read in the synagogues every sabbath day.

8. <u>Christian legalism brings many problems and temptations to those who try to meet the requirements of God through their own strength.</u> Because many authors write about the issues they have or are dealing with in their own lives, it is not surprising that the book of James, written by James the brother of Jesus, later in his life, gives us answers for addressing the problems caused by legalism in the Christian life. It is not clear that he ever completely escaped legalism in his own life, but at least he gives us his insights for coping with the inherent problems that legalistic Christians face. When we are told not to do something (the law) we are naturally tempted to do that very thing. The harder we try to defeat temptations in our own strength, the stronger the temptations become. James suggests that we see temptations as friends that will help us grow instead of trying to defeat them in our own strength.

Jas 1: 2 My brethren, count it all joy when ye fall into divers temptations;

3 Knowing this, that the trying of your faith worketh patience.

4 But let patience have her perfect work, that ye may be perfect and entire, wanting nothing.

9. <u>They must realize that their problems are caused by their own lust and not attempt to blame others when they fail to obey the law completely.</u> When we struggle in life trying to do what is right and fail, we tend to blame God for not helping us enough or the devil for tempting us. James suggests that the problem is our own lust. Legalists have tremendous problems with lust or unlimited selfish desires because they are relying on their own efforts (the flesh) to bring the flesh under control.

Jas 1:13 Let no man say when he is tempted, I am tempted of God: for God cannot be tempted with evil, neither tempteth he any man:

14 But every man is tempted, when he is drawn away of his own lust, and enticed.

15 Then when lust hath conceived, it bringeth forth sin: and sin, when it is finished, bringeth forth death.

10. <u>They must be careful to remain teachable and open to the Word of God.</u> Another temptation for legalists is to think that they have all the answers. Consequently, they rarely listen to others and are seldom open to learning from the Word of God. They are easily angered when others disagree with them.

Jas 1:19 Wherefore, my beloved brethren, let every man be swift to hear, slow to speak, slow to wrath:

20 For the wrath of man worketh not the righteousness of God.

11. <u>They must do everything to avoid hypocrisy; which is acting right on the outside but not truly fulfilling God's Word on the inside.</u> We need a cleansing of the filth inside through the engrafted Word and laying aside the evil we do. We must see through our facade and continue to live by the perfect law of liberty or God's miracle of grace that is motivated from within the person.

Jas 1:21 Wherefore lay apart all filthiness and superfluity of naughtiness, and receive with meekness the engrafted word, which is able to save your souls.

22 But be ye doers of the word, and not hearers only, deceiving your own selves.

25 But whoso looketh into the perfect law of liberty, and continueth therein, he being not a forgetful hearer, but a doer of the work, this man shall be blessed in his deed.

12. <u>They must successfully overcome envy and strife by applying the wisdom of God in their lives.</u> Since legalism is just a part of our attempt to meet our need to be secure and worthwhile by our own efforts, it leads directly to competition and envy. James suggests that the answer is understanding things from God's point of view (wisdom from above). This understanding will lead to peace instead of strife.

Jas 3:14 But if ye have bitter envying and strife in your hearts, glory not, and lie not against the truth.

15 This wisdom descendeth not from above, but is earthly, sensual, devilish.

16 For where envying and strife is, there is confusion and every evil work.

17 But the wisdom that is from above is first pure, then peaceable, gentle, and easy to be intreated, full of mercy and good fruits, without partiality, and without hypocrisy.

18 And the fruit of righteousness is sown in peace of them that make peace.

13. <u>They must avoid judging and condemning others.</u> Because legalistic people are proud of their efforts to obey the law, they naturally look down on others who fail to do so. James tells us that they are setting themselves up as judges instead of acknowledging that they are the ones who are to be obedient to the law. God is the only lawgiver and judge.

Jas 4:11 Speak not evil one of another, brethren. He that speaketh evil of his brother, and judgeth his brother, speaketh evil of the law, and judgeth the law: but if thou judge the law, thou art not a doer of the law, but a judge.

12 There is one lawgiver, who is able to save and to destroy: who art thou that judgest another?

14. <u>They must not be self-centered and attempt to direct their own lives.</u> Legalists will usually try to run and direct their own lives. They believe they have all the answers in the law and that is enough for them. James warns that since they do not even know what will happen tomorrow, they do not have enough information to direct their lives. They are to rely on God for the direction of their lives, or they are living in sin.

Jas 4:13 Go to now, ye that say, To day or to morrow we will go into such a city, and continue there a year, and buy and sell, and get gain:

14 Whereas ye know not what shall be on the morrow. For what is your life? It is even a vapour, that appeareth for a little time, and then vanisheth away.

17 Therefore to him that knoweth to do good, and doeth it not, to him it is sin.

15. <u>They must not be proud of their accomplishments or wealth.</u> If we obey the law and successfully make something of ourselves, we may think that we have something to boast about in our life. Instead, God uses our accomplishments and wealth as evidence of our selfishness and the manipulation we have used in obtaining these things.

Jas 5:1 Go to now, ye rich men, weep and howl for your miseries that shall come upon you.

2 Your riches are corrupted, and your garments are motheaten.

4 Behold, the hire of the labourers who have reaped down your fields, which is of you kept back by fraud, crieth: and the cries of them which have reaped are entered into the ears of the Lord of sabaoth.

Coping with Christian Legalism

1. Christian legalism is an attempt to make ourselves feel secure and successful as Christians by creating a black and white world based on our attempts to obey God's law and our own traditions by our own efforts.

2. Christian legalists view themselves as outstanding Christians while in fact they are motivated by selfish desires within their hearts. Others may view them as hypocritical.

3. Legalists tend to emphasize outward actions and performance rather than inward motivation as the key to the Christian life. God's method of righteousness is based on faith in His meeting our needs because of His grace and mercy, not our works.

4. Because Christian legalists trust in and rely on themselves, they struggle with many temptations and lusts. They become prideful, judgmental, and think they are better than others.

5. Legalists tend to be people pleasers, attempt to direct their own lives, think they have all the answers, and rely on themselves instead of God.

6. They must learn to listen, become teachable, and study the Word of God in order to understand again that we are saved by grace and not by anything that we have done or could do.

7. They must finally understand that it is the faith from within that is responsible for their right actions and that living the Christian life without a changed heart through faith is impossible.

PART V

Self-control—Knowing God as My Friend

Chapter 11

Internal Motivation through Grace All Things Are Lawful for Me

2 Pe 1:6 And to knowledge temperance; and to temperance patience; and to patience, godliness;

According to our text, the next step after knowledge is temperance. The word translated as temperance in the King James Bible is *egkrateia* which means "temperance or self-control; the ability to master one's desires and passions, especially sensual appetites." This is exactly the problem that we faced under the law—we could not, no matter how hard we tried; master our own desires and the passions of the flesh. That is what made us so miserable. Either we lied to ourselves and lowered our standards; or we had to admit that although we said we wanted to obey the law of God, we simply did not do it. This was especially true if we were willing to accept the even higher standard of Jesus' narration on the law in the Sermon on the Mount (Matthew Chapters 5-7). How many of us men have never looked at a woman with lust, or have always blessed those who cursed us, or have never failed to love our enemies?

Once we have been firmly educated and established in the law of God, we realize that we cannot obey it in our own strength. When we realize that nothing short of perfect obedience will please God, we come to a dead end. Most of us, at this stage, live in frustration deceiving ourselves and trying to do our best to hide, rationalize, or minimize our failures so that others (and God) will not think we have backslidden. We feel that God may even put up with us, but that He is definitely not pleased. Maybe because we are not that much worse than everyone else is and because we rely on the sacrifice of Jesus to get us into heaven, we may still make it—but barely with no crowns or fanfare. I heard one pastor who had fallen and had been publicly exposed; say to his congregation, "How can I tell you anything when I am such a lousy example of what a Christian should be!" We seem doomed to a life of trying to please God, but always coming short of the mark. One of my clients who never seemed able to please her mother, tragically and clearly put it this way, "Why would I want to have a relationship with God? He would just be someone else to disappoint!"

Once we have been confronted with this knowledge, we realize God must take the next step—for there is nothing that we can do. In fact, He has already taken this step—over 2000 years ago—but somehow we have just not gotten a revelation and understanding of what we so desperately need—His grace!

Grace

In Bible terms grace is the unmerited favor of God and sometimes the influence and power that He displays on our behalf due to His favor, mercy, and kindness.

1. <u>One of God's primary characteristics is grace or unmerited favor toward everyone.</u>

   Ne 9:31 Nevertheless for thy great mercies' sake thou didst not utterly consume them, nor forsake them; for thou art a gracious and merciful God.

   Ps 103:8 The LORD is merciful and gracious, slow to anger, and plenteous in mercy.

2. God's grace came to us through Jesus.

    Jo 1:14 And the Word was made flesh, and dwelt among us, (and we beheld his glory, the glory as of the only begotten of the Father,) full of grace and truth.

    17 For the law was given by Moses, but grace and truth came by Jesus Christ.

3. We are justified by grace.

    Ro 3:24 Being justified freely by his grace through the redemption that is in Christ Jesus:

4. Grace is a free gift that sets us free from the law and sin.

    Ro 5:15 But not as the offence, so also is the free gift. For if through the offence of one many be dead, much more the grace of God, and the gift by grace, which is by one man, Jesus Christ, hath abounded unto many.

    6:14 For sin shall not have dominion over you: for ye are not under the law, but under grace.

5. Grace is obtained through faith.

    Ro 5:2 By whom also we have access by faith into this grace wherein we stand, and rejoice in hope of the glory of God.

6. Grace sets us free from the legalistic requirements of the law, so that we can do whatever we wish, but we must be careful not to use grace as an occasion for the flesh because that will again bring us into bondage.

    1 Co 6:12 All things are lawful unto me, but all things are not expedient: all things are lawful for me, but I will not be brought under the power of any.

7. Grace cannot be obtained by works.

    Ro 11:6 And if by grace, then is it no more of works: otherwise grace is no more grace. But if it be of works, then is it no more grace: otherwise work is no more work.

8. Grace is supposed to result in good works.

    1 Co 15:10 But by the grace of God I am what I am: and his grace which was bestowed upon me was not in vain; but I laboured more abundantly than they all: yet not I, but the grace of God which was with me.

9. Trying to accomplish things in our own strength (the law) works against the grace of God and is called "falling from grace."

    Ga 2:21 I do not frustrate the grace of God: for if righteousness come by the law, then Christ is dead in vain.

    5:4 Christ is become of no effect unto you, whosoever of you are justified by the law; ye are fallen from grace.

10. <u>Grace functions best when we admit our inability and trust God to do His will.</u>

    2 Co 12:9 And he said unto me, My grace is sufficient for thee: for my strength is made perfect in weakness. Most gladly therefore will I rather glory in my infirmities, that the power of Christ may rest upon me.

11. <u>We must have a revelation of grace and understand how it sets us free.</u>

    Col 1:6 Which is come unto you, as it is in all the world; and bringeth forth fruit, as it doth also in you, since the day ye heard of it, and knew the grace of God in truth:

12. <u>We are saved by grace.</u>

    2 Ti 1:9 Who hath saved us, and called us with an holy calling, not according to our works, but according to his own purpose and grace, which was given us in Christ Jesus before the world began,

13. <u>God's grace results in sufficiency in everything.</u>

    2 Co 9:8 And God is able to make all grace abound toward you; that ye, always having all sufficiency in all things, may abound to every good work:

14. <u>Ministry comes by grace.</u>

    Eph 3:7 Whereof I was made a minister, according to the gift of the grace of God given unto me by the effectual working of his power.

15. <u>Grace gives us hope that God will work everything for our good.</u>

    2 Th 2:16 Now our Lord Jesus Christ himself, and God, even our Father, which hath loved us, and hath given us everlasting consolation and good hope through grace,

16. <u>Grace can give us strength.</u>

    2 Ti 2:1 Thou therefore, my son, be strong in the grace that is in Christ Jesus.

17. <u>Because of grace, we can approach God with full assurance in time of need.</u> When we rely on the grace of God instead of our own performance, we are assured that God will answer our prayers.

    Heb 4:16 Let us therefore come boldly unto the throne of grace, that we may obtain mercy, and find grace to help in time of need.

18. <u>Grace can be multiplied and grown as we know God and Jesus more.</u>

    2 Pe 1:2 Grace and peace be multiplied unto you through the knowledge of God, and of Jesus our Lord,
    3:18 But grow in grace, and in the knowledge of our Lord and Saviour Jesus Christ. To him be glory both now and for ever. Amen.

Pulling together what we have learned about grace and applying it to our lives, we must have a revelation of God's unmerited favor for us (grace) and our inability to save ourselves. Jesus fulfilled the law for us, died to provide forgiveness for all our sins and took the shame of our failures on the cross with Him. Consequently, we are now accepted and adored just the way we are—without any works on our part. No matter how well we perform or how miserably we fail, God will never condemn us. He will always love, adore, and work for our good, no matter what decisions we make. Of course, we will still receive the consequences of our actions, and, if necessary, He will still discipline us for our good. He will always love us no matter what happens, always work for our benefit in everything and always be on our side. Since we are "in Christ," He will accept Christ's perfect works in place of ours. Therefore, He will always answer our prayers even when the problems are of our own making. I have attempted to summarize this information on the chart on the following page.

A Difficult Transition

If the teenage years are one of the most challenging times in life, possibly the transition to adulthood is the most traumatic for many parents. What will happen when their son or daughter leaves the external control and the rules of their home and is totally free to do whatever they want to do? Usually one thing is for sure. They will not make all the same choices that their parents might have made for them in similar circumstances. Because of this, some parents make the mistake of still trying to control the decisions of their grown children and find that this leads to less and less influence in their children's lives or even to outright anger and separation.

In counseling parents, I suggest that they say something similar to this when their child turns 18 years of age. "Congratulations. You are now an adult. That means you are now free to make your own decisions and to receive the full consequences of those decisions. I will no longer tell you what you should do. In fact, even if you ask, I will only help you evaluate your options or alternatives, because they are your decisions to make. I will not get the consequences of your actions, you will. I will always love you, be there for you, pray for you, and have your best interests in mind no matter what you do and how life turns out for you. I will never do for you what you can do for yourself. It is up to you if you choose to continue to live with us for a few more years until you get your own life fully established, but if you do, we will work out a contract specifically stating your obligations and our expectations just as would be required if you were living at any apartment complex. If you are not willing to live up to whatever requirements we negotiate as adults, (and I believe we can offer you the best deal in town), you are free to find another place to live. You are expected to either find and hold a job or go full-time to college. If you choose to go to college, we are willing to provide a specific amount of additional support depending on what we can afford, although we have no obligation to do so. If you choose to accept this support which will last for no more than four years, we will make clear the requirements that go along with it, including a specific grade point average and an obligation to continue to attend church weekly. Of course, you are under no obligation to accept anything that we offer. It is your life and your choice. We love you very much. Again, we want to congratulate you at this very important time in your life."

Although this might seem somewhat harsh to some, I have found that this process produces excellent results and clarifies the new relationship that exists between parent and child.

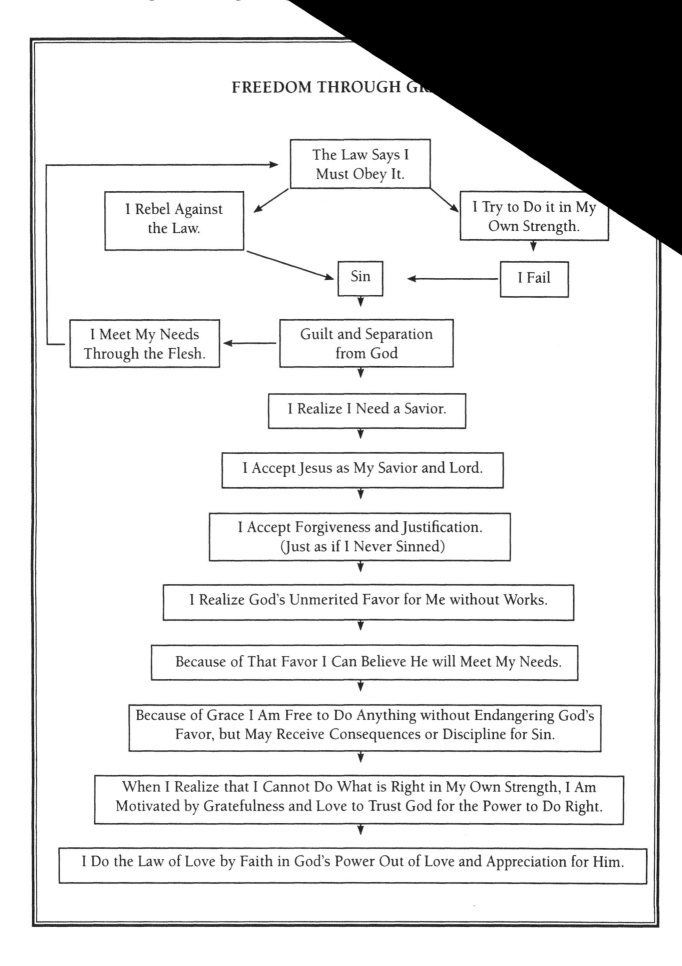

FREEDOM THROUGH GR...

The Law Says I Must Obey It.

I Rebel Against the Law.

I Try to Do it in My Own Strength.

Sin

I Fail

I Meet My Needs Through the Flesh.

Guilt and Separation from God

I Realize I Need a Savior.

I Accept Jesus as My Savior and Lord.

I Accept Forgiveness and Justification. (Just as if I Never Sinned)

I Realize God's Unmerited Favor for Me without Works.

Because of That Favor I Can Believe He will Meet My Needs.

Because of Grace I Am Free to Do Anything without Endangering God's Favor, but May Receive Consequences or Discipline for Sin.

When I Realize that I Cannot Do What is Right in My Own Strength, I Am Motivated by Gratefulness and Love to Trust God for the Power to Do Right.

I Do the Law of Love by Faith in God's Power Out of Love and Appreciation for Him.

He does not want a relationship with us
⌐ us to do what we do for Him, because we
⌐nts, I use the analogy of a bird in a cage. It

⌐ow one winter to see a bird shivering in the cold
⌐o means of healing its wing under these circum-
⌐t and bring it into the house, splint its wing, feed
⌐ird love and appreciate you for what you have done
⌐ealth? Of course, the answer is that we do not know. I
⌐ind out?" Most people will answer, "I guess you would

⌐d finds Himself in. He found us broken in our life of sin.
⌐ll that we needed. He sent his Son to do everything that was
provided a cage for us—the law. It kept us safe while we were
⌐nat we have a personal relationship with Him and have studied

healing ⌐
His Word to ⌐   ⌐, how will He (and us) ever know if we truly love and appreciate Him for what ⌐.   ⌐ave to set us free to see what we will do. Freedom is the necessary
ingredient for developing ⌐   ⌐or self-control. We have to be given the opportunity to choose what
we will do. We develop self-co⌐   ⌐ough experiencing negative consequences when we make the wrong
choices. How many of us still decia⌐ to put our hands on a hot stove? Because of our experiences growing
up, we choose not to do it. No one has to guard the stove anymore to prevent us from burning ourselves.

After the bird has been completely healed, setting it free can be a very dangerous time in its life. You can
never be absolutely sure what the bird may do after being locked in a cage for that long. The bird might attack you, attack the cat, make a mess, get killed by some predator, or fly away never to be seen again. Unless
you set the bird free, you will never find out if it likes and wants to be with you!

Just as in the bird illustration that we have been discussing, the transition from external control to internal control or self-discipline is possibly the most dangerous step in spiritual development. It is possible
to derail as we attempt to make our train turn completely around. In order to set us free, God has to give
us enough rope to hang ourselves. Possibly this is the reason that we hear so few sermons on this subject.
What if the pastor preaches a sermon on grace and members of his church run totally amuck in the flesh
when they realize they are no longer under the law and are free to do whatever they choose, knowing that
God will still love them? The Bible clearly warns us about this.

Ro 6:1 What shall we say then? Shall we continue in sin, that grace may abound?

15 What then? shall we sin, because we are not under the law, but under grace? God forbid.

Ga 5:13 For, brethren, ye have been called unto liberty; only use not liberty for an occasion to the
flesh, but by love serve one another.

How God Sets Us Free to Develop Self-control

God has provided all that we need to set us free to successfully develop a self-disciplined life in which
we want to do what is right, and in which we trust God to help us actually do it. The ingredients we need
to accomplish this are listed below:

1. <u>We need a desire within us to do what is right</u>. When we received the Holy Spirit at the point of our
   salvation, we received the desire to be holy. Spirits work continually to influence our will to yield to

them, so that they can make us like them. When we were saved and yielded ourselves to the Lordship of Jesus, He kindled this desire within us to want to do what is right.

Heb 8:10 For this is the covenant that I will make with the house of Israel after those days, saith the Lord; I will put my laws into their mind, and write them in their hearts: and I will be to them a God, and they shall be to me a people:

Php 2:13 For it is God which worketh in you both to will and to do of his good pleasure.

2. <u>We must know what is right and wrong.</u> This is the function of the law. When we know the will of God through His Word, we are equipped to be able to choose what is right.

    Ro 7:7 What shall we say then? Is the law sin? God forbid. Nay, I had not known sin, but by the law: for I had not known lust, except the law had said, Thou shalt not covet.

3. <u>We must have the revelation that we cannot obey the law in our own strength.</u> Without this revelation, we will continue in the curse of the law and fail in all of our attempts to obey it.

    Ro 7:18 For I know that in me (that is, in my flesh,) dwelleth no good thing: for to will is present with me; but how to perform that which is good I find not.

4. <u>We must have the ability to choose to do right.</u> When we were crucified with Christ, our old man who was hopelessly dominated with sin, died on the cross with Christ. Because Christ now lives within us, we have within us the power to choose to do right. However, since we still have a free will, we can still choose to serve sin and the devil.

    Ro 6: 6 Knowing this, that our old man is crucified with him, that the body of sin might be destroyed, that henceforth we should not serve sin.

    7 For he that is dead is freed from sin.

    11 Likewise reckon ye also yourselves to be dead indeed unto sin, but alive unto God through Jesus Christ our Lord.

    12 Let not sin therefore reign in your mortal body, that ye should obey it in the lusts thereof.

    13 Neither yield ye your members as instruments of unrighteousness unto sin: but yield yourselves unto God, as those that are alive from the dead, and your members as instruments of righteousness unto God.

5. <u>We must have a revelation of God's grace and unconditional acceptance.</u> Just as a healthy parent will always love and have his child's best interest at heart, so God, the perfect parent, unconditionally loves and accepts us no matter what we do. His love is not conditional or based on our works. He will always work for our good, even when we are failing Him.

    Ro 8:38 For I am persuaded, that neither death, nor life, nor angels, nor principalities, nor powers, nor things present (performance, approval, morals or circumstances), nor things to come,

    39 Nor height, nor depth, nor any other creature, shall be able to separate us from the love of God, which is in Christ Jesus our Lord.

6. <u>We must trust that God will meet our needs and answer our prayers even when we have failed Him.</u> God's love and care for us is not dependent on our works, but on the works of Jesus and His ongoing intercession for us.

Mt 6:30 Wherefore, if God so clothe the grass of the field, which to day is, and to morrow is cast into the oven, shall he not much more clothe you, O ye of little faith?

Ro 8:31 What shall we then say to these things? If God be for us, who can be against us?

32 He that spared not his own Son, but delivered him up for us all, how shall he not with him also freely give us all things?

7. <u>We must realize that we are not under the law because Jesus fulfilled the law.</u> We are part of His body and He dwells in us, therefore, we have fulfilled the law. However, this does not mean that we will not receive the consequences of our actions. As long as we are led by the Spirit, we are not under the law.

    Ro 7:4 Wherefore, my brethren, ye also are become dead to the law by the body of Christ; that ye should be married to another, even to him who is raised from the dead, that we should bring forth fruit unto God.

    1 Co 10:23 All things are lawful for me, but all things are not expedient: all things are lawful for me, but all things edify not.

    Ga 5:18 But if ye be led of the Spirit, ye are not under the law.

8. <u>We must realize that there is no condemnation to those who are in Christ Jesus.</u> Condemnation means that we are being judged in a negative sense. Because of God's grace, we are always favored by Him. Because Jesus died for our sins, they have been paid for in full.

    Ro 8:33 Who shall lay any thing to the charge of God's elect? It is God that justifieth.

    34 Who is he that condemneth? It is Christ that died, yea rather, that is risen again, who is even at the right hand of God, who also maketh intercession for us.

9. <u>We must know that we have been set free.</u> Without this revelation, we will continue to feel and act as those who are still in bondage. During the civil war, after the Emancipation Proclamation was signed, all the slaves in the South were free. However, most of them continued many more years acting like slaves until they had a revelation and realized that they were indeed free men.

    Jo 8:36 If the Son therefore shall make you free, ye shall be free indeed.

10. <u>We need to be careful not to get back into bondage.</u> It is interesting to see clients who fight against this concept of grace. For them it is too threatening to be fully responsible for themselves and to be responsible for making all of their own decisions. I actually had one client return to his old extremely legalistic church because he could not cope with the liberty he had in our church. He felt he could not function without the pastor providing external control by confronting him weekly to repent and change his ways.

    Ga 5:1 Stand fast therefore in the liberty wherewith Christ hath made us free, and be not entangled again with the yoke of bondage.

11. <u>We need to develop a life of obedience motivated by our gratitude and love for God.</u> God wants us to do what we do out of love and appreciation for what He has done for us. Love is the strongest and most effective motivation for obedience.

Jo 14:21 He that hath my commandments, and keepeth them, he it is that loveth me: and he that loveth me shall be loved of my Father, and I will love him, and will manifest myself to him.

12. <u>However, if we choose to use God's grace as an occasion for the flesh or an excuse to continue in sin, He will allow us to experience the full consequences of our choices</u>. Because He loves us so much and has our best interest in mind, He will do whatever it takes to help us learn from our mistakes. If we refuse to repent and choose to rebel against Him, we should expect the chastisement of our loving Father. Unfortunately, for some not even this is enough to bring them to repentance.

Heb 12:5 And ye have forgotten the exhortation which speaketh unto you as unto children, My son, despise not thou the chastening of the Lord, nor faint when thou art rebuked of him:

6 For whom the Lord loveth he chasteneth, and scourgeth every son whom he receiveth.

7 If ye endure chastening, God dealeth with you as with sons; for what son is he whom the father chasteneth not?

8 But if ye be without chastisement, whereof all are partakers, then are ye bastards, and not sons.

9 Furthermore we have had fathers of our flesh which corrected us, and we gave them reverence: shall we not much rather be in subjection unto the Father of spirits, and live?

10 For they verily for a few days chastened us after their own pleasure; but he for our profit, that we might be partakers of his holiness.

11 Now no chastening for the present seemeth to be joyous, but grievous: nevertheless afterward it yieldeth the peaceable fruit of righteousness unto them which are exercised thereby.

We must also deal with another aspect of the law—the shame that we feel because of our past failures and mistakes. While it is true that Christ took our shame on the cross and that we are no longer under the law but under grace, that does not automatically make us completely free from all the vestiges of shame in our life due to past experiences. We again need a full revelation that we are also free from shame because of what Christ has done for us and that there is no condemnation to them who are in Christ Jesus (Romans 8:1). We need to know how to deal with our present and past experiences so that we can remain free from shame, which can affect how we view ourselves.

Isa 50:6 I gave my back to the smiters, and my cheeks to them that plucked off the hair: I hid not my face from shame and spitting.

Heb 12:2 Looking unto Jesus the author and finisher of our faith; who for the joy that was set before him endured the cross, despising the shame, and is set down at the right hand of the throne of God.

The Example of the Prodigal Son

In the example of the parable of the Prodigal son, we have the conflict between the law and grace acted out. The younger son did not do well under the external control and direction of his father, knowing that his older brother would get the majority of the inheritance. In each of us is that rebellion of wanting to do things our way. Although the father had no obligation at all to give his son his inheritance before he died, he did not want his son to serve the family because he had to in order to get the inheritance. He wanted the son to want to serve the family simply because he loved them and wanted to be part of the family. The father knew that for the son to develop self-discipline, he would have to be set free.

Lu 15:11 And he said, A certain man had two sons:

12 And the younger of them said to his father, Father, give me the portion of goods that falleth to me. And he divided unto them his living.

When his son left, the father gave him complete liberty to choose what he would do and did nothing to bring him back home or to protect him from the consequences of his decisions.

Lu 15:13 And not many days after the younger son gathered all together, and took his journey into a far country, and there wasted his substance with riotous living.

14 And when he had spent all, there arose a mighty famine in that land; and he began to be in want.

17 And when he came to himself, he said, How many hired servants of my father's have bread enough and to spare, and I perish with hunger!

18 I will arise and go to my father, and will say unto him, Father, I have sinned against heaven, and before thee,

19 And am no more worthy to be called thy son: make me as one of thy hired servants.

It is clear that the Father loved the son unconditionally and had unmerited favor for the son, no matter what he did. When the son decided he wanted to come home and serve his father, the father was waiting for him with open arms. He restored him to full status as a son in spite of the fact that he had squandered all of his part of the father's inheritance.

Lu 15:20 And he arose, and came to his father. But when he was yet a great way off, his father saw him, and had compassion, and ran, and fell on his neck, and kissed him.

21 And the son said unto him, Father, I have sinned against heaven, and in thy sight, and am no more worthy to be called thy son.

22 But the father said to his servants, Bring forth the best robe, and put it on him; and put a ring on his hand, and shoes on his feet:

23 And bring hither the fatted calf, and kill it; and let us eat, and be merry:

24 For this my son was dead, and is alive again; he was lost, and is found. And they began to be merry.

The older brother, who served out of obligation for what he would inherit, was angry. Legalistic Christians who are trying to be good have a hard time understanding the grace of God and the transformation necessary to want to serve God out of appreciation and love. The youngest son had experienced the liberty of unconditional love and now, out of appreciation of the liberty that his father had given him, could serve his father joyfully out of gratitude and love.

Lu 15:25 Now his elder son was in the field: and as he came and drew nigh to the house, he heard musick and dancing.

26 And he called one of the servants, and asked what these things meant.

27 And he said unto him, Thy brother is come; and thy father hath killed the fatted calf, because he hath received him safe and sound.

28 And he was angry, and would not go in: therefore came his father out, and intreated him.

29 And he answering said to his father, Lo, these many years do I serve thee, neither transgressed I at any time thy commandment: and yet thou never gavest me a kid, that I might make merry with my friends:

30 But as soon as this thy son was come, which hath devoured thy living with harlots, thou hast killed for him the fatted calf.

The father understood that setting his youngest son free was a very dangerous thing to do, but realized that it was a necessary risk, which could possibly pay tremendous dividends. The father's actions showed the faith he had in his son. In the same way, God had tremendous faith in us when He sent His Son to set us free from the condemnation of sin, the law, and our own performance self-worth. Sometimes God has to lose us so that we can find Him in a completely new way. Only true love is willing to do this.

Lu 15:31 And he said unto him, Son, thou art ever with me, and all that I have is thine.

32 It was meet that we should make merry, and be glad: for this thy brother was dead, and is alive again; and was lost, and is found.

The Result: The law of Liberty

Possibly the most intriguing thing about this liberty that God has given us is the end result. When we have progressed to the point of using our liberty responsibly (and that is what it inherently leads to), we end up again fulfilling the very law from which we were set free. The difference is that this time we obey the intent of the law with little effort on our part because we want to do it.

1. The Bible talks about living according to the law of liberty which is to replace the moral and ceremonial law in the life of the Christian. The law of liberty is serving in the newness of the spirit rather than trying to obey the letter of the law. It is being so influenced by the Spirit that we want to obey the reason behind the law rather than trying to fulfill the letter of the law and avoid its real intent. When we obey God's will from our heart because we want to do it, it brings life to all we do. God praises and rewards those who want to serve Him.

    Ro 7:6 But now we are delivered from the law, that being dead wherein we were held; that we should serve in newness of spirit, and not in the oldness of the letter.

    2 Co 3:6 Who also hath made us able ministers of the new testament; not of the letter, but of the spirit: for the letter killeth, but the spirit giveth life.

    Ro 2:29 But he is a Jew, which is one inwardly; and circumcision is that of the heart, in the spirit, and not in the letter; whose praise is not of men, but of God.

2. The law of liberty brings blessing, mercy, and freedom. We are not judged by our performance or even how things turn out, but by our desires and the intents of our heart. God blesses us when we trust Him and do our best motivated by our love for Him.

    Jas 1:25 But whoso looketh into the perfect law of liberty, and continueth therein, he being not a forgetful hearer, but a doer of the work, this man shall be blessed in his deed.

    2:12 So speak ye, and so do, as they that shall be judged by the law of liberty.

3. Jesus clearly demonstrated this law while He was on earth, and as a result, was persecuted by the legalists who were still trying to obey the letter of the law to gain God's favor.

    Mr 2:23 And it came to pass, that he went through the corn fields on the sabbath day; and his disciples began, as they went, to pluck the ears of corn.

    24 And the Pharisees said unto him, Behold, why do they on the sabbath day that which is not lawful?

    27 And he said unto them, The sabbath was made for man, and not man for the sabbath:

    28 Therefore the Son of man is Lord also of the sabbath.

Mr 3:6 And the Pharisees went forth, and straightway took counsel with the Herodians against him, how they might destroy him.

4. <u>The law of liberty is based on love.</u> All of the moral law had only one intent, that we would always have God and our neighbor's best interest in mind. The law of liberty goes one step further. Since God has loved us and set us free, we are to not only have our neighbors' best interest in mind but also actually love them, deeply care for them, and do it because we want to do it.

Ga 5:14 For all the law is fulfilled in one word, even in this; Thou shalt love thy neighbour as thyself.

My Experience

From the time I truly gave my heart to Christ, through my period of discipleship and well into my ministry I tried as much as I felt possible to live the Christian life. I read again and again many of the deeper Christian classics. Some of my favorites were Watchman Nee's *The Spiritual Man, The Normal Christian Life,* and *The Release of the Spirit, Knowing God* by J. I. Packer, and *The Pursuit of God* by Tozer. It seemed that even these wonderful insights were just not enough for me to live a consistent Christian life of the caliber that I believed God had provided for me. No matter how hard I tried, I would periodically focus on desiring the things of this world, recognize that I was more interested in accomplishing for God than truly loving people, and find myself on an emotional roller coaster dependent on my performance and what others thought of me. I did not realize it at this time, but I was still trying to obey the law.

Possibly, my first breakthrough occurred while I was trying to address the problem of low self-image that I had struggled with earlier in my life and that seemed so prominent in my clients. I realized that my worth was not dependent on my performance, the approval of others, or even my moral behavior, but simply on the love of God. I began to understand that all my efforts to "be somebody" were worthless and that God loves me for who I am—His child—rather than what I have done. I realized that I had only changed from attempting to please people by what I did, to attempting to please God so that He would like and approve of me. No, He made me in His image and said I was very good; and He would not change His mind. There was nothing that I could do to make myself more worthwhile or less worthy in His sight. In fact, because I was His son, there was not even anything I could do on earth to make myself more significant. It was all because of what He did, and had nothing at all to do with my performance or my works. He just wanted me to do what He asked me to do, the best I could trusting in His strength. He would do the rest.

As I became more deeply involved in counseling, it became clear to me that almost everyone I met (including many pastors and church leaders) were struggling with different issues in their lives. Most of them were frustrated trying to pray more, study more, and worship more, so that they could find victory in their lives. Of course, I usually saw them when they had just had a crisis or failure. The fact was that none of us can make it by trying harder.

My next breakthrough came when I heard evangelist Duncan Filmore preach a series of sermons on grace (2002). His previous attempts to obey the law and live the Christian life made my efforts look like child's play. He had done everything to the extreme including several 40 day fasts and isolating himself in a closet reading the Bible for days on end. Nothing worked until he got a revelation of the grace of God. I finally realized that God loved me; He really loved me, and it had nothing to do with my performance. God had unmerited favor for me and the only thing I had to do to get it was "to be unmerited." I qualified! I had known this all to some degree in my mind, but now somehow, during one of his sermons it had gotten through to my spirit. I was free from the law! Because I was not under the law, I could do anything I chose to do but as the Apostle Paul said, "all things are not expedient." (1 Corinthians 6:12, 10:23) I also realized that no matter what I did, God would never condemn me. (Romans 8:1, 33, 34) If I made a bad choice, it was too bad that I had not done better (and would get the consequences of what I had just done); but God still loved me, approved of me (but not necessarily of my actions), would forgive me when I repented and asked for His forgiveness, and was still on my side rooting for me as one of His favorite kids.

Something very interesting happened. Because I was now free to do anything, and there was no longer anyone saying I could not do it, I was now freed from the curse of wanting to do what would not be good for me. It suddenly dawned on me that God had given me enough rope to hang myself and I had to decide if I was stupid enough to do it. I could if I wanted to. I was now responsible for myself, and no one was going to make me do what was right. I had to take personal responsibility for myself and there was no one else to blame. I would decide my future and choose my consequences.

Because I was free, I could now freely evaluate a situation, decide what was the right thing to do for everyone involved and do it with God's help. Of course, I could still use my new freedom to indulge the lust of the flesh. But even if I did, God was not going to condemn me. I would just have to learn by the consequences that followed that it was not a wise thing to do. The more I really appreciated how much trust God had placed in me and the freedom He had purchased for me with the blood of Christ, the more I wanted to do only that which was right.

Because I was free, I could also choose to walk according to the Spirit or according to the flesh. It depended on the focus of my life. If I fed my spirit through the spiritual disciplines of Bible meditation, prayer, fasting, and quiet time with God, I would reap the fruit of the Spirit and if I chose to indulge in the things of the flesh, I would reap the manifestations of the flesh. Is that what I really wanted for my life? I had to decide, not based on obligation, but because that is what I really wanted in life. God loved me so much that He would let me choose what I wanted my life to be like. No matter what I did, He would always love me.

If I did make a mistake, choose to do something that I would later regret, or even fail at something, "There is therefore now no condemnation to them which are in Christ Jesus, who walk not after the flesh, but after the Spirit."(Romans 8:1)," and I was not to condemn myself either. If I made a mistake, I was to learn from it, and choose to do differently the next time. I could now get off the emotional roller coaster of shame and guilt. No matter what happened; God loved me and I was okay. That does not mean, of course, that it was okay for me to continue in sin. "God forbid." (Romans 6:1-2) But I no longer have to defend myself or be tempted to blame others for my mistakes. As the Apostle Paul stated, I should take pleasure in my weaknesses so that God would receive the glory. (2 Corinthians 12:9-10)

I have to admit, I did test my newfound wings a bit. I was shocked to find the extent of some of the things that I had been trying to control externally. Being set free from all external restraint reveals what is really in our hearts and how much we are still controlled by our own flesh and our selfish desires. When I quit trying in my own strength to keep everything under control and simply trusted God for help, He never failed me. It is amazing how easily God can step in and deal with things that we have been struggling with for years. But even when I made mistakes, I no longer felt condemnation. In fact, I just appreciated the freedom and mercy of God more.

When I began to apply these principles in my counseling, I found out that they could produce dramatic results, especially in the areas of addictions and lust. I remember one young man who was addicted to visiting adult bookstores. When we finally reached this phase in our counseling, I remember telling him, "Now that you are free you can visit every single adult book store in this town if you want to before driving home and God will still love you. It's your choice; just so that you are willing to accept the consequences of your actions and that this is the kind of life you want." That day he did not visit a single adult bookstore.

Another aspect of this freedom was that when I would start getting stressed with all the things I was supposed to do, I would just say to myself, "You don't have to do anything." God would still love me even if I did not accomplish everything I was "supposed" to do. In fact, all that God wanted me to do was what He asked me to do—not all the other things I had added into my life. It was all about Him and His kingdom and not about me. I was just one of His kids.

Possibly the greatest benefit of this transformation was that I finally realized it was okay for me to just be me. I did not have to act a certain way or meet a certain set of expectations to impress anyone. It was okay to be and feel just the way I felt at that time and to have whatever desires I had. God loved me and accepted me just the way I was.

Finally, I came to a full conviction that, "Surely goodness and mercy shall follow me all the days of my life: and I will dwell in the house of the LORD for ever." (Psalms 23:6) My future and God's acceptance is not based on my performance—only on what Jesus has done for me. I am part of the body of Christ and He is victorious in everything He does.

A Letter from God.

In the beginning of this chapter, I presented a sample letter that I sometimes recommend to parents when their children reach the age of 18. Here is a letter that I believe God would like us to have as we reach adult maturity in our Christian lives:

"Congratulations. You are now a Christian man or woman. That means you are now free to make your own decisions and to receive the full consequences of those decisions. We (the Trinity) will no longer tell you what you should do unless you ask us. In fact, even if you ask, we will not make your decisions for you, but will make it clear what Our perfect will is for you. These are your decisions to make. We will not get the consequences of your actions; you will. We will always love you, be there for you, pray for you (Jesus intercedes for us, Romans 8:34), and have your best interest in mind no matter what you do and how life turns out for you. We will never do for you what you can do for yourself. It is up to you to find a church so that you can grow and contribute to Our kingdom. We do not have any secret service Christians. If you wish, we will make it clear which specific church We would like you to attend. It is your job to be faithful in all that We have called you to do. If you do so, We will make clear to you Our specific call on your life. It is your job to prepare yourself for that ministry, whatever it may be. We will never make you do anything and if you choose to reject Our call on your life, that is up to you. As you know, 'Many are called and few are chosen.' (Matthew 22:14) It is and always will be Our deepest desire that your life count significantly in Our Kingdom, but that is also up to you. We will always provide all you need for what We have called you to do as long as you obey and do not use what We give you for your personal gain. Of course, you are under no obligation to accept anything that We offer. It is your life and your choice. We love you very much. Again, We want to congratulate you at this very important time in your life."

Chapter 12

Escaping Legalism
(The Apostle Paul)

It is not the will of God that Christians remain in legalism throughout their lifetime. If we examine the Bible as a whole, we will not find a better example of how to escape from legalism than that of the story of the life of Saul, who was later called the Apostle Paul. As he testified, he was one of the strictest of the Pharisees, was extremely legalistic, and even became a persecutor of the early church when it dared to challenge his ideas. Our story begins with the arrest of Stephen and his trial before the Sanhedrin.

1. <u>One of the main characteristics of legalism is that it resists the Holy Spirit and will persecute anyone who opposes it.</u> Stephen directly accused the Jews in the Sanhedrin and their forefathers of always resisting the Holy Spirit, persecuting the prophets, and killing Jesus. When Stephen suggested that they had not kept the law, they turned on him.

   Ac 7:51 Ye stiffnecked and uncircumcised in heart and ears, ye do always resist the Holy Ghost: as your fathers did, so do ye.

   52 Which of the prophets have not your fathers persecuted? and they have slain them which shewed before of the coming of the Just One; of whom ye have been now the betrayers and murderers:

   53 Who have received the law by the disposition of angels, and have not kept it.

   54 When they heard these things, they were cut to the heart, and they gnashed on him with their teeth.

2. <u>Because legalists are primarily trying to make their own lives secure, they are not open to the truth, hearing from God, or spiritual revelation.</u> They were outraged at Stephen's vision, just at they had been unable to accept the miracles of Jesus. They "stopped up their ears" because they did not want to hear.

   Ac 7:55 But he, being full of the Holy Ghost, looked up stedfastly into heaven, and saw the glory of God, and Jesus standing on the right hand of God,

   56 And said, Behold, I see the heavens opened, and the Son of man standing on the right hand of God.

   57 Then they cried out with a loud voice, and stopped their ears, and ran upon him with one accord,

3. <u>Legalists are so sure that what they are doing is right, they will do everything they can to resist God and think they are doing it in the name of God.</u> This is because any threat against the law is seen as threatening their own personal security. In Acts 5:38-39 Gamaliel warned them about this: "And now I say unto you, Refrain from these men, and let them alone: for if this counsel or this work be

of men, it will come to nought: But if it be of God, ye cannot overthrow it; lest haply ye be found even to fight against God." In this case, Saul (who would later be called Paul) was so convinced that he was right that he acted as one of the official witnesses of the execution of Stephen.

Ac 7:58 And cast him out of the city, and stoned him: and the witnesses laid down their clothes at a young man's feet, whose name was Saul.

59 And they stoned Stephen, calling upon God, and saying, Lord Jesus, receive my spirit.

60 And he kneeled down, and cried with a loud voice, Lord, lay not this sin to their charge. And when he had said this, he fell asleep.

4.   It is the fear deep within the legalist that they could be wrong, that fuels the anger that leads to persecution of anyone that opposes them. Saul was possibly shaken by the way Stephen died, forgiving even his executioners. Instead of admitting that they could be wrong, legalists will become more and more angry against any opposition until they become violent.

Ac 8:3 As for Saul, he made havock of the church, entering into every house, and haling men and women committed them to prison.

Ga 1:13 For ye have heard of my conversation in time past in the Jews' religion, how that beyond measure I persecuted the church of God, and wasted it:

14 And profited in the Jews' religion above many my equals in mine own nation, being more exceedingly zealous of the traditions of my fathers.

5.   The legalist has a difficult time justifying what he is doing; because if he were honest with himself, he knows that it does not truly bring life. Saul means "asked of God" or someone who is questioning God, and Damascus means "sackful of blood or silent is the sackcloth weaver." These meanings suggest either guilt over what is being done (sackful of blood) or attempts to remain silent when one knows that something is wrong (silent is the sackcloth weaver).

Ac 9:1 And Saul, yet breathing out threatenings and slaughter against the disciples of the Lord, went unto the high priest,

2 And desired of him letters to Damascus to the synagogues, that if he found any of this way, whether they were men or women, he might bring them bound unto Jerusalem.

6.   In order to escape from legalism, we need a revelation of the grace and character of God. It took a miracle to convert Saul, and it usually takes some profound event to shake the legalist from his mistaken beliefs. The phrase, "it is hard to kick against the pricks," refers to an ox kicking against an ox goad. The legalist constantly has to fight off the convictions of God that something is wrong until he finally will be open to correction.

Ac 9:3 And as he journeyed, he came near Damascus: and suddenly there shined round about him a light from heaven:

4 And he fell to the earth, and heard a voice saying unto him, Saul, Saul, why persecutest thou me?

5 And he said, Who art thou, Lord? And the Lord said, I am Jesus whom thou persecutest: it is hard for thee to kick against the pricks.

Ga 1:11 But I certify you, brethren, that the gospel which was preached of me is not after man.

12 For I neither received it of man, neither was I taught it, but by the revelation of Jesus Christ.

7. <u>The legalist must repent and be willing to hear and do God's will no matter what the cost.</u> Deliverance usually comes as a personal revelation and, therefore, is not usually perceived by those around him.

Ac 9:6 And he trembling and astonished said, Lord, what wilt thou have me to do? And the Lord said unto him, Arise, and go into the city, and it shall be told thee what thou must do.

7 And the men which journeyed with him stood speechless, hearing a voice, but seeing no man.

8. <u>He must seek God and be open to a fuller revelation of God's grace in his life.</u>

Ac 9:8 And Saul arose from the earth; and when his eyes were opened, he saw no man: but they led him by the hand, and brought him into Damascus.

9 And he was three days without sight, and neither did eat nor drink.

9. <u>The legalist's eyes must be opened so that he can understand the grace of God and be filled with the Holy Ghost.</u> He must be baptized, which symbolizes turning away from and dying to the sin in his life.

Ac 9:17 And Ananias went his way, and entered into the house; and putting his hands on him said, Brother Saul, the Lord, even Jesus, that appeared unto thee in the way as thou camest, hath sent me, that thou mightest receive thy sight, and be filled with the Holy Ghost.

18 And immediately there fell from his eyes as it had been scales: and he received sight forthwith, and arose, and was baptized.

10. <u>This new-found revelation must be strengthened and shared with others for it to firmly be established in the life of the believer.</u> Others may be astonished at the changes in the life of the transformed legalist.

Acts 9:20 And straightway he preached Christ in the synagogues, that he is the Son of God.

22 But Saul increased the more in strength, and confounded the Jews which dwelt at Damascus, proving that this is very Christ.

Ga 1:15 But when it pleased God, who separated me from my mother's womb, and called me by his grace,

16 To reveal his Son in me, that I might preach him among the heathen; immediately I conferred not with flesh and blood:

17 Neither went I up to Jerusalem to them which were apostles before me; but I went into Arabia, and returned again unto Damascus.

11. <u>Those that escape legalism must be careful not to be brought again under its power.</u> The Jewish legalists did not want Paul preaching about the grace of Christ so he was forced to escape, not by his own efforts, but with the assistance of others. In the same way, the escaped legalist must be assisted in his efforts and accepted into the fellowship of believers.

Ac 9:23 And after that many days were fulfilled, the Jews took counsel to kill him:

24 But their laying await was known of Saul. And they watched the gates day and night to kill him.

25 Then the disciples took him by night, and let him down by the wall in a basket.

26 And when Saul was come to Jerusalem, he assayed to join himself to the disciples: but they were all afraid of him, and believed not that he was a disciple.

27 But Barnabas took him, and brought him to the apostles, and declared unto them how he had seen the Lord in the way, and that he had spoken to him, and how he had preached boldly at Damascus in the name of Jesus.

28 And he was with them coming in and going out at Jerusalem.

12. <u>He must understand that he is free from the law; because Christ fulfilled it and that he is now one with Christ.</u> Christ has fulfilled the law for us. If salvation or wholeness can come through legalism, than Christ did not have to die!

Ga 2:16 Knowing that a man is not justified by the works of the law, but by the faith of Jesus Christ, even we have believed in Jesus Christ, that we might be justified by the faith of Christ, and not by the works of the law: for by the works of the law shall no flesh be justified.

21 I do not frustrate the grace of God: for if righteousness come by the law, then Christ is dead in vain.

13. <u>Only the Spirit can bring life, transform us, and provide the power of God.</u>

Ga 3:2 This only would I learn of you, Received ye the Spirit by the works of the law, or by the hearing of faith?

3 Are ye so foolish? having begun in the Spirit, are ye now made perfect by the flesh?

14. <u>Those who try to obey the law in their own strength are under a curse because the flesh cannot and will never obey the law perfectly.</u> We can only be delivered by Christ through faith.

Ga 3:10 For as many as are of the works of the law are under the curse: for it is written, Cursed is every one that continueth not in all things which are written in the book of the law to do them.

11 But that no man is justified by the law in the sight of God, it is evident: for, The just shall live by faith.

15. <u>After we escape legalism by receiving a revelation of the truth of the grace of God, we must stand firm in this liberty so that we are not again entangled in bondage.</u> It is something that we must actively do since it is easy to slip back into legalism and rely again on our own efforts. Even a single act of attempting to obey the law (like circumcision) puts us under the law requiring us to obey all of it again.

Ga 5:1 Stand fast therefore in the liberty wherewith Christ hath made us free, and be not entangled again with the yoke of bondage.

2 Behold, I Paul say unto you, that if ye be circumcised, Christ shall profit you nothing.

3 For I testify again to every man that is circumcised, that he is a debtor to do the whole law.

16. <u>We must be careful not to go to the other extreme and use the grace of God for an occasion for the flesh.</u> We must focus on walking according to the Spirit and loving others instead of using grace as an excuse to fulfill the flesh

Ga 5:13 For, brethren, ye have been called unto liberty; only use not liberty for an occasion to the flesh, but by love serve one another.

17. <u>However, if we, like the Apostle Paul, allow legalists to influence us in order to keep the peace, they will get us into trouble.</u> When the Apostle Paul brought his gift for the church in Jerusalem, he was influenced by James to follow the Jewish tradition of purification so that the legalists would not be offended. The implication here is that although the Gentile Christians were exempt from the law, Jewish Christians were still required to obey it. This compromise led directly to Paul's capture, imprisonment and appeal to be tried before Caesar in order to save his life. As God promises, He even turned this incident around for the good, using it as part of His plan to have Paul witness for Christ in Rome.

Ac 21:23 Do therefore this that we say to thee: We have four men which have a vow on them;

24 Them take, and purify thyself with them, and be at charges with them, that they may shave their heads: and all may know that those things, whereof they were informed concerning thee, are nothing; <u>but that thou thyself also walkest orderly, and keepest the law.</u>

27 And when the seven days were almost ended, the Jews which were of Asia, when they saw him in the temple, stirred up all the people, and laid hands on him.

Escaping Legalism

1. In order to escape from legalism, we must have a revelation of the grace of God.

2. After we have been trapped into trying to obey the law by our own efforts, we will need the help of others to hold us accountable and to keep us from again falling into bondage.

3. In order to fully appreciate the grace of God, we will have to study and meditate on its implications until they become part of our spirit.

4. Until we experience the freedom from the law, act accordingly in all circumstances, and appreciate what God has done for us we have not yet been set free.

5. We do not fall from grace by sinning, but by again trying to obey the law by our own efforts or by trying to rely on the flesh to transform us into better people.

6. We must be fully convinced that we can only be saved and transformed through the Spirit, by faith through grace, and not by works.

7. We must not try to use our newfound liberty as an occasion for the flesh.

8. We must be careful not to compromise even a little with legalism or we will again come under bondage and receive its consequences in our lives.

PART VI

Perseverance—Knowing God as My Father

Chapter 13

Accepting Responsibility
I Am God's Child

2 Pe 1:6 And to knowledge temperance; and to temperance patience; and to patience, godliness;

After making the switch from external to internal control, we must learn to do what is right consistently and under all circumstances. The word translated in verse 6 as patience is the Greek word *hupomone*. It can also be translated as endurance or perseverance. It means "patient continuance, steadfastness, and constancy." It is characteristic of a man who is not swerved from his deliberate purpose and his loyalty to faith and piety by even the greatest trials and sufferings. It is not enough to win periodic victories over the flesh. We must get to the place where under the most difficult circumstance we will continue to persist in doing what is right. It is only when we get a revelation of our complete identification with Christ and the fact that we are truly a child of God that we will unswervingly be committed to doing what is best for the Kingdom of God without reservation.

In order to accomplish this, these established facts must become truth to our spirit. Watchman Nee says it best when he states in *Sit, Walk, Stand,* "Most Christians make the mistake of trying to walk in order to sit, but that is the reversal of the true order… If at the outset we try to do anything, we get nothing; if we seek to attain something, we miss everything. For Christianity begins not with a big DO, but with a big DONE…Whereas God worked six days and then enjoyed the Sabbath rest, Adam began his life with the Sabbath (having been created on the 6th day); for God works before He rests, while man must first enter into God's rest, and then alone can he work" (1957, pp. 11-13)

Neil Anderson in his *Overcomer's Covenant in Christ* states: "I gladly embrace the truth that I am now a child of God who is unconditionally loved and accepted. I reject the lie that I have to perform to be accepted. I also reject my fallen and natural identity, which was derived from the world. I know that it is not what I do that determines who I am, but who I am that determines what I do." (1996)

This is an important point. Who we perceive we are will determine what we do. In the end, we will act according to who we think we are. Our identity is an extremely effective change agent in counseling. As an example, a client who was addicted to the high he received from breathing toxic fumes quit when he realized that his addiction was controlling him. He saw himself as someone in control, not someone who was controlled by an outside force. A lady had a tendency to get into a pity party when things did not go her way and would begin to feel suicidal. I suggested that since she was bought by God for a price she did not belong to herself; and, therefore, if she killed herself, she would be a murderer. She was able to avoid her suicidal thoughts, because she did not perceive herself as a murderer. There is a powerful potential in realizing that we are one with Christ, part of His body, and that we have been adopted as sons and daughters into the Kingdom of God.

Our Identification with Christ

Possibly, for Westerners, no area of the Bible is harder to grasp than that of our position in or identification with Christ. We are so time-oriented that we find it hard to grasp that God operates outside of time and to Him it is as if everything in the future has already taken place. If we truly believe what the Word of God says and act accordingly, these realities become manifested. By faith, God spoke the world into existence; and if we can learn to truly take God at His Word, through faith we can experience the future that God has already provided for us. Because we act according to our perceptions, tremendous change can occur if we simply line up our perceptions about ourselves and our circumstances with what God has already spoken. We must remember that God cannot lie and what He says is truly reality. God's truth must win out over what we have previously believed to be the facts in our lives.

1. <u>We must accept the fact that to God everything in the future has already been accomplished even before it happens.</u> All we need to do is to believe what God says and act on our belief. God calls things that are not as if they are.

    Ro 4:17 (As it is written, I have made thee a father of many nations,) before him whom he believed, [even] God, who quickeneth the dead, and calleth those things which be not as though they were.

2. <u>We have been adopted as sons and daughters.</u>

    Ro 8:15 For ye have not received the spirit of bondage again to fear; but ye have received the Spirit of adoption, whereby we cry, Abba, Father.

3. <u>He is in us.</u>

    Jo 17:21 That they all may be one; as thou, Father, [art] in me, and I in thee, that they also may be one in us: that the world may believe that thou hast sent me.

4. <u>We are in Him.</u>

    1 Jo 4:13 Hereby know we that we dwell in him, and he in us, because he hath given us of his Spirit.

5. <u>We are justified.</u>

    Tit 3:7 That being justified by his grace, we should be made heirs according to the hope of eternal life.

6. <u>We are sanctified.</u>

    1 Co 1:30 But of him are ye in Christ Jesus, who of God is made unto us wisdom, and righteousness, and sanctification, and redemption:

7. <u>We are glorified.</u>

    Ro 8:30 Moreover whom he did predestinate, them he also called: and whom he called, them he also justified: and whom he justified, them he also glorified.

8. <u>We are the righteousness of God in Him.</u>

    2 Co 5:21 For he hath made him [to be] sin for us, who knew no sin; that we might be made the righteousness of God in him.

9. <u>We are kings and priests.</u>

    Re 5:10 And hast made us unto our God kings and priests: and we shall reign on the earth.

10. <u>We have power over all the power of the enemy.</u>

    Lu 10:19 Behold, I give unto you power to tread on serpents and scorpions, and over all the power of the enemy: and nothing shall by any means hurt you.

11. <u>We are complete in Him through co-identification; because we are in Him, and He in us.</u>

    Col 2:10 And ye are complete in him, which is the head of all principality and power:

12. <u>We are more than conquerors in Him.</u>

    Ro 8:37 Nay, in all these things we are more than conquerors through him that loved us.

13. <u>We are joint heirs with Jesus.</u>

    Ro 8:17 And if children, then heirs; heirs of God, and joint-heirs with Christ; if so be that we suffer with [him], that we may be also glorified together.

14. <u>We are seated with Christ in heavenly places.</u>

    Eph 2:5 Even when we were dead in sins, hath quickened us together with Christ, (by grace ye are saved;)

    6 And hath raised [us] up together, and made [us] sit together in heavenly [places] in Christ Jesus:

15. <u>God has provided for all our needs.</u>

    Php 4:19 But my God shall supply all your need according to his riches in glory by Christ Jesus.

In *Hudson Taylor's Spiritual Secret*, he expresses the results of this full identification with God using the biblical example of the vine and the branches, which is then directly related to being a son in the household of God.

As I thought on the Vine and the branches, what light the blessed Spirit poured direct into my soul! How great seemed my mistake in wishing to get the sap, the fullness out of Him! I saw not only that Jesus will never leave me, but that I am a member of His body, and His flesh and of His bones. The vine is not the root merely, but all—root, stem, branches, twigs, leaves, flowers, fruit… Think what this involves… Could a bank clerk say to a customer, "It was only your hand, not you that wrote that check" or "I cannot pay this sum of money to your hand, but only to yourself." No more can your prayers or mine be discredited if offered in the name of Jesus… But if we ask anything according to his will … we know that we have the petitions that we desired of him. (Taylor, 1939. p. 161)

Now let us examine the verses Hudson Taylor is referring to:

Jo 15:4 Abide in me, and I in you. As the branch cannot bear fruit of itself, except it abide in the vine; no more can ye, except ye abide in me.

5 I am the vine, ye are the branches: He that abideth in me, and I in him, the same bringeth forth much fruit: for without me ye can do nothing.

Hudson continues by saying,

The sweetest part… is the rest which full identification with Christ brings. I am no longer anxious about anything, as I realize this; for He, I know is able to carry out His will, and His will is mine. It makes no matter where He places me, or how. That is rather for Him to consider than me; for in the easiest position He must give me His grace; and in the most difficult His grace is sufficient… And His resources are mine, for He is mine, and is with me and dwells in me… And since Christ has thus dwelt in my heart by faith, how happy I have been!… (Taylor, p. 162-163)

Our Adoption in Christ

Probably the easiest part of our identification in Christ for us to understand is the fact that God has adopted us into His family. The best way I know of explaining the significance of our adoption into God's family is a story of unknown origin that I once heard after I committed my life to Christ.

There was a very young boy living on the streets of a very large city who had lost his parents. He was surviving by gathering food from garbage cans. Because the garbage of rich citizens usually provided more tasty foods, he was drawn to an area of large mansions surrounded by gardens, tall fences and gates. One day as he was passing a particularly impressive mansion a thought came to him, "I wonder if the lady of that house might want a boy like me?" In an impetuous manner that only a naïve child could muster, he walked up to the gate, let himself in, and walked straight up to the huge entrance doors and rang the doorbell. When the lady of the house came to the door, he looked up straight into her eyes and asked, "Lady, would you like to have a boy like me?" The lady was overcome with compassion, let him in, and gave him some food that was better than he had ever experienced. He was thrilled at the great house, the bright lights and all the servants. He was eventually adopted into the family.

Something drastic changed the day that this boy was adopted. All of a sudden, he was no longer a destitute street kid, but the heir of a great fortune. One day no one cared for him, the next he was part of a loving family. One day he had almost nothing to eat; now he could have anything he wanted to eat. The problem was that somehow he had to be convinced that all this was really his and he was now a member of a prominent family. Initially the servants would find him looking in the garbage for something to eat. No, he did not have to eat out of garbage cans anymore. All he had to do was ask, and they would prepare him anything he wanted. In fact, it would be a great embarrassment to the family if someone saw him eating garbage. He needed to understand that he was now a member of a prominent family, not a street kid.

This is not only the story of an orphan who was adopted into a prominent family—it is also our story. We were destitute in the world of sin eating out of the garbage can of the flesh. One day we were drawn to the greatest mansion of all and adopted into the family of the King of Kings. One minute we were hopeless and unloved, and now we are unconditionally loved by the King of Love. One minute we had only a few worldly trinkets, and now we are joint heirs with Jesus Christ who will inherit the entire universe. One minute we were fighting with the other rats to make something of ourselves, and now we can have anything that is good for us just for the asking.

There is more. When the child finally realized who he was, he also realized that certain obligations went along with the privileges. Now that he was a member of a prominent family, he could not just do whatever he wanted; or he would tarnish that great reputation. Everyone was watching and whatever he did might be front-page news the next day. He also had a place in managing and expanding the family fortune. He was not like a servant building somebody else's business. Now he was a son working directly for his father, and what he did would affect his entire family and determine his future.

In the same way, when we finally receive a revelation that we truly are the adopted children of the King of Kings, we also realize that we have certain responsibilities. By our actions we can tarnish the name of the King, and by our actions we can further His kingdom. We work directly for God so we should not be concerned with other things. Whatever we do for the Kingdom of God we are actually doing for ourselves, because we are joint heirs with Jesus. When we face tribulation, persecution or struggles, we cannot quit; because we are sons, not servants. We are in this for the long haul.

What the Bible Says about Adoption

1. <u>We are adopted and born again as we are led by the Spirit of God.</u>

    Ro 8:11 But if the Spirit of him that raised up Jesus from the dead dwell in you, he that raised up Christ from the dead shall also quicken your mortal bodies by his Spirit that dwelleth in you.

    14 For as many as are led by the Spirit of God, they are the sons of God.

2. <u>If we are born of the Spirit, we are no longer to live after the flesh.</u>

    Ro 8:12 Therefore, brethren, we are debtors, not to the flesh, to live after the flesh.

    13 For if ye live after the flesh, ye shall die: but if ye through the Spirit do mortify the deeds of the body, ye shall live.

3. <u>Because we are children of God, we have nothing to fear.</u>

    Ro 8:15 For ye have not received the spirit of bondage again to fear; but ye have received the Spirit of adoption, whereby we cry, Abba, Father.

    16 The Spirit itself beareth witness with our spirit, that we are the children of God:

4. <u>If we are adopted, we are joint-heirs with Christ.</u>

    Ro 8:17 And if children, then heirs; heirs of God, and joint-heirs with Christ; if so be that we suffer with him, that we may be also glorified together.

5. <u>Being part of the family of God includes suffering for the furtherance of the Kingdom of God.</u>

    Ro 8:18 For I reckon that the sufferings of this present time are not worthy to be compared with the glory which shall be revealed in us.

    19 For the earnest expectation of the creature waiteth for the manifestation of the sons of God.

6. <u>A key part of adoption is knowing that God will take care of us in every circumstance.</u>

Ro 8:28 And we know that all things work together for good to them that love God, to them who are the called according to his purpose.

7. Adoption guarantees our transformation.

    Ro 8:29 For whom he did foreknow, he also did predestinate to be conformed to the image of his Son, that he might be the firstborn among many brethren.

    30 Moreover whom he did predestinate, them he also called: and whom he called, them he also justified: and whom he justified, them he also glorified.

8. If we are adopted, no one can prevail against us.

    Ro 8:31 What shall we then say to these things? If God be for us, who can be against us?

    32 He that spared not his own Son, but delivered him up for us all, how shall he not with him also freely give us all things?

9. We will not be condemned, even if we fail.

    Ro 8:33 Who shall lay any thing to the charge of God's elect? It is God that justifieth.

    34 Who is he that condemneth? It is Christ that died, yea rather, that is risen again, who is even at the right hand of God, who also maketh intercession for us.

10. No matter what happens, we can never be separated from God's love.

    Ro 8:35 Who shall separate us from the love of Christ? shall tribulation, or distress, or persecution, or famine, or nakedness, or peril, or sword?

    36 As it is written, For thy sake we are killed all the day long; we are accounted as sheep for the slaughter.

11. We are more than conquerors.

    Ro 8:37 Nay, in all these things we are more than conquerors through him that loved us.

    38 For I am persuaded, that neither death, nor life, nor angels, nor principalities, nor powers, nor things present, nor things to come,

    39 Nor height, nor depth, nor any other creature, shall be able to separate us from the love of God, which is in Christ Jesus our Lord.

Progressing from Servants to Sons

About 30 years ago there was a controversy among some churches concerning servanthood and sonship. Those that professed servanthood emphasized all the work they did for God and those that professed sonship emphasized the many privileges that sonship or being a "Kings Kid" entailed. Although these contrasts are artificial, they do make a point. We are to progress from being servants under the law to the liberty of sons. God wants us to grow from just serving Him out of obligation, to working with Him as sons because we want to and because we have a vested interest in His Kingdom. The distinction between servants and sons is made clear in the following verses:

1. <u>Servants are evaluated and rewarded by how much they gain for their lord in relation to their talents.</u>

   Lu 19:15 And it came to pass, that when he was returned, having received the kingdom, then he commanded these servants to be called unto him, to whom he had given the money, that he might know how much every man had gained by trading.

   17 And he said unto him, Well, thou good servant: because thou hast been faithful in a very little, have thou authority over ten cities.

2. <u>Servants are punished if they do not perform.</u>

   Mt 25:26 His lord answered and said unto him, Thou wicked and slothful servant, thou knewest that I reap where I sowed not, and gather where I have not strawed:

   30 And cast ye the unprofitable servant into outer darkness: there shall be weeping and gnashing of teeth.

   Lu 12:47 And that servant, which knew his lord's will, and prepared not himself, neither did according to his will, shall be beaten with many stripes.

3. <u>The master does not confide in servants but only in friends and sons.</u>

   Jo 15:15 Henceforth I call you not servants; for the servant knoweth not what his lord doeth: but I have called you friends; for all things that I have heard of my Father I have made known unto you.

4. <u>We are sons not servants.</u>

   Ga 4:5 To redeem them that were under the law, that we might receive the adoption of sons.

5. <u>Servants are told what to do; sons are allowed to choose what they do.</u>

   Ga 4:1 Now I say, That the heir, as long as he is a child, differeth nothing from a servant, though he be lord of all;

   2 But is under tutors and governors until the time appointed of the father.

   3 Even so we, when we were children, were in bondage under the elements of the world:

   4 But when the fulness of the time was come, God sent forth his Son, made of a woman, made under the law,

   5 To redeem them that were under the law, that we might receive the adoption of sons.

6. <u>Now we can appeal directly to daddy.</u> Sons even have a right to interrupt their parents at work without making an appointment. Servants have to wait for their master to have time for them.

   Ga 4:6 And because ye are sons, God hath sent forth the Spirit of his Son into your hearts, crying, Abba, Father.

7. <u>Sons are heirs and interested in the future of the family.</u>

   Ga 4:7 Wherefore thou art no more a servant, but a son; and if a son, then an heir of God through Christ.

8. <u>We are to be holy (set apart)</u>

Eph 1:4 According as he hath chosen us in him before the foundation of the world, that we should be holy and without blame before him in love:

5 Having predestinated us unto the adoption of children by Jesus Christ to himself, according to the good pleasure of his will,

9. <u>We are to be separate from the world.</u>

2 Co 6:17 Wherefore come out from among them, and be ye separate, saith the Lord, and touch not the unclean thing; and I will receive you,

18 And will be a Father unto you, and ye shall be my sons and daughters, saith the Lord Almighty.

10. <u>Because we are sons, we are to cleanse ourselves from the things of world so that we can represent God without any blame.</u>

Php 2:14 Do all things without murmurings and disputings:

15 That ye may be blameless and harmless, the sons of God, without rebuke, in the midst of a crooked and perverse nation, among whom ye shine as lights in the world;

11. <u>Sons will be disciplined.</u>

Heb 12:7 If ye endure chastening, God dealeth with you as with sons; for what son is he whom the father chasteneth not?

8 But if ye be without chastisement, whereof all are partakers, then are ye bastards, and not sons.

12. <u>The ultimate goal of sonship is to be like the father.</u>

1 Jo 3:1 Behold, what manner of love the Father hath bestowed upon us, that we should be called the sons of God: therefore the world knoweth us not, because it knew him not.

2 Beloved, now are we the sons of God, and it doth not yet appear what we shall be: but we know that, when he shall appear, we shall be like him; for we shall see him as he is.

The Prodigal Son Revisited

In concluding this step, let us revisit the story of the prodigal son because here we will again see the contrast between a son and a servant. First, as a son he had an inheritance coming. None of the servants had any rights outside of a salary, meals, and servant's quarters. The son was free to make his own decisions concerning his own life.

Lu 15:11 And he said, A certain man had two sons:

12 And the younger of them said to his father, Father, give me the portion of goods that falleth to me. And he divided unto them his living.

13 And not many days after the younger son gathered all together, and took his journey into a far country, and there wasted his substance with riotous living.

14 And when he had spent all, there arose a mighty famine in that land; and he began to be in want.

In the foreign land, the prodigal son had no special rights and so became a servant. He had no one who really loved him and cared for him when he was hungry. He realized that even his father's servants were better off than he was. At least they all had enough to eat. He also realized that as a son, he had had a responsibility not to defame his father's name. He had failed his father and his family.

Lu 15:15 And he went and joined himself to a citizen of that country; and he sent him into his fields to feed swine.

16 And he would fain have filled his belly with the husks that the swine did eat: and no man gave unto him.

17 And when he came to himself, he said, How many hired servants of my father's have bread enough and to spare, and I perish with hunger!

18 I will arise and go to my father, and will say unto him, Father, I have sinned against heaven, and before thee,

19 And am no more worthy to be called thy son: make me as one of thy hired servants.

When he arrived home, he was immediately welcomed and given the privileges of a son; because sonship was not based on performance but on who he was. The best robe, ring, and shoes belonged to him even if he failed, because his worth was based on the unconditional love of the father. Yes, the eldest son was unhappy about how he had acted, but that did not change the prodigal son's status—he was still a son! It was now time for him to learn what it meant to be a son in this family and to start acting like it.

Lu 15:20 And he arose, and came to his father. But when he was yet a great way off, his father saw him, and had compassion, and ran, and fell on his neck, and kissed him.

21 And the son said unto him, Father, I have sinned against heaven, and in thy sight, and am no more worthy to be called thy son.

22 But the father said to his servants, Bring forth the best robe, and put it on him; and put a ring on his hand, and shoes on his feet:

23 And bring hither the fatted calf, and kill it; and let us eat, and be merry:

24 For this my son was dead, and is alive again; he was lost, and is found. And they began to be merry.

25 Now his elder son was in the field: and as he came and drew nigh to the house, he heard musick and dancing.

26 And he called one of the servants, and asked what these things meant.

27 And he said unto him, Thy brother is come; and thy father hath killed the fatted calf, because he hath received him safe and sound.

28 And he was angry, and would not go in: therefore came his father out, and intreated him.

31 And he said unto him, Son, thou art ever with me, and all that I have is thine.

My Experience

The process of change from attempting to fulfill the law in our own strength to finding full liberty and self-discipline in Christ can take some time. Through trial and error, we begin to realize that since we are not under the law, we are free to do anything; but doing some things can bring significant consequences. During this time, the focus is on taking responsibility for how we want our lives to turn out. This alone can be enough to spur us into a life of self-control and a desire to win the victory over sin consistently. However,

God wants this inner desire to do right to be based on a more noble goal—our identification with Him, His glory, and His kingdom.

Soon after I fully committed my life to Christ, I began reading Watchman Nee's three volume book, *The Spiritual Man* (1968). I recognized the significance and the depth of his insight into the spiritual world, but I had a hard time grasping it and understanding how to apply it to my life. Much later in my life after I started counseling, I began using Neil Anderson's *Freedom from Addiction* program for clients who had a solid spiritual foundation. Its strong emphasis and excellent presentation on achieving freedom in Christ through identification with Him added to my understanding of this subject.

When I realized that I truly was a son of the King of Kings, I began to understand the obligations that came along with the privileges. Yes, I was free to do anything, but if I did do something, how would that affect the Kingdom of God, my church, and my ministry? It was time for me seriously to refocus on what I could do for the good of the kingdom that I would one day inherit with Christ. Did it make any sense at all to dabble in things that would defame God's kingdom or assist the devil in resisting God's power? No, it was time to get serious about being holy, both because it was what I desired, and because it was what the Kingdom of God needed—another dedicated and sanctified son who was completely focused on furthering the Kingdom of God.

Chapter 14

Life as a Child of God
(Jesus the Christ)

Our ability to achieve this step of perseverance depends on our position in Christ as an adopted son of God. Christ was to be the "firstborn of many brethren." Therefore, it only makes sense that Jesus Christ Himself should be our model for achieving the full revelation of what it means to be sons and daughters of the living God. In fact, Jesus is the perfect model of what we are to become (Hebrews 12:2).

1. <u>We must realize that even before we were born, we were called to be sons and daughters of God.</u> Just as Jesus was called to be the Son of God through the Spirit, each of us have been called to be God's adopted sons and daughters when we accept the Spirit of Christ into our hearts.

    Lu 1:35 And the angel answered and said unto her, The Holy Ghost shall come upon thee, and the power of the Highest shall overshadow thee: therefore also that holy thing which shall be born of thee shall be called the Son of God.

    Ga 4:5 To redeem them that were under the law, that we might receive the adoption of sons.

2. <u>When we become a son or daughter of God and are filled with the Spirit of God, we have all of the power available to us that was in Christ.</u> Just as all the fullness of the Godhead dwelt in Christ when He was here on earth, when we are in Christ, we have all of that same potential within us. This is critical because if Christ relied on His eternal power when He was here on earth, then we have no hope of being transformed into His likeness. However, the Scriptures assure us that we have been risen with and are "complete in Him."

    Col 2:9 For in him dwelleth all the fulness of the Godhead bodily.

    10 And ye are complete in him, which is the head of all principality and power:

3. <u>As children of God, we, like Christ, must be willing to humble ourselves to do whatever is necessary for the good of the Kingdom of God.</u> Employees can quit and contractors can claim they have not agreed to do something, but those in the family must be willing to do whatever it takes for the good of the family. God's kingdom must be our highest priority and obligation. Christ was even willing to die on the cross for the good of the Kingdom of God.

    Php 2:5 Let this mind be in you, which was also in Christ Jesus:

    6 Who, being in the form of God, thought it not robbery to be equal with God:

    7 But made himself of no reputation, and took upon him the form of a servant, and was made in the likeness of men:

    8 And being found in fashion as a man, he humbled himself, and became obedient unto death, even the death of the cross.

4. <u>We must follow Christ's example and do whatever we are asked without murmuring or complaining.</u>

    Php 2:15 That ye may be blameless and harmless, the sons of God, without rebuke, in the midst of a crooked and perverse nation, among whom ye shine as lights in the world;

    16 Holding forth the word of life; that I may rejoice in the day of Christ, that I have not run in vain, neither laboured in vain.

5. <u>We must have the revelation in our hearts that we are indeed sons and daughters of the living God and that we are part of His eternal family.</u> Just as Jesus had to believe the prophecies concerning Himself, we must believe that God has adopted us into His family and that we are saved.

    Mt 1:23 Behold, a virgin shall be with child, and shall bring forth a son, and they shall call his name Emmanuel, which being interpreted is, God with us.

    Ga 4:5 To redeem them that were under the law, that we might receive the adoption of sons.

6. <u>We must believe in our heart the same evidence that Jesus did, that God confirmed His calling at His baptism when the Spirit came upon Him.</u> In the same way, we can know that we are sons and daughters by the fact that we receive the Spirit when we are saved.

    Lu 3: 21 Now when all the people were baptized, it came to pass, that Jesus also being baptized, and praying, the heaven was opened,

    22 And the Holy Ghost descended in a bodily shape like a dove upon him, and a voice came from heaven, which said, Thou art my beloved Son; in thee I am well pleased.

    2 Co 1:22 Who hath also sealed us, and given the earnest of the Spirit in our hearts.

7. <u>Just as the devil tempted Jesus Christ, our status as a son or daughter of God will be challenged</u> We must know who we are in Christ, or we will not have the power to carry out our calling in the Kingdom of God. Note that the devil preceded the temptations of Christ with the challenge, "If you are the Son of God…" He tempted Jesus to use His ministry for His own needs, to use it to get power for Himself, and to tempt God instead of submit to God's plan for His life. We may also be tempted in these areas. If we are not totally sure we are a child of God, we will probably not persevere when things become difficult or major sacrifices are required of us.

    Lu 4:3 And the devil said unto him, If thou be the Son of God, command this stone that it be made bread.

    4 And Jesus answered him, saying, It is written, That man shall not live by bread alone, but by every word of God.

    5 And the devil, taking him up into an high mountain, shewed unto him all the kingdoms of the world in a moment of time.

    6 And the devil said unto him, All this power will I give thee, and the glory of them: for that is delivered unto me; and to whomsoever I will I give it.

    7 If thou therefore wilt worship me, all shall be thine.

    8 And Jesus answered and said unto him, Get thee behind me, Satan: for it is written, Thou shalt worship the Lord thy God, and him only shalt thou serve.

    9 And he brought him to Jerusalem, and set him on a pinnacle of the temple, and said unto him, If thou be the Son of God, cast thyself down from hence:

    10 For it is written, He shall give his angels charge over thee, to keep thee:

11 And in their hands they shall bear thee up, lest at any time thou dash thy foot against a stone.

12 And Jesus answering said unto him, It is said, Thou shalt not tempt the Lord thy God.

13 And when the devil had ended all the temptation, he departed from him for a season.

8. <u>We are called to preach, heal, and deliver just as Jesus was called to do these thing.</u> Whatever our elder brother Jesus has been called to do, we are called to assist Him in doing the same things.

Lu 4:17 And there was delivered unto him the book of the prophet Esaias. And when he had opened the book, he found the place where it was written,

18 The Spirit of the Lord is upon me, because he hath anointed me to preach the gospel to the poor; he hath sent me to heal the brokenhearted, to preach deliverance to the captives, and recovering of sight to the blind, to set at liberty them that are bruised,

19 To preach the acceptable year of the Lord.

20 And he closed the book, and he gave it again to the minister, and sat down. And the eyes of all them that were in the synagogue were fastened on him.

21 And he began to say unto them, This day is this scripture fulfilled in your ears.

9. <u>Just as Jesus' ministry was confirmed through signs, wonders, and miracles, we are to prove our calling to the world by the things that God is able to accomplish through us.</u>

Heb 2:3 How shall we escape, if we neglect so great salvation; which at the first began to be spoken by the Lord, and was confirmed unto us by them that heard him;

4 God also bearing them witness, both with signs and wonders, and with divers miracles, and gifts of the Holy Ghost, according to his own will?

Jo 5:36 But I have greater witness than that of John: for the works which the Father hath given me to finish, the same works that I do, bear witness of me, that the Father hath sent me.

14:12 Verily, verily, I say unto you, He that believeth on me, the works that I do shall he do also; and greater works than these shall he do; because I go unto my Father.

10. <u>Because God has predestinated us to be conformed to the image of Jesus, we have a clear model of what we are to do and how we are to act.</u> The popular phrase, "What would Jesus do?" applies.

Ro 8:29 For whom he did foreknow, he also did predestinate to be conformed to the image of his Son, that he might be the firstborn among many brethren.

Eph 4:13 Till we all come in the unity of the faith, and of the knowledge of the Son of God, unto a perfect man, unto the measure of the stature of the fulness of Christ:

Ga 2:20 I am crucified with Christ: nevertheless I live; yet not I, but Christ liveth in me: and the life which I now live in the flesh I live by the faith of the Son of God, who loved me, and gave himself for me.

11. <u>We are to act like sons and daughters of God, not servants.</u>

Jo 8:28 Then said Jesus unto them, When ye have lifted up the Son of man, then shall ye know that I am he, and that I do nothing of myself; but as my Father hath taught me, I speak these things.

8:35 And the servant abideth not in the house for ever: but the Son abideth ever.

12. <u>The basic principle for being part of the family of God is submission to the Father.</u> Although it meant unspeakable agony even to think about it, Christ willingly went to the cross because it was the will of the Father.

Lu 22:42 Saying, Father, if thou be willing, remove this cup from me: nevertheless not my will, but thine, be done.

43 And there appeared an angel unto him from heaven, strengthening him.

44 And being in an agony he prayed more earnestly: and his sweat was as it were great drops of blood falling down to the ground.

13. <u>We are to follow Jesus' example and look forward to what God will do through us in order to be joyfully obedient to Him—even if it means going to the cross.</u> This steadfastness even under the most severe trial is what the Bible calls perseverance. We are to follow in His footsteps.

Heb 12:1 Wherefore seeing we also are compassed about with so great a cloud of witnesses, let us lay aside every weight, and the sin which doth so easily beset us, and let us run with patience the race that is set before us,

2 Looking unto Jesus the author and finisher of our faith; who for the joy that was set before him endured the cross, despising the shame, and is set down at the right hand of the throne of God.

14. <u>The blessings and rewards of being part of the family of God are beyond human comprehension.</u>

1 Co 2:9 But as it is written, Eye hath not seen, nor ear heard, neither have entered into the heart of man, the things which God hath prepared for them that love him.

Re 21:7 He that overcometh shall inherit all things; and I will be his God, and he shall be my son.

Becoming a Son or Daughter of God

1.   We must realize that we have been called and predestined to be the adopted children of God.

2.   We must be willing to humble ourselves to do whatever is needed for the Kingdom of God, just as Jesus humbled Himself by becoming human and dying on the cross.

3.   We must develop faith and have a revelation in our hearts that we are truly children of the living God. We can know that this is true by the Spirit of God that lives within us. We must know and act like we are sons and daughters and not servants.

4.   We should see Jesus as our example of the life of a son or daughter in the service of our God. With Jesus as our elder brother, we are called to assist Him in doing whatever the Father requests.

5.   We must be willing to sacrifice anything that we have, even our lives for the Kingdom of God.

6.   Since we are to be conformed to the image of our elder brother Jesus, we should ask the question, "What would Jesus do?"

7.   If we persevere as children of God, we can expect rewards and an inheritance far beyond anything that we can imagine or think.

PART VII

Godliness—Knowing God as the Spirit of Holiness

Chapter 15

Dying to Self-life
The Spirit Overcomes the Flesh

2 Pe 1:6 And to knowledge temperance; and to temperance patience; and to patience godliness;

Once we are consistently obedient, we are finally in a position to really do God's will, maintain constant fellowship with God, and really get to know and worship Him as He really is. The word interpreted as godliness or holiness is *eusebeia* and means "reverence, respect, or piety towards God or godliness." This suggests becoming like God and developing godly character. According to John 14:21, God manifests Himself to those who obey Him: "He that hath my commandments, and keepeth them, he it is that loveth me: and he that loveth me shall be loved of my Father, and I will love him, and will manifest myself to him." As we commune with God, we are changed from glory to glory. We become more like Him and begin to display more of His character and power. We exchange our life for His life.

If, in this step, we are to take on the character of God Himself, then we must be led by the Spirit of God, be obedient to the will of the Father, take on the identity of Christ, overcome the lust of the flesh and its stronghold in our lives, and have a pure heart. This requires achieving victory in our lives in a number of critical areas. Several have already been partially achieved at this point in our spiritual development and a number have not yet been addressed. They are: 1. Giving the Spirit priority in our lives. (Virtue or making Jesus Lord) 2. Obedience to the law of God. (Self-control) 3. Establishing our identity in Christ. (Perseverance) 4. Dying to the self-life. 5. Mortifying the flesh. 6. Overcoming the strongholds in our lives through the Spirit. 7. Purifying our hearts. In the remainder of this section, I will discuss how each of these is to be firmly established in our lives.

Exchanging Our Life for His Life

Possibly the clearest verse that describes this step of godiness is found in Galatians Chapter 2. The idea presented here is that we are now one with Christ and Christ lives in us. As we yield more and more of our selfish desires to God, He is able to express more of Himself through us. In one of his Sunday School classes D. L. Moody held up a glass and asked the class "How can I get the air out of this glass? The answer, of course, was to fill the glass with water and automatically it would displace the air. (Tan, 1988, #2233) In the same way, we need to be filled with the Spirit of God to displace our own fleshly and selfish desires so that we can be transformed into His image. This is what has been termed "life exchange."

> Ga 2:20 I am crucified with Christ: nevertheless I live; yet not I, but Christ liveth in me: and the life which I now live in the flesh I live by the faith of the Son of God, who loved me, and gave himself for me.

Before continuing, it is important that we understand what the Bible means when it calls on us to "die to the self-life" (Matthew 16:25, Mark 8:35, Luke 9:24, 17:33) and to "mortify the flesh" (Romans 8:13) In the verses concerning dying to our self-life, it is clear that those who save their self-life, will lose God's abundant or eternal life. This "life-exchange" deals with giving the spirit priority in our lives, over the needs of the self, which include self-worth, significance, security, and love. Only by giving priority to the things of God can we acquire the life of God. Romans 8:13 states that "if ye through the Spirit do mortify the deeds of the body, ye shall live." This makes it clear that our efforts to meet our needs through our own strength or the flesh must die. Instead, we must rely on God to meet our needs. We, therefore, die to the self by giving greater priority to the things of the Spirit and the Kingdom of God; and we die to the flesh by giving up our attempts to meet our own needs by our own efforts.

Walking According to the Spirit

God has an overall plan for developing godliness in us. Instead of a negative plan of trying to make us give up something that we want to keep, it is a positive plan of giving us something better. He wants us to learn to walk according to the Spirit instead of focusing on our own selfish desires and attempting to meet these desires by relying on our flesh.

To walk according to the Spirit means to live a life directed by, obedient to, and relying on the Spirit of God. It requires that we yield our will completely to the will of God as we effectively discern the leading of God's Spirit, and act accordingly. This is a learned process. It is essential to living a holy, sanctified Christian life. Watchman Nee states, "Nothing is more vital to the Christian life than to walk daily after the spirit. It is this that maintains the Christian in a constant spiritual state, delivers him from the power of the flesh, assists him to obey God's will always, and shields him from the assault of Satan." (Nee, 1968, Vol. Two. P. 129)

1. <u>God has a plan for our lives, to motivate us through the Spirit to do His will.</u>

   Eze 36:27 And I will put my spirit within you, and cause you to walk in my statutes, and ye shall keep my judgments, and do [them].

2. <u>He has put aside our offenses.</u> If we will walk after His Spirit, we will not feel condemned and will be able to have a loving relationship with Him.

   Ro 8:1 [There is] therefore now no condemnation to them which are in Christ Jesus, who walk not after the flesh, but after the Spirit.

3. <u>This inner law frees us to make right choices that lead to life and not sin and death.</u> We are transformed from the inside out through our spiritual relationship with God.

   Ro 8:2 For the law of the Spirit of life in Christ Jesus hath made me free from the law of sin and death.

4. <u>Now through what Jesus has done, we have the power to obey the law of God through the Spirit.</u>

   Ro 8:3 For what the law could not do, in that it was weak through the flesh, God sending his own Son in the likeness of sinful flesh, and for sin, condemned sin in the flesh:

   4 That the righteousness of the law might be fulfilled in us, who walk not after the flesh, but after the Spirit.

5. <u>We walk according to the Spirit by focusing our life on spiritual things.</u>

   Ro 8:5 For they that are after the flesh do mind the things of the flesh; but they that are after the Spirit the things of the Spirit.

6. <u>We must rely on the Spirit, in order to die to the flesh, so that we can have God's abundant life.</u>

    Ro 8:13 For if ye live after the flesh, ye shall die: but if ye through the Spirit do mortify the deeds of the body, ye shall live.

7. <u>This new spiritual life is based on a personal, intimate relationship with God.</u>

    Ro 8:14 For as many as are led by the Spirit of God, they are the sons of God.

    15 For ye have not received the spirit of bondage again to fear; but ye have received the Spirit of adoption, whereby we cry, Abba, Father.

    16 The Spirit itself beareth witness with our spirit, that we are the children of God:

8. <u>As we become identified with the body of Christ and are willing to suffer with Him, we will be rewarded together with Him.</u>

    Ro 8:17 And if children, then heirs; heirs of God, and joint-heirs with Christ; if so be that we suffer with [him], that we may be also glorified together.

9. <u>As we walk according to the Spirit, we are delivered from the bondage of the lusts of the flesh, so that we can live a righteous life.</u>

    Ga 5:16 [This] I say then, Walk in the Spirit, and ye shall not fulfil the lust of the flesh.

    17 For the flesh lusteth against the Spirit, and the Spirit against the flesh: and these are contrary the one to the other: so that ye cannot do the things that ye would.

Dying to Our Self-life

Self-centeredness or selfishness is the underlying basis of the sin problem. As I have stated before, the psychological needs of the self are the need to feel worthwhile, to be significant, to feel secure, and to be loved. Our self-life is the life we live that is focused on meeting the needs of our self. In secular counseling, the goal is to help the client to better meet the needs of the self through the flesh in a more socially acceptable and effective way. Without faith, it is impossible to die to our self-life or to overcome the problem of the selfishness within us. Through faith, God calls us to give up focusing on meeting our selfish desires through the flesh, in order to give priority to and receive the far greater rewards of the Kingdom of God, through the Spirit. These principles of dying to our self-life lead us to serve God and the interests of others more and more as we grow in faith, knowing that God will take care of our needs because He loves us. The more we trust God, the more we will be willing to give up our attempts to meet our needs through relying on the flesh. The flesh can never overcome our selfish desires. They can only be overcome through the Spirit, as we count the things of God as more important and exchange one life for the other.

In the Greek there is a very important distinction between the words that the King James Bible translates as life. The first word is *psuche* which means "our soul" or self-life which tries to meet the needs of the self by relying on the flesh. It includes self-admiration, self-assertion, self-centeredness, self-conceit, self-confidence, self-control, self-determination, self-devotion, self-desire, self-expression, self-importance, self-indulgence, self-interest, self-pity, self-preservation, self-regard, self-righteousness, self-satisfaction, self-seeking, self-serving, self-sufficiency, self-sustaining, self-will, and many more. The second word is *zoe*, which is many times translated as eternal or everlasting life. It actually refers to the quality and length of spiritual life that God lives. It is sometimes also translated as the abundant life. It can be described by replacing the word "self" with the word "spirit" in the list above. Therefore, in the verses that follow, we are enjoined to give up our soul or self-life, in exchange for the type and quality of spiritual life that God lives. Jim Elliott, who was martyred as a missionary in South America, put it this way: "He is no fool who gives up what he cannot keep to have that which he cannot lose." (Tan, 1988, #5219)

1. Man looks at his self or natural life as something to be nurtured and preserved.

    Eph 5:29 For no man ever yet hated his own flesh; but nourisheth and cherisheth it...

2. The world is motivated through its attempts to meet the needs of the self.

    Php 2:21 For all seek their own, not the things which are Jesus Christ's.

3. This striving to meet the needs of the self results in the evil symptoms of self-focus or selfishness. This is the basis of lust and evil in the world.

    2 Ti 3:2 For men shall be lovers of their own selves, covetous, boasters, proud, blasphemers, disobedient to parents, unthankful, unholy,

    3 Without natural affection, trucebreakers, false accusers, incontinent, fierce, despisers of those that are good,

    4 Traitors, heady, highminded, lovers of pleasures more than lovers of God; (AV)

4. If Christ died for us, we should be willing to give up our self-life to live for Him.

    2 Co 5:15 And [that] he died for all, that they which live should not henceforth live unto themselves, but unto him which died for them, and rose again.

5. When we get our eyes off our needs through faith we can focus on the needs of others.

    Php 2:3 [Let] nothing [be done] through strife or vainglory; but in lowliness of mind let each esteem other better than themselves.

    4 Look not every man on his own things, but every man also on the things of others.

6. We must die to soulish affection.

    Mt 10:37 He that loveth father or mother more than me is not worthy of me: and he that loveth son or daughter more than me is not worthy of me.

    38 And he that taketh not his cross, and followeth after me, is not worthy of me.

    39 He that findeth his life shall lose it: and he that loseth his life for my sake shall find it.

7. We must die to self-will.

    Mt 16:24 Then said Jesus unto his disciples, If any [man] will come after me, let him deny himself, and take up his cross, and follow me.

    25 For whosoever will save his life shall lose it: and whosoever will lose his life for my sake shall find it.

    26 For what is a man profited, if he shall gain the whole world, and lose his own soul? or what shall a man give in exchange for his soul? (AV)

8. <u>This dying to self must be done on a daily basis.</u>

    1 Co 15:31 I protest by your rejoicing which I have in Christ Jesus our Lord, I die daily.

9. <u>Dying to the self is our reasonable service and is necessary for fulfilling God's purpose in our lives.</u>

    Ro 12:1 I beseech you therefore, brethren, by the mercies of God, that ye present your bodies a living sacrifice, holy, acceptable unto God, [which is] your reasonable service.

    2 And be not conformed to this world: but be ye transformed by the renewing of your mind, that ye may prove what [is] that good, and acceptable, and perfect, will of God.

10. <u>If we seek the best interests of the Kingdom of God first, God will meet all our needs.</u> If we seek to meet our needs directly ourselves, our lives will become selfish and we will fail in our attempt to satisfy our needs.

    Mt 6:31 Therefore take no thought, saying, What shall we eat? or, What shall we drink? or, Wherewithal shall we be clothed?

    33 But seek ye first the kingdom of God, and his righteousness; and all these things shall be added unto you.

11. <u>We must learn to esteem riches and possessions lightly.</u>

    Mt 19:23 Then said Jesus unto his disciples, Verily I say unto you, That a rich man shall hardly enter into the kingdom of heaven.

    24 And again I say unto you, It is easier for a camel to go through the eye of a needle, than for a rich man to enter into the kingdom of God.

12. <u>We must choose not to love the world, but the love the Father instead.</u>

    1 Jo 2:15 Love not the world, neither the things [that are] in the world. If any man love the world, the love of the Father is not in him.

    16 For all that [is] in the world, the lust of the flesh, and the lust of the eyes, and the pride of life, is not of the Father, but is of the world.

    17 And the world passeth away, and the lust thereof: but he that doeth the will of God abideth for ever.

13. <u>We must die to our soul-life in order to produce the fruit of eternal life.</u>

    Jo 12:24 Verily, verily, I say unto you, Except a corn of wheat fall into the ground and die, it abideth alone: but if it die, it bringeth forth much fruit.

    25 He that loveth his life shall lose it; and he that hateth his life in this world shall keep it unto life eternal.

14. <u>We must be more concerned about honoring God, than being concerned about what men think about us.</u>

    Mr 8:38 Whosoever therefore shall be ashamed of me and of my words in this adulterous and sinful generation; of him also shall the Son of man be ashamed, when he cometh in the glory of his Father with the holy angels.

It is important to realize that our outer man (the soul) with its desires must be broken in order for our inner man (the spirit) to be released. As long as our soul, dominated by the flesh will not yield to our spirit and the Spirit of God, we will not be able to walk effectively according to the Spirit. Consequently, this is a growing cyclical type of action. As we learn to walk according to the Spirit, we displace the self and our reliance on the flesh. This weakens their influence on us, so that we desire more of the Spirit and are able to yield ourselves in a greater measure to walk according to the Spirit. Eventually our spirit gains influence and our flesh and self decrease, until we are able to more fully and consistently walk according to the Spirit of God as it influences our spirit.

Dying to the Flesh

The first result of concentrating on spiritual things (dying to the self-life), is that we rely less and less on the carnal or fleshly things of this life to meet our needs. Either we walk according to the Spirit and get our needs met through the Spirit, or we walk according to the flesh and try to get our needs met through relying on the flesh. We cannot have both because they war against each other for the control of our soul.

1. <u>Carnal Christians are Christians who continue to rely on the flesh in order to meet the needs of the self.</u>

    1 Co 3:3 For ye are yet carnal: for whereas [there is] among you envying, and strife, and divisions, are ye not carnal, and walk as men?

    4 For while one saith, I am of Paul; and another, I [am] of Apollos; are ye not carnal?

2. <u>The Spirit resists the control of the flesh and the flesh resists the Spirit.</u>

    Ga 5:16 This I say then, Walk in the Spirit, and ye shall not fulfil the lust of the flesh.

    17 For the flesh lusteth against the Spirit, and the Spirit against the flesh: and these are contrary the one to the other: so that ye cannot do the things that ye would.

3. <u>Relying on the flesh will result in the evil manifestations of the flesh in our lives.</u>

    Ga 5:19 When you follow the desires of your sinful nature, your lives will produce these evil results: sexual immorality, impure thoughts, eagerness for lustful pleasure,

    20 idolatry, participation in demonic activities, hostility, quarreling, jealousy, outbursts of anger, selfish ambition, divisions, the feeling that everyone is wrong except those in your own little group,

    21 envy, drunkenness, wild parties, and other kinds of sin. Let me tell you again, as I have before, that anyone living that sort of life will not inherit the Kingdom of God. (NLT)

4. <u>The fruits of the Spirit are the direct opposites to the manifestation of the flesh.</u> Therefore, if we cultivate the fruit of the Spirit, we are working directly in opposition to the control of the flesh in our lives.

    Ga 5:22 But when the Holy Spirit controls our lives, he will produce this kind of fruit in us: love, joy, peace, patience, kindness, goodness, faithfulness,

    23 gentleness, and self-control. Here there is no conflict with the law. (NLT)

5. <u>The gifts of the Spirit are given to us to overcome the domination of the flesh in our lives.</u> They are spiritual tools that provide the power to directly oppose the destructive power of the flesh in our lives.

> 1 Co 12:7 But the manifestation of the Spirit is given to every man to profit withal.
>
> 8 For to one is given by the Spirit the word of wisdom; to another the word of knowledge by the same Spirit;
>
> 9 To another faith by the same Spirit; to another the gifts of healing by the same Spirit;
>
> 10 To another the working of miracles; to another prophecy; to another discerning of spirits; to another divers kinds of tongues; to another the interpretation of tongues:
>
> 11 But all these worketh that one and the selfsame Spirit, dividing to every man severally as he will.

6. <u>It is our job to crucify our reliance on the flesh, by choosing instead to rely more and more on the Spirit.</u>

> Ga 5:24 And they that are Christ's have crucified the flesh with the affections and lusts.

7. <u>We must realize that our actions will determine whether the spirit or flesh wins out in our lives.</u> The more we focus and rely on spiritual things, the more our spirit prospers, and the more we rely on the flesh to meet our needs, the more it will dominate in our lives.

> Ga 6:7 Be not deceived; God is not mocked: for whatsoever a man soweth, that shall he also reap.
>
> 8 For he that soweth to his flesh shall of the flesh reap corruption; but he that soweth to the Spirit shall of the Spirit reap life everlasting.

My experience

From my reading of *The Spiritual Man* (Nee, 1968) I understood the need to walk according to the Spirit of God. I did what I could to try to walk according to the Spirit, with mixed results. Probably my greatest hindrance was that I still had a tendency to want to perform and accomplish things for God in my own strength, rather than desiring to spend intimate time with Him in order to strengthen my spiritual walk. I realized that men (as opposed to women) tend to build relationships through working and doing things together but my greater need was to develop a much closer personal relationship with God. My greatest success in walking according to the Spirit would come when I dedicated an entire Saturday to just spend time with God and tried to do whatever I felt He was telling me to do, through the inner voice of my spiritual intuition. I could connect better with Him when my time was completely dedicated to my relationship with Him.

I have to admit that I was more like an Old Testament saint. I related directly with God as to the affairs of my life, but I was not consistently walking according to the Spirit. In fact, I would tend to switch between a focus on accomplishing things that I needed to do in this life and focusing on the things of God. As I ministered or studied for sermons, I was intensely involved in the things of God; and when I focused on my secular work, I was intensely involved in it. After retirement from the United States Air Force and entry into full time ministry, a large majority of my time was now spent on the things of God. However, I felt His presence only on a periodic basis, mostly as part of a powerful praise service or when I was intently seeking God's guidance for the answer to some important question. I prayed when important concerns required it, insured a certain amount of spiritual input by reading the daily segment of the *One Year Bible* (1991), and listened to the Bible as I drove in my vehicle. I was in a maintenance mode of spirituality.

At times, I had a deep desire to completely refocus my entire life on spiritual things, but the "thorns of the cares of this world" eventually choked out the desire and I found myself back in the daily grind of life. This was especially true when I was focused on another project, which I felt I just had to get done. Somehow, I had to find a way out of this carnal rut. I knew that I needed to die to the flesh and my soul-life, but I did not know how to do it.

One day as I was lecturing on spiritual growth at Word of Life Institute, I began seeing a link between walking in the Spirit, dying to the self-life, and dying to the flesh. Later, as I was preparing for the next class, I realized that the fruit and gifts of the Spirit and the manifestations of the flesh were opposites. Could it be that walking in the Spirit was the key to dying to the soul-life and mortifying the flesh? I made a chart and mapped one against the other. I now knew how to do it, but I still needed the desire to do it.

No matter how hard I tried, I had been unable to walk consistently according to the Spirit. I now realized that I would have to do this in order to win the battle over the self and the flesh. It seemed I was at a dead end. No matter how much I wanted to, I just could not move to this next level of spiritual growth. I just could not do it.

The answer finally came when I again realized a fundamental principle of spiritual change. Each step requires a revelation that we cannot do it in our own strength. Just as I realized that I could not direct my life and that I could not obey the law, I had to come to the revelation that I could not, in my own strength, walk consistently in the Spirit, die to my self-life or to the flesh. If we believe we can do something, we will attempt to do it in the flesh; and the flesh is definitely not interested in or capable of dying to the self-life or to the flesh! I had to turn it completely over to God and rely on the Spirit to do it. I cried out to Him to "consume me with spiritual desire" and take full control of all of my life. I still lacked one piece of the puzzle.

As I prepared to preach a series of sermons on the rebuilding of the Temple and the walls of Jerusalem, I realized the connection between rebuilding the city of peace (Jerusalem) and the establishment of godliness in our lives. If I wanted to develop the character of Jesus (godliness), the Spirit of Christ would have to control my heart fully. Only when this occurred, would I experience the peace of God in my spirit. If there remained any of the vestiges of the conflict between the Spirit and the flesh, I could not be at peace in my spirit. In order to continually have peace in my spirit, I would have to purify my heart and exclude all fleshly strongholds (lust, fear, and selfish desires) from my life that might disturb that peace. This, in practical application, is dying to the self and the flesh. I could not have any mixture of the things of the world and the things of God in my life and still maintain God's peace. I needed to let the peace of God rule in my life (Colossians 3:15) and exclude everything that disturbed that peace. Through faith, all anxiety, conflict, and other disturbances of the flesh would have to be overcome and excluded forever.

Chapter 16

Overcoming the Flesh
(The Model of Esther)

In attempting to achieve godliness in our lives, possibly the most difficult task is that of successfully overcoming our reliance on the flesh. The flesh, motivated by the self, attempts to meet our needs in our own strength, and in our way. The war between the flesh and the spirit is one of the most predominant themes in the Bible and one that constantly disturbs our peace. Once our reliance on the flesh has become solidly established, it is very difficult to overcome. This conflict accounts for most of the backsliding among church members and many of the failures in Christian ministry. All of us begin the process of salvation, meeting most of our needs relying on the flesh. If we do not overcome our reliance on the flesh, the flesh will continue to manifest itself and dominate our lives; and we will remain carnal Christians. The manifestations of the flesh usually result in boundary violations and the abuse of others.

In the book of Exodus, as they prepared to enter the Promised Land, Israel fought and won a battle against the Amalikites. According to *Wilson's Dictionary of Bible Types* (1957) Amalek is a type of the flesh. The battle was won only after Aaron and Hur supported Moses' arms, as he held up the staff of God's authority. When they did, the Israelite army, led by Joshua, was finally able to win the victory. The text declares that God would have war with Amalek from generation to generation (Exodus 17:16). God takes our battle to overcome the flesh in our lives very seriously. King Saul was removed as king when he refused to totally destroy the Amalekites (the flesh). (1 Samuel 28:18)

One of the most intriguing stories in the Bible is that of Esther. I have to admit that I pondered this story for years until the Holy Spirit helped me to understand its significance in helping clients overcome the domination of the flesh in their lives. Because of the large number of verses involved, I will briefly explain the meaning of this story as I interpret it and only quote those scriptures that are necessary to get a complete understanding of the process for overcoming the flesh in our lives.

Esther Chapter 1 one through Chapter 3 gives us a broad history of the conflict between the flesh and the Spirit. Ahasuerus, whose name means prince, represents God. He is married to Queen Vashti, whose name means "beautiful woman." I believe she represents the natural person of creation. Just like Adam and Eve, she refused to obey King Ahasuerus when he called her to the banquet, and, therefore, was not suited to reign with him. Ahasuerus, therefore, replaced Vashti with Esther who represents the spiritual person (Esther's other name is Hadassah meaning "myrtle" which stands for the Christian life). Mordecai (which means "little man" or our spirit) was the uncle who raised Esther. Haman (which means "celebrated man") was an Amalekite. This tribe stands for the flesh. He (the flesh) was put in charge of the kingdom, just as the natural man in Adam is ruled by the flesh and was originally commissioned by God to carry out His will on earth. The flesh (Haman) desired to be worshipped but the spirit (Mordecai) refused. The flesh, therefore, wanted to kill the spirit and all spiritual men, so it attempted to do so with the law. The law is the downfall of every person who tries to obey it in his own strength. The king (God) made an edict that all who do not completely obey the law (the Jews) must die. The spiritual man had no other option but to appeal to God for help, just as we have no other option except to appeal to God for a Savior because no one of us is able on our own ability to obey the law completely. Esther's appeal to the king (God) to overcome the flesh provides the basis of a model that can guide us on our quest to overcome the flesh in our own lives.

1. <u>The spiritual person must realize that the flesh is not an ally, but an enemy that intends to kill him and therefore should appeal to God for help.</u> Esther (the spiritual person) was informed by Mordecai (our spirit) that Haman (the flesh) had succeeded in obtaining a decree (the law) for the destruction of all the Jews (spiritual people). Until the client realizes that being controlled by the flesh can and will destroy his relationship with God and result in significant consequences, he will not be able to make any progress in his spiritual walk. Sin has pleasure for a season. He must realize that the flesh intends to kill his spiritual man and that he cannot conquer it in his own strength.

2. <u>The spiritual person must take action against the flesh or the evil will overcome him.</u> Overcoming the flesh is not an automatic result of spiritual birth. The flesh wars against the Spirit in its battle to remain the dominant influence over the soul. The Holy Spirit draws the soul to desire holiness and a spiritual walk with God. The spiritual person must act or his flesh will continue to dominate his soul and, ultimately, bring his destruction. He will not escape. We have all come to the Kingdom of God to assist in the destruction of our flesh and become effective spiritual men and women.

    Es 4:13 Then Mordecai commanded to answer Esther, Think not with thyself that thou shalt escape in the king's house, more than all the Jews.

    14 For if thou altogether holdest thy peace at this time, [then] shall there enlargement and deliverance arise to the Jews from another place; but thou and thy father's house shall be destroyed: and who knoweth whether thou art come to the kingdom for [such] a time as this?

3. <u>The first step in breaking the power of the flesh is to fast.</u> Fasting helps us concentrate on spiritual things and breaks the power of the flesh. Without fasting, it is usually more difficult to hear from God. According to Isaiah Chapter 58, fasting moves the hand of God in difficult situations.

    Es 4:15 Then Esther bade [them] return Mordecai [this answer],

    16 Go, gather together all the Jews that are present in Shushan, and fast ye for me, and neither eat nor drink three days, night or day: I also and my maidens will fast likewise; and so will I go in unto the king, which [is] not according to the law: and if I perish, I perish.

4. <u>We must be willing to die to ourselves, accept our position in Christ, and boldly enter into His presence believing that God will favor and help us.</u> God always favors the spiritual person, since only spiritual people can and will obey Him. Jesus provided the way, through the veil that was ripped in two when He died on the cross, so that we can enter boldly into His presence at any time that we choose. However, we are the ones who must choose to come and request His assistance in overcoming the flesh.

    Es 5:1 Now it came to pass on the third day, that Esther put on [her] royal [apparel] (The robe of Jesus' righteousness), and stood in the inner court of the king's house, over against the king's house: and the king sat upon his royal throne in the royal house, over against the gate of the house.

    2 And it was so, when the king saw Esther the queen standing in the court, [that] she obtained favour in his sight: and the king held out to Esther the golden sceptre that [was] in his hand. So Esther drew near, and touched the top of the sceptre.

5. <u>Spiritual feeding is essential because the spiritual man must be strong in order to confront the flesh.</u> Esther met with the king and Haman two times before exposing Haman. We must remember that Haman was the second ruler of the entire kingdom and had great influence. Similarly, the flesh is the main method of functioning for most persons and has significant dominance over the soul, prior to salvation. As we minister and commune with God, our trust that He will meet our needs, even without the assistance of the flesh, grows. The banquet of wine stands for spiritual communion and intimacy.

Es 5:4 And Esther answered, If [it seem] good unto the king, let the king and Haman come this day unto the banquet that I have prepared for him.

6 And the king said unto Esther at the banquet of wine (spirit), What [is] thy petition? and it shall be granted thee: and what [is] thy request? even to the half of the kingdom it shall be performed.

7 Then answered Esther, and said, My petition and my request [is];

8 If I have found favour in the sight of the king, and if it please the king to grant my petition, and to perform my request, let the king and Haman come to the banquet that I shall prepare for them, and I will do to morrow as the king hath said.

6. <u>God favors the spirit because it is on His side and commands the flesh to honor it.</u> Because the spirit (Modecai) had helped Ahasuerus (God), by revealing the plot of the door keepers, He wanted to honor Modecai, and directed Haman (the flesh) to do so. God wants our flesh to line up and support the influence of our spirit. Although this is the last thing the flesh wants, it has no choice if the spirit becomes dominant over the soul.

Es 6:10 Then the king said to Haman, Make haste, [and] take the apparel and the horse, as thou hast said, and do even so to Mordecai the Jew, that sitteth at the king's gate: let nothing fail of all that thou hast spoken.

7. <u>The deeds of the flesh must be exposed.</u> Esther exposed the fact that Haman was trying to kill her and all the Jews (spiritual men). When the client chooses to expose the flesh as his enemy and asks God for deliverance, the flesh quickly loses its power.

Es 7: 3 Then Esther the queen answered and said, If I have found favour in thy sight, O king, and if it please the king, let my life be given me at my petition, and my people at my request:

4 For we are sold, I and my people, to be destroyed, to be slain, and to perish. But if we had been sold for bondmen and bondwomen, I had held my tongue, although the enemy could not countervail the king's damage.

5 Then the king Ahasuerus answered and said unto Esther the queen, Who is he, and where is he, that durst presume in his heart to do so?

6 And Esther said, The adversary and enemy [is] this wicked Haman. Then Haman was afraid before the king and the queen.

8. <u>When exposed, we can count on God's wrath against the flesh to end its power.</u> God Himself, who will not override our will, will quickly execute judgment on the flesh in favor of our spirit, when we truly want and desire deliverance. To God, the domination of the flesh over the spiritual person is the equivalent of rape!

Es 7:7 And the king arising from the banquet of wine in his wrath [went] into the palace garden: and Haman stood up to make request for his life to Esther the queen; for he saw that there was evil determined against him by the king.

8 Then the king returned out of the palace garden into the place of the banquet of wine; and Haman was fallen upon the bed whereon Esther [was]. Then said the king, Will he force the queen also before me in the house? As the word went out of the king's mouth, they covered Haman's face.

9.   The flesh must be hung based on its own inability to obey God. Haman attempted to use the law to destroy both Modecai and the Jews, but the inability of the flesh to obey the law itself requires the destruction of the flesh. Five stands for the weakness of every human being and ten stands for man's infirmity and failure. It is these fifty cubit high gallows (The flesh's weakness and inability to obey God) from which the flesh must be hung. They who are dominated by the flesh cannot please God. When this reality becomes a revelation in our spirit, we will immediately agree that we must mortify (kill) the flesh in our lives.

Es 7:9 And Harbonah, one of the chamberlains, said before the king, Behold also, the gallows fifty cubits high, which Haman had made for Mordecai, who had spoken good for the king, standeth in the house of Haman. Then the king said, Hang him thereon.

10 So they hanged Haman on the gallows that he had prepared for Mordecai. Then was the king's wrath pacified.

10.   We must realize that God has given the spiritual man (the Christian) power over all the resources of the flesh. With the death of the flesh, all the resources of the soul become available for the use of the spiritual person.

Es 8:1 On that day did the king Ahasuerus give the house of Haman the Jews' enemy unto Esther the queen. And Mordecai came before the king; for Esther had told what he [was] unto her.

11.   God has taken from the flesh all authority to rule men and has given it to the spirit. Therefore, we must place the spirit in charge of all that we have. The signet ring, in those days, provided absolute authority; since it was used to sign official decrees. After the flesh is overcome, the spirit filled with the Spirit of God, has absolute authority to act for God Himself and has absolute power over all the resources of the flesh.

Es 8:2 And the king took off his ring, which he had taken from Haman, and gave it unto Mordecai. And Esther set Mordecai over the house of Haman.

12.   The very law that was against our spiritual man is now for us, because Christ has fulfilled the law; and through the power of the Spirit we can now obey the law. God, through Jesus, has reversed the curse of the law that was against us, because through the spirit we now can and want to obey the law—not in our own strength—but in His.

Es 8:5 And said, If it please the king, and if I have found favour in his sight, and the thing [seem] right before the king, and I [be] pleasing in his eyes, let it be written to reverse the letters devised by Haman the son of Hammedatha the Agagite, which he wrote to destroy the Jews which [are] in all the king's provinces:

13. <u>We must work together to use the authority God has given us and the power of the Spirit to destroy all the power of the flesh in our lives.</u> The Jews gathered together to defend themselves according to the edict of the king. In the same way, the entire host of God's angels joins with the Christian who dares to take a stand against the flesh and the world, and all the forces of evil against him.

> Es 9:2 The Jews gathered themselves together in their cities throughout all the provinces of the king Ahasuerus, to lay hand on such as sought their hurt: and no man could withstand them; for the fear of them fell upon all people.
>
> 3 And all the rulers of the provinces, and the lieutenants, and the deputies, and officers of the king, helped the Jews; because the fear of Mordecai fell upon them.
>
> 4 For Mordecai [was] great in the king's house, and his fame went out throughout all the provinces: for this man Mordecai waxed greater and greater.
>
> 5 Thus the Jews smote all their enemies with the stroke of the sword, and slaughter, and destruction, and did what they would unto those that hated them.

Perhaps the most crucial part of this battle over the flesh is convincing the client that his flesh is his enemy and that it is plotting his destruction. Once the client sees the flesh as his enemy, he must build his faith that God will meet all of his needs through the Spirit in a more wonderful and greater way than he has ever experienced in his more carnal days. This faith must be built experientially. As his spirit becomes more dominant, the client will have a greater desire for the things of the Spirit, will meet more of his needs through the Spirit, and will stand stronger against the temptation of the flesh until complete victory is won. The ultimate in God is then a life of walking according to the direction of the Spirit, as described in Romans Chapter 8. Of course, this fight may need to be repeated as the faith-life ebbs and flows from time to time in the life of the individual believer.

Overcoming the Flesh

1. We must realize that the flesh is our enemy. If we rely on the flesh to meet our needs, it will destroy our lives.

2. Begin with fasting and prayer.

3. We must confess our inability, without God's help, to overcome our reliance on the flesh. We must determine to rely on God instead of on ourselves to meet our needs.

4. We must use our position in Christ to approach God in faith for help.

5. We must strengthen our spiritual life through the spiritual disciplines and spending quality time with Him.

6. We must use God's authority to overcome the flesh by exposing the works of the flesh, trusting God to meet all of our needs according to the Spirit, and choosing to die to our self-life by putting God first in our lives.

7. We must remain in a loving, focused, favored position with God, and do God's will by walking according to and relying on the Spirit.

Chapter 17

Establishing the Control of the Spirit in Our Hearts
(Rebuilding the Temple by Ezra)

One of the most crucial issues in developing godliness is establishing spiritual control in our hearts. Although our spiritual life had dominance in the garden, when Adam and Eve ate of the tree of good and evil, our spirits were deposed from their rightful position. When we rely on the flesh to meet our needs, it will eventually dominate our hearts and we will backslide.

The rule of the spirit in our hearts is symbolized in the Bible by the temple of God. The temple is where God dwells; therefore, it can refer to the universal church, an individual church, the body of the individual Christian, our soul, or our spirit. In a direct analogy to the ancient temple, the Outer Place is our body, the Holy Place is our soul, and the Holy of Holies is our spirit in which the Holy Spirit is to dwell. When Jesus stated that God would destroy this temple and raise it again in three days, He was referring to His body (Mark 14:58). When He cleansed the temple, He was figuratively cleansing the heart of the deeds of the flesh (Matthew 21:12). When the veil of the temple was ripped in two when Jesus died (Mark 15:38), it indicated that the spirit and soul were no longer separated and that our spirit controlled by the Holy Spirit, was again to be predominant in our heart.

There are many reasons why the temple of our hearts, where our spirit resides, can be destroyed or left in ruin. In the case of the children of Israel, it was due to pride, prolonged sin, and a refusal to repent. After God added 15 years to Hezekiah's life, he became prideful and showed all of his treasures to Babylonian emissaries. (2 Kings 20 and Isaiah 39) The Babylonians later destroyed the temple and the city of Jerusalem. Jerusalem means "city of peace" and Babylon means "confusion due to mixing." When we are tempted by pride and think our success is of our own doing (rely on the flesh) and when we begin to compromise in our lives with the lust of the flesh and sin, our lives become confused, as the flesh and the spirit struggle for predominance. Eventually, if the flesh wins over our spirit for the control of our soul, the temple of our heart will be left in disrepair and may even be destroyed.

Nebuchadnezzar means "the God Nebo is the protector against misfortune." It is the role of the self to protect us against misfortune. He was the Babylonian King who captured the nation of Israel and Judah and took the Israelites away to Babylon (confusion). He destroyed the temple building and the walls of Jerusalem. When the self becomes dominant in our soul and we rely on the flesh, it destroys our peace and brings confusion to our heart. When we come to Christ, we are all still self-centered. Since we are motivated by the self, we are by nature, selfish. Our flesh, which serves the self, can never bring life, only a confused attempt to meet our own needs in our own strength at the expense of others. This is not God's will. The Bible tells us that the Branch (Jesus) was to rebuild the temple (Zechariah 6:12). In truth, He has: body, soul, and spirit. He has provided all that we need.

The only answer to this confusion is to re-establish the control of the spirit in our lives. This is God's will since only the spirit will obey God and carry out His directions. In practical application, this is the establishment of the spirit as director of the soul after salvation or the rededication and restoration of a Christian, whose life has been overcome by selfishness and reliance on the flesh. Of course, if the person has never been saved, leading him to a personal relationship with Christ is the first step. Our story begins in Ezra Chapter 1.

A. We Must Become Tired of the Confusion in our Lives and Strongly Desire to have Peace.

1. <u>We must accept God's will in our lives.</u> It is God's will that the temple of our spirit be rebuilt and be established as the ruler of our soul, so that we can have peace in our hearts. I believe that, in this case, Cyrus, whose name means "possessor of the sun and ruler of a pure kingdom" (Persia), represents God, who wishes to carry out the prophesies of Jeremiah that the children of Israel would be returned to their land after 70 years of captivity in Babylon (confusion). According to Wilson (1957, p. 443) the sun often represents God who gives light and life.

   Ez 1:1 Now in the first year of Cyrus (possess thou the furnace or sun) king of Persia (" pure" or "splendid"), that the word of the LORD by the mouth of Jeremiah might be fulfilled, the LORD stirred up the spirit of Cyrus king of Persia, that he made a proclamation throughout all his kingdom, and put it also in writing, saying,

   2 Thus saith Cyrus king of Persia, The LORD God of heaven hath given me all the kingdoms of the earth; and he hath charged me to build him an house at Jerusalem, which is in Judah.

   3 Who is there among you of all his people? his God be with him, and let him go up to Jerusalem, which is in Judah, and build the house of the LORD God of Israel, (he is the God,) which is in Jerusalem.

2. <u>Those who are saved, who wish to become special to God, and who will praise Him, must rise up to do the work with the assistance of those around them.</u> When we are saved, God draws us to Him ("whose spirit God had raised"), and we desire to grow in our relationship with God. Because we all have been affected by the fall of Adam and Eve, we must all rebuild our temple. The temple at Jerusalem that had previously existed was now destroyed. The first step is to decide to do it. Others willingly offered silver, gold, goods, and beasts for the work. We must allow others to participate in the rebuilding of the temple of our spirit. Note that this list is identical to the list of items provided by Cyrus (God), suggesting that God has already provided what we need for this task. A counselor with his own spiritual relationship with God can be of great assistance.

   Ez 1:4 And whosoever remaineth in any place where he sojourneth, let the men of his place help him with silver, and with gold, and with goods, and with beasts, beside the freewill offering for the house of God that is in Jerusalem.

   5 Then rose up the chief of the fathers of Judah (praise) and Benjamin (son of the right hand or those who want to be special to God), and the priests, and the Levites, with all them whose spirit God had raised, to go up to build the house of the LORD which is in Jerusalem (peace).

3. <u>In order to rebuild our spiritual life, we need to be tired of the confusion in our lives, desire to be so close to God that we are scorched by Him, have Jesus and the Holy Spirit as our helpers, respect and fear God, make Him ruler of our lives, have a willing spirit and a controlled tongue, know the Word of God, be happy, compassionate, and humble.</u> Of course, these are also the fruits of the Spirit and are available to us from God. They are included in the steps for spiritual growth, as previously discussed, and form the prerequisites for achieving this step of godliness.

Ez 2:1 Now these are the children of the province that went up out of the captivity, of those which had been carried away, whom Nebuchadnezzar the king of Babylon (confusion by mixing) had carried away unto Babylon, and came again unto Jerusalem and Judah, every one unto his city;

2 Which came with Zerubbabel (scorched by fire): Jeshua (Jesus), Nehemiah (Jehovah comforts or the Holy Spirit), Seraiah (Jehovah is ruler), Reelaiah (Jehovah causes trembling or a bearer of Jehovah), Mordecai (little man or spirit), Bilshan (slander or son of the tongue—Smith's Dictionary, 1970), Mispar (number or writing—all the People), Bigvai (happy or the people), Rehum (compassion), Baanah (affliction or humbling). The number of the men of the people of Israel:

B. We Must Rebuild the Altar.

4. <u>We must rebuild our altar of worship to God through a strong desire to enter the presence of God and to meet with God again.</u> The first step is to set up the altar of sacrifice in our hearts, recognizing the sacrifice of Jesus for our sins and be willing to sacrifice ourselves for God (Romans 12:1). The altar was rebuilt by Jeshua (Jesus) and Zerubbabel the son of Shealtiel. Zerubbabel means "scorched by fire," showing a strong desire to get very close to God (symbolized by fire). Shealtiel means "this is what we have desired of God." Therefore, these verses are telling us that if we want to rebuild the temple of God in our hearts, the first requirement is to have a burning desire to draw close to God. It also suggests that we need the help of Jesus (Jeshua) to accomplish this task.

Ez 3:1 And when the seventh month was come, and the children of Israel were in the cities, the people gathered themselves together as one man to Jerusalem.

2 Then stood up Jeshua (Jesus the Savior) the son of Jozadak (Jehovah is righteous), and his brethren the priests, and Zerubbabel the son of Shealtiel (I have asked of God), and his brethren, and builded the altar of the God of Israel, to offer burnt offerings thereon, as it is written in the law of Moses the man of God.

5. <u>We must show our appreciation for all that God has done for us, by giving offerings and serving Him.</u> The client must again begin to give tithes and offerings in order to begin to break down his self-centeredness.

Ez 3:5 And afterward offered the continual burnt offering, both of the new moons, and of all the set feasts of the LORD that were consecrated, and of every one that willingly offered a freewill offering unto the LORD.

6 From the first day of the seventh month began they to offer burnt offerings unto the LORD. But the foundation of the temple of the LORD was not yet laid.

C. We Must Rebuild the Foundation.

6. <u>We must rebuild the foundation of our temple by rededicating our lives and all that we have to God.</u> We must sing, praise, and thank Him that His mercy endures forever and that He has seen fit to reconcile us to Himself.

Ez 3:10 And when the builders laid the foundation of the temple of the LORD, they set the priests in their apparel with trumpets, and the Levites the sons of Asaph with cymbals, to praise the LORD, after the ordinance of David king of Israel.

11 And they sang together by course in praising and giving thanks unto the LORD; because he is good, for his mercy endureth for ever toward Israel. And all the people shouted with a great shout, when they praised the LORD, because the foundation of the house of the LORD was laid.

D. We Must Build the Walls of the Temple to Provide for the Priority of the Spirit.

7. <u>If we are not careful, it is very easy to move on to taking care of our pressing needs, to such an extent, that the spiritual foundation that was laid never results in full spiritual restoration.</u> The rebuilding of the temple was stopped for 16 years because of an accusation that they were actually rebuilding the city instead. This was considered rebellion since rebuilding the city had not yet been ordered by the king. In actuality, if we make the mistake of restoring the soul out of its confusion without reestablishing the spiritual life of the client, we are simply producing a more functional sinner who will remain in rebellion against God and will easily revert to attempting to meet his needs through the flesh.

Ez 4:11 This is the copy of the letter that they sent unto him, even unto Artaxerxes the king; Thy servants the men on this side the river, and at such a time.

12 Be it known unto the king, that the Jews which came up from thee to us are come unto Jerusalem, building the rebellious and the bad city, and have set up the walls thereof, and joined the foundations.

13 Be it known now unto the king, that, if this city be builded, and the walls set up again, then will they not pay toll, tribute, and custom, and so thou shalt endamage the revenue of the kings.

21 Give ye now commandment to cause these men to cease, and that this city be not builded, until another commandment shall be given from me.

24 Then ceased the work of the house of God which is at Jerusalem. So it ceased unto the second year of the reign of Darius king of Persia.

8. <u>Without the restoration of the spiritual life, nothing else will work.</u> We need to consider our ways and insure that our spiritual restoration and the needs of the Kingdom of God come first. This is dying to the self. During the years after the foundation of the temple was laid, the people had begun again to focus on their own needs and homes, but with little results.

Hag 1:3 Then came the word of the LORD by Haggai the prophet, saying,

4 Is it time for you, O ye, to dwell in your cieled houses, and this house lie waste?

5 Now therefore thus saith the LORD of hosts; Consider your ways.

6 Ye have sown much, and bring in little; ye eat, but ye have not enough; ye drink, but ye are not filled with drink; ye clothe you, but there is none warm; and he that earneth wages earneth wages to put it into a bag with holes.

7 Thus saith the LORD of hosts; Consider your ways.

9. <u>If we will obey and walk according to the Spirit, God will be with us and will motivate us and others in the things of God that bring life and peace.</u>

Hag 1:14 And the LORD stirred up the spirit of Zerubbabel the son of Shealtiel, governor of Judah, and the spirit of Joshua the son of Josedech, the high priest, and the spirit of all the remnant of the people; and they came and did work in the house of the LORD of hosts, their God,

E. We Must Welcome the Holy Spirit Back in Control of Our Lives as We Learn to Walk According to the Spirit.

10. <u>Once we have re-established a place for the Holy Spirit in our lives, He will come to dwell in us.</u> Ezra's character is described through his ancestry. It is a clear description of the Holy Spirit. He was sent by the king (God) when the temple was completed. He is our helper, He represents God as our ruler, He helps God, and He protects us.

    Ez 7:1 Now after these things, in the reign of Artaxerxes king of Persia, Ezra (helper) the son of Seraiah (Jehovah is ruler), the son of Azariah (Jehovah has helped), the son of Hilkiah (Jehovah is protection or my portion is Jehovah),

    6 This Ezra (helper) went up from Babylon; and he was a ready scribe in the law of Moses, which the LORD God of Israel had given: and the king granted him all his request, according to the hand of the LORD his God upon him.

F. We Must Study and Meditate on the Word of God in Order to Know His Will and to Have Faith to Rely on Him to Meet our Needs.

11. <u>Once the Spirit of God has been re-established in control, the Holy Spirit will help us apply ourselves to fasting, studying, and meditating on the Word of God.</u> When the Spirit of God rules within us, we will be motivated to do these things. It is the peace of God that comes from studying His Word that helps us stand strong in the face of the tribulations in this life.

    Ez 7:10 For Ezra had prepared his heart to seek the law of the LORD, and to do it, and to teach in Israel statutes and judgments.

    8:21 Then I proclaimed a fast there, at the river of Ahava, that we might afflict ourselves before our God, to seek of him a right way for us, and for our little ones, and for all our substance.

G. We Must Make a Covenant to Remove the Things from Our Heart That Will Fight Against Our Spirit and Steal our Peace.

12. <u>For the spirit to rule and bring us peace, we cannot be joined in any way to psychological strongholds, the world, the self, or the flesh.</u> They must be removed! We will have to make some hard decisions. The Israelites had inter-married with the people who had remained in the land. These stand for the strongholds that will resist the things of the Spirit and will again bring us into bondage. These are some of the most serious problems that keep us from continually walking according to the Spirit and having peace in our lives. We must overcome low self-worth, fear, lack of boundaries, abusiveness, selfish desires, lust, things of the world, and our desire for prominence in order to have peace in our lives. The Holy Spirit (Ezra) is exceedingly grieved when we allow these things to be part of our lives. We must have nothing to do with them, or they will destroy our peace! Following an explanation of the meanings of each of these enemies of our peace, I have provided a number of verses that provide biblical answers for overcoming each one in our lives.

    Ez 9:1 Now when these things were done, the princes came to me, saying, The people of Israel, and the priests, and the Levites, have not separated themselves from the people of the lands, doing according to their abominations, even of the Canaanites (low self-worth), the Hittites (fear), the Perizzites (lack of boundaries), the Jebusites (abuse), the Ammonites (selfish desires), the Moabites (lust), the Egyptians (world), and the Amorites (prominence).

2 For they have taken of their daughters for themselves, and for their sons: so that the holy seed have mingled themselves with the people of those lands: yea, the hand of the princes and rulers hath been chief in this trespass.

3 And when I heard this thing, I rent my garment and my mantle, and plucked off the hair of my head and of my beard, and sat down astonied.

4 Then were assembled unto me every one that trembled at the words of the God of Israel, because of the transgression of those that had been carried away; and I sat astonied until the evening sacrifice.

a. <u>Fear is the greatest enemy of peace.</u> We cannot be afraid and be at peace at the same time. God offers to give us the gift of peace if we will choose to trust Him.

    Jo 14:27 Peace I leave with you, my peace I give unto you: not as the world giveth, give I unto you. Let not your heart be troubled, neither let it be afraid.

b. <u>A lack of boundaries leads to a chaotic life, offenses, and conflict, which take away our peace.</u> We must allow peace to rule in our lives to warn us when our boundaries are being violated. Letting peace rule in our hearts suggests that we are to do nothing that disturbs the peace we have in our spirit. If our spirit is disturbed, we know that something is not right within us. We need to find whatever it is and correct it.

    Col 3:15 And let the peace of God rule in your hearts, to the which also ye are called in one body; and be ye thankful.

c. <u>Abuse occurs when we offend others.</u> It makes us feel ashamed, and shame takes away our peace. We must deal with the shame, ask for forgiveness, and seek peace. One way that God chastens us is to remove peace from our lives when we do what is wrong. When we correct the problem, we again have peace.

    Heb 12:11 Now no chastening for the present seemeth to be joyous, but grievous: nevertheless afterward it yieldeth the peaceable fruit of righteousness unto them which are exercised thereby.

d. <u>Lust provides a short term good feeling, but results in long term losses and feelings of shame.</u> It never truly satisfies, so we always want more. We cannot have peace as long as we allow even the smallest amount of lust in our lives. We must flee lust as if it is poison to our soul. Having a pure heart is critical to having peace in our lives.

    2 Ti 2:22 Flee also youthful lusts: but follow righteousness, faith, charity, peace, with them that call on the Lord out of a pure heart.

e. <u>Selfish desires draw our focus away from God and onto the world.</u> This leads to a carnal mind, which brings death. The world cannot bring peace. We must focus on the things of the Spirit and trust God to meet our needs through the power of the Holy Ghost.

    Ro 8:6 For to be carnally minded is death; but to be spiritually minded is life and peace

    15:13 Now the God of hope fill you with all joy and peace in believing, that ye may abound in hope, through the power of the Holy Ghost.

f. <u>The world cannot bring us peace.</u> We cannot love both God and the things of the world. Through Christ, we must overcome the world. We must put the things of God first.

Mt 6:24 No man can serve two masters: for either he will hate the one, and love the other; or else he will hold to the one, and despise the other. Ye cannot serve God and mammon.

1 Jo 2:15 Love not the world, neither the things that are in the world. If any man love the world, the love of the Father is not in him.

g. <u>Low self-worth leads to a struggle to make ourselves something in the eyes of the world.</u> This struggle takes away our peace. When we understand that we have been justified by faith, we can finally find peace with God.

Ro 5:1 Therefore being justified by faith, we have peace with God through our Lord Jesus Christ:"

h. <u>Our attempt to be prominent or important in life leads to competition which takes away our peace.</u> When we follow God's plan for our lives and work for His kingdom, we find peace. His yoke is easy and His burden is light.

Mt 11:28 Come unto me, all ye that labour and are heavy laden, and I will give you rest.

29 Take my yoke upon you, and learn of me; for I am meek and lowly in heart: and ye shall find rest unto your souls.

30 For my yoke is easy, and my burden is light.

13. <u>We must make a covenant with God to put all these things out of our lives.</u> We must also put off all of their offspring (sins).

Ez 10:3 Now therefore let us make a covenant with our God to put away all the wives, and such as are born of them, according to the counsel of my lord, and of those that tremble at the commandment of our God; and let it be done according to the law.

5 Then arose Ezra, and made the chief priests, the Levites, and all Israel, to swear that they should do according to this word. And they sware.

H. If We Will Diligently Pursue Godliness by Establishing Our Spirit in Control of our Heart, We Will be Blessed Beyond Anything That We Can Imagine, as We Experience Peace in Our Lives.

14. <u>If we will rebuild the dominance of the Spirit in our lives, God will increase it far beyond our original salvation experiences and will replace our confusion with peace.</u>

Hag 2:9 The glory of this latter house shall be greater than of the former, saith the LORD of hosts: and in this place will I give peace, saith the LORD of hosts.

Zec 4:6 Then he answered and spake unto me, saying, This is the word of the LORD unto Zerubbabel, saying, Not by might, nor by power, but by my spirit, saith the LORD of hosts.

7 Who art thou, O great mountain? before Zerubbabel thou shalt become a plain: and he shall bring forth the headstone thereof with shoutings, crying, Grace, grace unto it.

Establishing the Control of the Spirit in Our Hearts

1. Rebuild the altar—Have a deep desire to be restored in the spirit, draw close to God, be delivered from the confusion in our lives, and have peace.

2. Rebuild the foundation—Rededicate all of ourselves to God. Accept the sacrifice of Jesus for our sins and offer ourselves and all we have as a living sacrifice for Him.

3. Rebuild the walls of the temple—Repent of our past failures and determine that we will do whatever it takes, no matter how much it costs us, to restore the priority of the Spirit in our lives until our hearts have again become fully the temples of God.

4. Realize that without the direction of the Spirit of God, nothing will work in our lives as long as we attempt to rely on the flesh to meet our needs.

5. Be careful not to despise the time of small beginnings, become impatient with our progress, and again attempt to meet our needs of the self through the flesh.

6. Strengthen our spiritual walk by studying and meditating on the Word of God, fasting, spending quiet time with God in prayer, thanksgiving, praise, and worship.

7. Make a covenant with God to permanently remove the things of this world, low self-worth, fear, lack of boundaries, abuse, selfish desires, lust, and drive for prominence from our lives.

8. If we truly seek Him with all of our heart, He will restore our spiritual walk far beyond anything that we have previously experienced and bless our lives with abundant peace.

Chapter 18

Purifying Our Hearts
(Rebuilding the Walls of Jerusalem)

Without a pure heart, we can never achieve true godliness since God is without corruption. The weeds of this world, the self, and the flesh will cause conflict, steal our peace, and choke out our fruitfulness. (Matthew 13:22) Consequently, after the Spirit is established in control of our heart, we must be careful to purify our hearts from anything that would challenge the control of our spirit or take peace from our lives. It is clear that it is those with a pure and undivided heart who are able to draw near and fully experience God (Psalms 24, Matthew 5:8). God's final goal for us is love manifested from a pure heart (1 Timothy 1:5). For those who have lived most of their lives self-centered and dominated by the flesh, even after rebuilding their spirit, purifying their hearts will not be an easy task.

Peace in our spirit can only result in our lives when the flesh, motivated by the self, has been completely overcome by the spirit and our hearts are pure. Consequently, a lack of peace can serve as a warning that something that conflicts with the Spirit has been allowed to enter into our hearts or lives. The Bible tells us to "let the peace of God rule in our hearts." (Colossians 3:15) We should never make a decision or do anything in our lives unless we have the peace of God concerning it. We are to do everything we can to exclude those things from our hearts that will challenge the dominance of the Spirit and take away our peace.

Peace means more than a lack of conflict or confusion. It is a state and condition of general order and tranquility. (The New International Webster's Dictionary of the English Language, 1997, edited by Sidney Landau) In the Hebrew, the word translated as peace, *shalom*, means "completeness, soundness, welfare, safety, health, prosperity, quietness, tranquility, contentment, and friendship." It was used as a greeting to mean that the person was wishing all of this for the person greeted. Consequently, as we discuss the restoration of the temple and the city of Jerusalem (the city of peace) in our lives, we must understand the full meaning of peace as I have just described it.

After the temple (of the spirit) was restored in 458 BC (a type of our initial salvation experience and the development or rebuilding of our spiritual life), it was now time for the walls of the city (the soul) to be rebuilt in 444 BC. Without the walls of a set identity and the gates of effective boundaries, the spirit will continually be affected by outside influences that will try to defeat its control of the soul and destroy our peace.

Our identity in Christ is represented by the fixed boundaries of the walls of Jerusalem. An identity is "the state of being exactly that which has been claimed, asserted, or described. The distinctive character belonging to an individual" (The New International Webster's Dictionary of the English Language, 1997, edited by Sidney Landau) People without identities are constantly changing how they act and what they stand for, to comply with their circumstances. They are in a constant state of change and turmoil. Our identity is to be that of Christ. In the previous step of perseverance, we established that we are now children of God, and that Christ is in us and we are in Him. Consequently, we can ask anything according to His will and He will give it to us. Now, we must so solidly believe this that it becomes a wall against any attack from the outside that tries to change or compromise our character. If we have established our identity in Christ, we will act like Christ.

Our will is represented by the gates. The doors of the gates stand for our personal choices as to whether we will open or shut the gate to particular influences or events. These choices determine what we will allow into our heart and what we will exclude from our hearts. In order to keep our hearts pure, we will have to make very wise choices and make full use of the gates and doors of our heart. (Later in this chapter, I will discuss the meaning of each of the gates of Jerusalem in detail.)

In my book *Transformation!,* I have previously discussed the model of Nehemiah as symbolizing the establishing of personal boundaries to deal with the chaos in the lives of dysfunctional people. At this point, I intend to examine this story as it relates to the development of godliness. In both situations, this story of the rebuilding of the walls of Jerusalem clearly relates to re-establishing and maintaining peace in our lives; and, of course, there will be many similarities in these discussions. However, in order to maintain our godliness, a much higher level of spiritual development and purity will be required. In order to more clearly discuss the issues involved, I have taken the liberty to group similar events in this story together rather than to strictly follow the verse by verse order of the book of Nehemiah. We begin our study of the rebuilding of the defenses of Jerusalem in Nehemiah Chapter 1:

A. We must recognize and confess our lack of identity and boundaries, and have a desire to rebuild them.

1. <u>We must first recognize that restoration is required.</u> It is the Holy Spirit's job, with the help of God's grace, to bring restoration. Nehemiah means "Jehovah comforts" or "the comforter," another name for the Holy Spirit. His father's name, Hachaliah, means "whom Jehovah enlightens" which is one of the functions of the Holy Spirit. The news that Jerusalem's walls and gates were broken down was brought to Nehemiah by his brother, Hanani, which means "gracious," one of the main characteristics of the Holy Spirit.

   Ne 1:2 That Hanani, one of my brethren, came, he and certain men of Judah; and I asked them concerning the Jews that had escaped, which were left of the captivity, and concerning Jerusalem.

   3 And they said unto me, The remnant that are left of the captivity there in the province are in great affliction and reproach: the wall of Jerusalem also is broken down, and the gates thereof are burned with fire.

   4 And it came to pass, when I heard these words, that I sat down and wept, and mourned certain days, and fasted, and prayed before the God of heaven,

2. <u>We need to ask for God's help to rebuild our personalities and purify our hearts.</u> Even Nehemiah (the Holy Spirit) had to go to the king (God) and ask assistance to rebuild Jerusalem. In the same way, without God the Father's help, we will not succeed because, without trusting Him, our flesh will prevail; and it was our flesh that allowed the boundaries (or walls) to be pulled down by our self (Nebuchadnezzar) in the first place.

   Ne 2:3 And said unto the king, Let the king live for ever: why should not my countenance be sad, when the city, the place of my fathers' sepulchres, lieth waste, and the gates thereof are consumed with fire?

   4 Then the king said unto me, For what dost thou make request? So I prayed to the God of heaven.

   5 And I said unto the king, If it please the king, and if thy servant have found favour in thy sight, that thou wouldest send me unto Judah, unto the city of my fathers' sepulchres, that I may build it.

B. We need to recognize our enemies and realize that our effort to keep our hearts pure will be resisted.

3. <u>We should expect resistance from our lust and our selfish desires.</u> They do not want to be limited in their activities, which bring chaos into our lives. They were "exceedingly grieved."

Ne 2:10 When Sanballat (strong), the Horonite (Moabite or lust), and Tobiah (Jehovah is good) the servant, the Ammonite, (selfish desires) heard of it, it grieved them exceedingly that there was come a man to seek the welfare of the children of Israel.

Although they have all not yet been introduced in this verse, I have listed the enemies of our peace below. Each will appear later in this discussion, along with the strategies that they employ to prevent us from establishing adequate boundaries in our lives in order to maintain our peace.

a. <u>Strong lust</u>—Sanballat (strong or strength), the Moabite (lust)
b. <u>Good, but selfish desires</u>—Tobiah (Jehovah is good), the Ammonite (selfish desires)
c. <u>Unfruitful, overwhelming emotions</u>—Geshem (rainstorm), the Arabian (unfruitful)
d. <u>Strongholds</u>—Ashdodites (stronghold), the Canaanite city that worshiped Dagon, the fertility or sex god.
e. <u>Fear</u>—Shemaiah (heard of Jehovah, the fearful prophet.)

C. We must understand and resist the tactics that will be used against us to discourage us and stop us from rebuilding our city of peace.

4. <u>They will tell us, "It cannot be rebuilt."</u> We must rely on God and not allow the size of the task to stop us. Feeling inadequate to establish boundaries is the first type of resistance usually encountered. We must not let this unfruitful emotion (Geshem) or the unfruitfulness of past efforts (Arabians), or the size of the job stop us. Sanballat, Tobiah, and Geshem did everything they could to resist the rebuilding of the walls. Initially, they even laughed at the idea that the city could be rebuilt. We, like Nehemiah, must ignore our fears and rely on God, not the flesh, to accomplish this.

Ne 2:19 But when Sanballat the Horonite (lust), and Tobiah the servant, the Ammonite (good selfish desires), and Geshem (rainstorm) the Arabian (step-dweller or sterility, unfruitfulness), heard it, they laughed us to scorn, and despised us, and said, What is this thing that ye do? will ye rebel against the king?

20 Then answered I them, and said unto them, The God of heaven, he will prosper us; therefore we his servants will arise and build: but ye have no portion, nor right, nor memorial, in Jerusalem.

5. <u>They tell us, "Our boundaries will not be strong enough."</u> We may fear that our identity in Christ and our will cannot be strong enough to stop our lust, selfish desires, and overwhelming emotions from stealing our peace. Sanballat (strong lust) was joined by the Arabians (overwhelming unfruitful emotions) and the Ammonites (selfish desires) in the resistance. Our lust and selfish desires will not easily submit to a new identity in Christ.

Ne 4:1 But it came to pass, that when Sanballat heard that we builded the wall, he was wroth, and took great indignation, and mocked the Jews.

2 And he spake before his brethren and the army of Samaria (false religion), and said, What do these feeble Jews? will they fortify themselves? will they sacrifice? will they make an end in a day? will they revive the stones out of the heaps of the rubbish which are burned?

3 Now Tobiah the Ammonite was by him, and he said, Even that which they build, if a fox go up, he shall even break down their stone wall.

6 So built we the wall; and all the wall was joined together unto the half thereof: for the people had a mind to work.

6. They tell us, "Our strongholds, lust, selfish desires, and unfruitful emotions will destroy us if we exclude them from our lives." We may fear that because of the strongholds in our lives, we cannot live without the "enjoyment" that our lust, selfish desires, and unfruitful emotions provide. These enemies of our peace understand that when our new identity becomes a revelation to our spirit (or subconscious reality), it will be hard to overcome. We must rely on God, be watchful, and realize that this fear is an attempt to take away our peace. Strongholds like codependency and addictions will resist boundaries at all costs. Most addicts fear giving up their "best friend."

Ne 4:7 But it came to pass, that when Sanballat, and Tobiah, and the Arabians, and the Ammonites, and the Ashdodites (strongholds), heard that the walls of Jerusalem were made up, and that the breaches began to be stopped, then they were very wroth,

8 And conspired all of them together to come and to fight against Jerusalem, and to hinder it.

9 Nevertheless we made our prayer unto our God, and set a watch against them day and night, because of them.

11 And our adversaries said, They shall not know, neither see, till we come in the midst among them, and slay them, and cause the work to cease.

7. They tell us, "You have too many other important things to do." Lust and unproductive emotions will resist our efforts to finish the work by trying to get us involved in other things, acting like they are our friends. As the Christian begins to recover, he many times is tempted to get involved in too many other activities. Even stress from doing good things can lead again to a chaotic life and affect our focus on the things of the spirit and our peace. Over-extending one's self is also a self-boundary violation. Sanballat asked for a meeting on the plain of Ono, which means "vigor or strength." Nehemiah refused, saying that he could not leave the work.

Ne 6:2 That Sanballat and Geshem sent unto me, saying, Come, let us meet together in some one of the villages in the plain of Ono (vigorous, strength or might). But they thought to do me mischief.

3 And I sent messengers unto them, saying, I am doing a great work, so that I cannot come down: why should the work cease, whilst I leave it, and come down to you?

8. They tell us, "It is too dangerous." Fear is the greatest enemy of peace and of our desire to walk according to the Spirit. If we run from our fears, they increase. Although Shemaiah was a prophet, he was used by Sanballat to try to make Nehemiah afraid so that he would be hindered in his work. In the same way Satan will even use fearful Christian friends to hinder our efforts of rebuilding boundaries in our lives. Going into the temple to protect himself represents succumbing to fear and emotionally withdrawing. Nehemiah even suggested that it would be a sin to withdraw from the work out of fear. Unfortunately, even other Christians can lead us to fear the enforcement of effective boundaries in our lives.

Ne 6:10 Afterward I came unto the house of Shemaiah (heard of Jehovah) the son of Delaiah (Jehovah has drawn) the son of Mehetabeel, (favored of God) who was shut up; and he said, Let us meet together in the house of God, within the temple, and let us shut the doors of the temple: for they will come to slay thee; yea, in the night will they come to slay thee.

11 And I said, Should such a man as I flee? and who is there, that, being as I am, would go into the temple to save his life? I will not go in.

12 And, lo, I perceived that God had not sent him; but that he pronounced this prophecy against me: for Tobiah and Sanballat had hired him.

13 Therefore was he hired, that I should be afraid, and do so, and sin, and that they might have matter for an evil report, that they might reproach me.

D. We must use the weapons that God has given us to resist efforts to stop the work.

9. We must not be afraid to use the weapons that God has given us to defend ourselves from further boundary violations and abuse. Offenses and emotional conflicts can easily steal our peace. Watchfulness and strong initial boundaries in the weakest areas are important to insure that the abuse does not continue. It is easy for the client to fall into the old way of doing things. Under Nehemiah, half of the people stood guard in preparation for an attack while the other half worked. Here we have identified three weapons: the Word of God, the power of God, and the strength of God. The Word of God tells us what is right or wrong to allow into our city and gives us peace as we meditate on it. The power that God has given us gives us power over all the power of the enemy (Luke 10:19), and we can rely on His strength to accomplish what we cannot do (Philippians 4:13).

Ne 4:12 And it came to pass, that when the Jews which dwelt by them came, they said unto us ten times, From all places whence ye shall return unto us they will be upon you.

13 Therefore set I in the lower places behind the wall, and on the higher places, I even set the people after their families with their swords (Word of God), their spears (power of God), and their bows (strength of God).

14 And I looked, and rose up, and said unto the nobles, and to the rulers, and to the rest of the people, Be not ye afraid of them: remember the Lord, which is great and terrible, and fight for your brethren, your sons, and your daughters, your wives, and your houses.

15 And it came to pass, when our enemies heard that it was known unto us, and God had brought their counsel to nought, that we returned all of us to the wall, every one unto his work.

10. When under attack, we must declare God's Word as well as use our faith and the armor of God for our defense. When attacked, Nehemiah was to blow the trumpet as an alarm to draw defenders to that particular place in the wall. We must declare God's Word of truth (the trumpet) in order to stand against any attack, and we must use our faith (the shield) to cast our cares upon God in order to overcome the fear and anxiety that steals our peace. (1 Peter 5:7)

Ne 4:16 And it came to pass from that time forth, that the half of my servants wrought in the work, and the other half of them held both the spears (power of God), the shields (faith), and the bows (strength of God), and the habergeons (armor or lance); and the rulers were behind all the house of Judah.

17 They which builded on the wall, and they that bare burdens, with those that laded, every one with one of his hands wrought in the work, and with the other hand held a weapon.

18 For the builders, every one had his sword (Word of God) girded by his side, and so builded. And he that sounded the trumpet (declaring the Word) was by me.

11. <u>We must be so diligent in defending our identity and boundaries that we never let down our guard or allow our character to slip.</u> Nehemiah asked everyone to lodge within Jerusalem day and night. We must be solidly committed to maintain our peace as much as possible. They were so involved that they did not even take off their clothes except to wash. In the same way, a Christian must learn to always wear and not take off Christ's character or the armor of God, and be fully committed to a life of peace in the Holy Spirit.

Ne 4:22 Likewise at the same time said I unto the people, Let every one with his servant lodge within Jerusalem, that in the night they may be a guard to us, and labour on the day.

23 So neither I, nor my brethren, nor my servants, nor the men of the guard which followed me, none of us put off our clothes (character), saving that every one put them off for washing.

E. We must learn to make good choices as to what we allow in and what we exclude from our lives and respect the boundaries of others.

12. <u>When establishing boundaries, respect for the boundaries of others is equally important.</u> We must learn to respect other's boundaries if we want others to respect ours. Some of those building the walls had taken advantage of the other builders. Nehemiah immediately put a stop to this. Unfortunately, boundaries can be used selfishly. The Christian must be as careful not to violate other people's boundaries as he is defending his own. When they learn about boundaries, many clients initially use them excessively as a method of control. A respect for all boundaries is the basis of what is called assertiveness training today. Quickly resolving any conflicts in our lives and forgiving the offender is essential to maintaining our peace.

Ne 5:1 And there was a great cry of the people and of their wives against their brethren the Jews.

7 Then I consulted with myself, and I rebuked the nobles, and the rulers, and said unto them, Ye exact usury, every one of his brother. And I set a great assembly against them.

13. <u>We must make good choices as to what we allow and what we exclude from our lives.</u> Establishing an identity in Christ (the fixed walls) is not sufficient to maintain our peace. Flexible boundaries are the gates and our choices are the doors. If we make poor choices and allow the enemies of our peace into our heart, they will steal our peace.

Ne 6:1 Now it came to pass, when Sanballat, and Tobiah, and Geshem the Arabian, and the rest of our enemies, heard that I had builded the wall, and that there was no breach left therein; (though at that time I had not set up the doors upon the gates;)

Referring back to Nehemiah Chapter 3, we have a listing of the gates as they were being rebuilt. The gates define the selective or complex boundaries, which determine what we will allow and prohibit into our hearts. They help us identify the most important choices that we make in our lives that affect our peace. We must use them effectively to keep the bad out and let the good in. Allowing the bad into our lives at each of these gates will lead to specific problems. Sometimes the existence of these problems in our lives will help us realize that this specific gate needs rebuilding or that we need to learn to make better choices in a specific area. The verses that follow give us God's answer for repairing each of these gates in order to exclude the things that are stealing our peace. Here is the symbology as I best understand it: First, I will list the typical problem that results from a lack of adequately controlling this part of our life, then the name of the gate, followed by what I believe the gate symbolizes. Finally, I will give verses that I believe help explain the meaning of the gate followed by verses suggesting answers for dealing with these kinds of problems in our lives.

a. <u>Depressing thoughts—The Valley Gate controls the low experiences, sorrows, perplexities or failures in our lives.</u> Unless we trust that God will work even these things for our good, we will be overcome with fear of failure, feelings of inadequacy, and anxiety. We must not let them discourage us, try to deny them, build defenses to ensure that they never happen again, or let them lead to depression or pessimism. Instead, we must embrace our low experiences, sorrows, perplexities, and failures, so that we can overcome them through faith as we rely more and more on Christ and less on ourselves. They are never to be allowed in as lies concerning our self-worth or our significance in life. They must be processed until they become our allies instead of our enemies. Theophostic Ministry (Smith, 1966) is an effective way to process these past negative experiences.

Ps 23:4 Yea, though I walk through the valley of the shadow of death, I will fear no evil: for thou art with me; thy rod and thy staff they comfort me.

Php 4:8 Finally, brethren, whatsoever things are true, whatsoever things are honest, whatsoever things are just, whatsoever things are pure, whatsoever things are lovely, whatsoever things are of good report; if there be any virtue, and if there be any praise, think on these things.

b. <u>Legalism and hypocrisy—The Fountain Gate controls the spiritual experiences of life.</u> It must be wide open to all valid spiritual experiences and shut closed against all pretense, hypocrisy, false religion, or superficiality. Keeping this gate wide open to the Spirit of God must be a priority in our lives. It is our faith that overcomes the fears of our lives that try to steal our peace.

Jo 4:14 But whosoever drinketh of the water that I shall give him shall never thirst; but the water that I shall give him shall be in him a well of water springing up into everlasting life.

Ps 24:3 Who shall ascend into the hill of the LORD? or who shall stand in his holy place?

4 He that hath clean hands, and a pure heart; who hath not lifted up his soul unto vanity (worshipped idols), nor sworn deceitfully.

c. <u>Bitterness—The Sheep Gate controls our relationships with other people.</u> We are never to allow the offenses or actions of others to take away our peace. We must rely on God to meet our needs instead. We are to allow others into our lives to the degree they are trustworthy and exclude those that are dangerous and abusive. Conflict and confrontation easily take away our peace. We are to forgive them for their offenses, but set reasonable boundaries on our relationships. We are to have the best interests of everyone else in mind and love them unconditionally, but allow them to learn from their own choices and consequences.

Jo 10:14 I am the good shepherd, and know my sheep, and am known of mine.

1 Pe 1:22 Seeing ye have purified your souls in obeying the truth through the Spirit unto unfeigned love of the brethren, see that ye love one another with a pure heart fervently:

d. <u>Stress—The Fish Gate controls worldly physical and psychological nourishment.</u> Our needs must be met in order to survive physically and live a full life psychologically, but we must rely on God, instead of our flesh to meet these needs. We must trust God to meet all of our needs. We must clearly understand which things of this world are good for us and which are bad. We are to allow the good in and exclude the bad. We have been called to be fishers of men, instead of fishers of fish.

Mr 6:41 And when he had taken the five loaves and the two fishes, he looked up to heaven, and blessed, and brake the loaves, and gave them to his disciples to set before them; and the two fishes divided he among them all.

Jas 4:8 Draw nigh to God, and he will draw nigh to you. Cleanse your hands, ye sinners; and purify your hearts, ye double minded.

e. <u>Stagnation—The Old Gate controls our past experiences, traditions, or ways of doing things.</u> Because we tend to revert back to or favor our old ways of doing things, we must be careful not to allow our old ways or traditions to hinder what God is trying to do in our lives. Since they can greatly influence what we will do in the future, we must be careful to let them only influence us for the good and exclude or work through all past experiences that might influence us negatively.

Mt 13:52 Then said he unto them, Therefore every scribe which is instructed unto the kingdom of heaven is like unto a man that is an householder, which bringeth forth out of his treasure things new and old.

Lu 5:37 And no man putteth new wine into old bottles; else the new wine will burst the bottles, and be spilled, and the bottles shall perish.

39 No man also having drunk old wine straightway desireth new: for he saith, The old is better.

f. <u>Shame—The Dung Gate controls the detestable evil ways, bad habits, and worthless things of this world that lead to guilt and shame in our lives.</u> Through this gate the dung was thrown out of the city of Jerusalem. We must similarly throw these things out of our lives. Because Jesus took our shame on the cross, we are not to allow it to influence or defile our lives. There is no condemnation for us in Christ Jesus. (Romans 8:1) We are especially to never allow it to affect our self-image or lead to being defensive, critical, or judgmental of others. We are simply to give it to Jesus and put it under the blood. Shame is one of the building blocks of addictions.

Php 3:8 Yea doubtless, and I count all things but loss for the excellency of the knowledge of Christ Jesus my Lord: for whom I have suffered the loss of all things, and do count them but dung, that I may win Christ,

2 Co 7:1 Having therefore these promises, dearly beloved, let us cleanse ourselves from all filthiness of the flesh and spirit, perfecting holiness in the fear of God.

g. <u>Emptiness—The Water Gate controls the things that bring physical and spiritual life to us.</u> Jesus came to give us life and life more abundantly (John 10:10b), but we must be careful to discern which things of life are truly life-giving and which are not really good for us in the long run. Water also represents the Holy Spirit and the Word of God. We must let only those things in that truly give spiritual life. If instead of relying on the things of God for our nourishment, we attempt to rely on the world, we will feel empty.

Jo 4:14 But whosoever drinketh of the water that I shall give him shall never thirst; but the water that I shall give him shall be in him a well of water springing up into everlasting life.

Eph 5:26 That he might sanctify and cleanse it with the washing of water by the word,

h. <u>Arrogance—The Horse Gate controls our capacity to accomplish things.</u> We must not over-rely on our own talents or capabilities but realize our limitations and trust in God to make us sufficient for every good work. (2 Corinthians 9:8) We must not let this desire to do things or develop capabilities become the basis for meeting our needs for worth or significance, or to bring stress into our lives. Stress, which results from our drive to accomplish worldly things, is a significant threat to our peace. We must not let the urgent things of life prioritize or overshadow the truly important spiritual things of life. Those who rely on their own capabilities may become prideful, judgmental, and arrogant.

Ps 20:7 Some trust in chariots, and some in horses: but we will remember the name of the LORD our God.

i. <u>Hopelessness—The East Gate controls the expectations for our future, dreams, visions, and hopes.</u> Since the sun rises in the east it is usually associated with the advent of new things to come in our lives. Christ is to return through the East Gate of Jerusalem. We must be careful not to desire what God has not planned for our lives or covet the things of this world. If we chose to pursue selfish desires or lusts, we will destroy our future and our peace. Only the perfect will of God can lead to the peace of God.

Eze 43:4 And the glory of the LORD came into the house by the way of the gate whose prospect is toward the east.

j. <u>Codependency—The Miphkad Gate controls the influence of other people in our lives.</u> This word means "to register or command." Possibly this gate was the location where a census of the people was taken. We must choose which people we will allow to speak into our lives and to what degree we will rely on them. Codependency results when we excessively rely on others or ourselves. These choices will have a very significant influence on us. Do we listen and rely on our pastor, elders, counselor, parents, Christian friends, or do we listen and rely on our worldly friends, secular professors, television commentators, and Hollywood producers? Choosing to rely excessively on the wrong persons in our circle of friends can destroy our peace. Christ must be more important than our friends and families.

Lu 14:26 If any man come to me, and hate not his father, and mother, and wife, and children, and brethren, and sisters, yea, and his own life also, he cannot be my disciple

Jas 3:17 But the wisdom that is from above is first pure, <u>then peaceable</u>, gentle, and easy to be intreated, full of mercy and good fruits, without partiality, and without hypocrisy

k. <u>Dissipation—The Ephraim Gate controls the fruitfulness and productivity in our lives.</u> Ephraim means "double ash heap" or "I will be doubly fruitful." Our lives and our resources will either result in a double ash heap if we serve the world or double fruitfulness if they are used for the Kingdom of God and not solely for our own selfish desires and fulfillment. Without abiding in God we can do nothing. (John 15:5) What does it profit a man if he gains the whole world and loses his own soul? (Matthew 16:26) We will only find peace in the center of God's will and purpose for our lives.

Ge 41:52 And the name of the second called he Ephraim: For God hath caused me to be fruitful in the land of my affliction.

Ac 15:9 And put no difference between us and them, purifying their hearts by faith.

l. <u>Bondage—The Prison Gate controls what we allow in our lives in the way of bondages, lusts, and addictions.</u> These are to be excluded from the city of peace. If they are not, we will never be able to maintain our peace or have a happy, abundant life.

> 2 Ti 2:22 Flee also youthful lusts: but follow righteousness, faith, charity, peace, with them that call on the Lord out of a pure heart.

14. <u>Although it might take a long time to finish the task, in the end even the heathen will give God the glory for our identity in Christ and the establishment of effective boundaries.</u> The establishment of a healthy Christ-like identity and personality give glory to God. When the walls were finished, everyone realized that it had been done by God. Clearly, we can never in our own efforts establish our identity in Christ without what Christ has done for us, and we cannot find the balance needed to establish effective boundaries without His help.

> Ne 6:15 So the wall was finished in the twenty and fifth day of the month Elul, in fifty and two days.
>
> 16 And it came to pass, that when all our enemies heard thereof, and all the heathen that were about us saw these things, they were much cast down in their own eyes: for they perceived that this work was wrought of our God.

F. **Our newly established boundaries must be exercised to maintain the rule of the Spirit in our hearts through grace.**

15. <u>Once the identity and boundaries are established, the new personality must be ruled by the grace of God. We must believe in God's favor to meet all of our needs (faith).</u> Hanani (grace) and Hananiah (Jehovah has favored) were appointed rulers. We must practice grace or unmerited favor when we use boundaries in our relations with others and not use them for selfish purposes.

> Ne 7:1 Now it came to pass, when the wall was built, and I had set up the doors, and the porters and the singers and the Levites were appointed,
>
> 2 That I gave my brother Hanani, and Hananiah the ruler of the palace, charge over Jerusalem: for he was a faithful man, and feared God above many.

16. <u>When established, the new boundaries must be exercised to keep the good in and the bad out.</u> The gates were even guarded in broad daylight when they were open. Some of the most important self-boundary areas to be controlled are mentioned in the final verses of the book of Nehemiah. They are discussed below.

> Ne 7:3 And I said unto them, Let not the gates of Jerusalem be opened until the sun be hot; and while they stand by, let them shut the doors, and bar them: and appoint watches of the inhabitants of Jerusalem, every one in his watch, and every one to be over against his house.

17. <u>We must invite the Word of God into our hearts so that we will know the good, which should be allowed in and the bad, which must be excluded from our hearts.</u> It is the Holy Spirit who illuminates the Word of God and gives us an understanding of how to use the boundaries in our lives.

> Ne 8:1 And all the people gathered themselves together as one man into the street that was before the water gate; and they spake unto Ezra (the Holy Spirit) the scribe to bring the book of the law of Moses, which the LORD had commanded to Israel.

8 So they read in the book in the law of God distinctly, and gave the sense, and caused them to understand the reading.

G. We must be willing to sacrifice the time necessary to exercise and maintain our boundaries which keep our hearts pure.

18. <u>We must purify ourselves and our boundaries from all evil and shame, giving thanks to God.</u> Shame and guilt are enemies of our peace. Unless they are excluded from our lives, we will be unable to maintain a life of peace.

    Ne 12:30 And the priests and the Levites purified themselves, and purified the people, and the gates, and the wall.

19. <u>At least ten percent of our time should be dedicated to maintaining healthy boundaries and peace in our lives.</u> Quiet time with God is essential in maintaining the peace of God in our hearts. It is too easy to get so involved in the things of life that they steal our peace.

    Ne 11:1 And the rulers of the people dwelt at Jerusalem: the rest of the people also cast lots, to bring one of ten to dwell in Jerusalem the holy city, and nine parts to dwell in other cities.

20. <u>Lust and selfish desires must be totally banned from our hearts forever.</u> They are never to be allowed into our lives again. Even the slightest opening that allows lust or selfish desires into our hearts will eventually lead to shame, which will destroy the peace in our lives.

    Ne13:1 On that day they read in the book of Moses in the audience of the people; and therein was found written, that the Ammonite (selfish desires) and the Moabite (lust) should not come into the congregation of God for ever;

21. <u>Boundaries must be used to limit how much we allow in our lives.</u> The Sabbath and the laws concerning not planting on the seventh year were limits on physical work. God expects us to place limits on what we agree to do. We are to use good choices to insure that we are not stressed beyond limit in this life. We are not to let excessive work or demands into our lives.

    Ne 13:19 And it came to pass, that when the gates of Jerusalem began to be dark before the sabbath, I commanded that the gates should be shut, and charged that they should not be opened till after the sabbath: and some of my servants set I at the gates, that there should no burden be brought in on the sabbath day.

How to Purify Our Hearts

1. Once the rule of the Spirit has been established in the temple of our hearts, it must be defended by establishing our identity in Christ and keeping out those things that would cause conflict with the Spirit and steal our peace.

2. We must first rebuild the fixed boundary walls of our identity by knowing who we are in Christ. If we are in Christ, we will only do the things that Jesus, our elder brother, would do. We can ask ourselves the question in each situation, "What would Jesus do?"

3. Letting the peace of God rule in our hearts (Colossians 3:15) requires that we purify them by excluding all things from our hearts that will take away the peace in our spirit.

4. We must learn to recognize the enemies of our peace: lust, selfish desires, unproductive emotions, and fear.

5. We must use the weapons that God has provided for us: the trumpet (declaring God's Word), the sword (the Word of God), the spear (the power of God), the shield (faith), the bow (God's strength), and the armor of God.

6. We must understand and defeat the strategies of our enemies: Telling ourselves it cannot be done, it will not really protect us, our enemies are too strong, we have more important things to do, we cannot live without lust, or it could hurt us in some way.

7. We must do everything we can to rebuild and defend the gates of our hearts, or we could end up depressed, hypocritical, bitter, stressed, stagnant, ashamed, empty, arrogant, hopeless, codependent, dissipated, or in bondage.

8. If we are successful in purifying our hearts, we will find that we really do not miss the things we have given up, as we experience the blessings of godliness in our lives.

PART VIII

Brotherly Kindness—Knowing Jesus as My Brother

Chapter 19

Accepting God's Kids
God Accepts Me as I Am

2 Pe 1:7 And to godliness, brotherly kindness; and to brotherly kindness charity.

Up until this point in spiritual development, we have been focused on achieving victory over ourselves. However, no matter how much we have been able to achieve self-control, perseverance and godliness in our lives; it must be expressed in the crucible of real life, among our Christian brethren and among the people that we meet in our day-to-day lives. We may be able to achieve peace in our lives when we are alone by ourselves, but can we continue to have that peace in our relations with truly dysfunctional and worldly people?

Our God is a relational God. If we are to truly become like Him, then we are going to have to care for others like He does. In fact, spiritual growth is movement from self-centeredness to other-centeredness. The word in verse 7, translated as brotherly kindness, is the Greek word *philadelphia*, which means "the love with which Christians cherish, appreciate, or have tender affection for each other as brethren." It has been translated in other verses as brotherly love, brotherly kindness and love of the brethren. In the New Testament, it is the love that Christians cherish for each other as brethren. It comes from the word *phileo*, which means "to love, to approve of, to like, sanction, to treat affectionately or kindly, to welcome, befriend, to show signs of love, to kiss." It is the word Peter used after his denial to describe his relationship with Jesus. He was fond, but not unconditionally committed to Jesus; because he was no longer sure he could fulfill any commitment he would make. As we walk with God and take on His character, we automatically begin to see Christ in other Christians; and we have brotherly kindness for them. As we work together shoulder to shoulder, a bond of affection is formed, and we begin to care for our Christian brothers deeply. The Bible tells us about relationships based on this kind of fondness.

1. <u>Fondness is based on what others have done for us and it can easily turn to hate if they work against us and become our enemies.</u>

    Pr 9:8 Reprove not a scorner, lest he hate thee: rebuke a wise man, and he will love thee.

    Mt 6:24 No man can serve two masters: for either he will hate the one, and love the other; or else he will hold to the one, and despise the other. Ye cannot serve God and mammon.

2. <u>Fondness has a lot to do with who we perceive is on our side.</u>

    Jo 15:19 If ye were of the world, the world would love his own: but because ye are not of the world, but I have chosen you out of the world, therefore the world hateth you.

    16:27 For the Father himself loveth you, because ye have loved me, and have believed that I came out from God.

3. <u>Fondness leads us to do nice things for others.</u>

    Jo 5:20 For the Father loveth the Son, and sheweth him all things that himself doeth: and he will shew him greater works than these, that ye may marvel.

4. <u>Jesus demonstrated fondness for Lazarus through the tears that He shed for him.</u>

    Jo 11:36 Then said the Jews, Behold how he loved him!

5. <u>John perceived that Jesus was fond of him.</u>

    Jo 20:2 Then she runneth, and cometh to Simon Peter, and to the other disciple, whom Jesus loved, and saith unto them, They have taken away the Lord out of the sepulchre, and we know not where they have laid him.

6. <u>We all should be fond or have affection for Jesus because of what He did for us.</u>

    1 Co 16:22 If any man love not the Lord Jesus Christ, let him be Anathema Maranatha.

7. <u>Because God is fond of us, He sometimes rebukes us.</u>

    Re 3:19 As many as I love, I rebuke and chasten: be zealous therefore, and repent.

8. <u>Fondness leads us to prefer others ahead of ourselves.</u>

    Ro 12:10 Be kindly affectioned one to another with brotherly love; in honour preferring one another;

9. <u>God expects His children to be fond of one another.</u>

    Heb 13:1 Let brotherly love continue.

10. <u>It is God who teaches us, by example, to be fond of one another.</u>

    1 Th 4:9 But as touching brotherly love ye need not that I write unto you: for ye yourselves are taught of God to love one another.

11. <u>It proves we are Christians.</u>

    1 Jo 3:14 We know that we have passed from death unto life, because we love the brethren. He that loveth not his brother abideth in death.
    4:20 If a man say, I love God, and hateth his brother, he is a liar: for he that loveth not his brother whom he hath seen, how can he love God whom he hath not seen?

12. <u>God commands us to have compassion on others, since He had compassion on us.</u>

    1 Pe 3:8 Finally, be ye all of one mind, having compassion one of another, love as brethren, be pitiful, be courteous:

Mt 18:33 Shouldest not thou also have had compassion on thy fellowservant, even as I had pity on thee?

13. <u>Because we love God, we should also love His children.</u>

1 Jo 4:21 And this commandment have we from him, That he who loveth God love his brother also.

14. <u>In order to develop brotherly love, we must purify our souls.</u> This purification process was previously discussed as a requirement for achieving godliness.

1 Pe 1:22 Seeing ye have purified your souls in obeying the truth through the Spirit unto unfeigned love of the brethren, see that ye love one another with a pure heart fervently:

15. <u>We can care for and give grace to others who are struggling, because we know what it is like to struggle in the flesh ourselves.</u>

Heb 5:2 Who can have compassion on the ignorant, and on them that are out of the way; for that he himself also is compassed with infirmity.

16. <u>Fondness is born out of relationships and common experiences.</u> Mary and Martha knew that Jesus cared for Lazarus because they had spent time together. The apostles grew fond of each other as they worked together for the sake of the gospel.

Jo 11:3 Therefore his sisters sent unto him, saying, Lord, behold, he whom thou lovest is sick.

Tit 3:15 All that are with me salute thee. Greet them that love us in the faith. Grace be with you all. Amen.

17. <u>God's love leads us to want to have compassion on and meet the needs of others.</u>

1 Jo 3:17 But whoso hath this world's good, and seeth his brother have need, and shutteth up his bowels of compassion from him, how dwelleth the love of God in him?

18. <u>Christian maturity requires the development of unconditional love—not just being fond of one another.</u> God wants us to love everyone, even those who are unkind to us.

Mt 5: 46 For if ye love them which love you, what reward have ye? do not even the publicans the same?

47 And if ye salute your brethren only, what do ye more than others? do not even the publicans so?

48 Be ye therefore perfect, even as your Father which is in heaven is perfect.

How God Sees and Values people

Many years ago, I remember a little vignette from one of Bob Mumford's teachings. He said that one day he was extremely frustrated in his dealings with other Christians, almost despairing of the incompetence that he saw all around him. He asked God, "Why did you choose to use people to establish your kingdom on earth?" God answered him in his spirit, "Because it is the greatest challenge!" Clearly, if God can win the battle over Satan in spite of all of the mistakes, backslidings, and the incompetence of His people, He definitely is a wise and powerful God beyond anything that we can comprehend.

The Bible gives us a perspective very different from the world on how we should view people. This perspective is important because in order to develop a fondness for all of God's children, we must learn to see them through His eyes.

1. <u>God values all of us equally.</u> He made each of us in His image, and we are all equal in His sight. If we accept Him, we are forgiven and part of the body of Christ. We cannot do anything to make ourselves of more worth; because everything we have, He has given us. We are all saved by His grace and not by works. God loved all of us while we were yet sinners.

    2 Ti 1:9 Who hath saved us, and called us with an holy calling, not according to our works, but according to his own purpose and grace, which was given us in Christ Jesus before the world began,

    Ro 5:8 But God commendeth his love toward us, in that, while we were yet sinners, Christ died for us.

2. <u>The Bible tells us there is nothing we can do to make ourselves more significant after we have accepted Jesus as our Savior and have been adopted into His family.</u> It says that all of our attempts to make ourselves righteous are filthy rags because they are motivated out of our selfishness. When we have been adopted and have become children of God and joint heirs with Christ, we are so significant that there is nothing we can do in our own strength that will make us more significant.

    Isa 64:6 But we are all as an unclean thing, and all our righteousnesses are as filthy rags; and we all do fade as a leaf; and our iniquities, like the wind, have taken us away.

3. <u>Each of us are given talents according to God's plan for our lives.</u> We do not choose our calling or our talents—God does. Therefore, just because we have certain talents we are not any better than anyone else. God expects us to use our talents, and He will reward us according to what we do with them. However, in the eyes of God the two talent person who made two talents is just as successful as the five talent person who made five talents. They received the same commendation.

    Mt 25:20 And so he that had received five talents came and brought other five talents, saying, Lord, thou deliveredst unto me five talents: behold, I have gained beside them five talents more.

    21 His lord said unto him, Well done, thou good and faithful servant: thou hast been faithful over a few things, I will make thee ruler over many things: enter thou into the joy of thy lord.

    22 He also that had received two talents came and said, Lord, thou deliveredst unto me two talents: behold, I have gained two other talents beside them.

    23 His lord said unto him, Well done, good and faithful servant; thou hast been faithful over a few things, I will make thee ruler over many things: enter thou into the joy of thy lord.

4. <u>God requires more of those who have been given more talents.</u> Those with more talents may possibly progress farther in life and accomplish more, but they will also face more difficult challenges.

    Mt 25:28 Take therefore the talent from him, and give it unto him which hath ten talents.

    29 For unto every one that hath shall be given, and he shall have abundance: but from him that hath not shall be taken away even that which he hath.

5. <u>Each of us are running different races according to our place in the body of Christ and our specific calling.</u> Consequently, we cannot compare ourselves with anyone else. If the person running the 50 yard dash tries to compare himself to one running the mile, he will think he is doing well, until he fades after the 50 yards and the miler continues running.

1 Co 12:14 For the body is not one member, but many.

15 If the foot shall say, Because I am not the hand, I am not of the body; is it therefore not of the body?

16 And if the ear shall say, Because I am not the eye, I am not of the body; is it therefore not of the body?

17 If the whole body were an eye, where were the hearing? If the whole were hearing, where were the smelling?

18 But now hath God set the members every one of them in the body, as it hath pleased him.

6. <u>Many who appear to be last in this life will be first in the Kingdom of God.</u> The things that make one first in this world are not the same things that make one first in God's Kingdom. John the Baptist is a good example of this. So are the many prayer intercessors that no one has ever heard of who have changed history through their prayers.

Mt 20:16 So the last shall be first, and the first last: for many be called, but few chosen.

7. <u>We will be held responsible for what we know.</u> Jesus condemned the people of Capernaum, because they had seen His miracles and did not repent. He said that it would be better for the people of Sodom and Gomorrah at the judgment day because, when they sinned and did not repent, they had not seen Jesus' miracles or known Him.

Mt 11:21 Woe unto thee, Chorazin! woe unto thee, Bethsaida! for if the mighty works, which were done in you, had been done in Tyre and Sidon, they would have repented long ago in sackcloth and ashes.

22 But I say unto you, It shall be more tolerable for Tyre and Sidon at the day of judgment, than for you.

23 And thou, Capernaum, which art exalted unto heaven, shalt be brought down to hell: for if the mighty works, which have been done in thee, had been done in Sodom, it would have remained until this day.

8. <u>We are to measure ourselves by the measuring rod of faith.</u> As I have discussed before, since faith is the basis of our righteousness "from first to last," it is the measure of a Christian. God does not primarily judge us by how much we have accomplished, how many talents we have, or what positions we have held. God is more interested in our character than our success.

Ro 1:17 For in the gospel a righteousness from God is revealed, a righteousness that is by faith from first to last, just as it is written: "The righteous will live by faith." (NIV)

12:3 For I say, through the grace given unto me, to every man that is among you, not to think of himself more highly than he ought to think; but to think soberly, according as God hath dealt to every man the measure of faith. (AV)

9. <u>God looks at the heart rather that the outside appearance.</u> That is why He chose David to be king over all of his brethren.

> 1 Sa 16:7 But the LORD said unto Samuel, Look not on his countenance, or on the height of his stature; because I have refused him: for the LORD seeth not as man seeth; for man looketh on the outward appearance, but the LORD looketh on the heart.

If we put this all together, we get a very different view of how God perceives the members of the body of Christ. What we need to grasp is that God values all His children equally, but judges their works based on the talents He gave them and what He called them to do. We might see the pastor as the most important in a particular church, those who are very talented second, those who help the most third, and so on until we come to those who struggle to function or might even appear to be handicapped. From the principles above, some unknown prayer warrior or some new convert who has few talents but a real heart for God might be considered greater in God's eyes than the pastor who has many more talents. God wants us to be fond of each and every one of His children, without passing judgment of any kind. To do so, we need to put aside our own human prejudices, and value each one as a unique child of God who has a special place in the Kingdom of God. (For more on this topic see my book *Faith Therapy*.)

My Experience

Learning to value people for who they are rather than for what they can accomplish in life required a significant transformation in my life, because in my earlier years I was so strongly driven to be successful. At each of the earlier steps to spiritual maturity, God chipped away at my heart. When I made Jesus Lord and looked for His direction, He started directing me toward unconditionally valuing people. As I began ministering to people and began to counsel them, God spread His love abroad in my heart, so that I learned more and more to truly care and value my clients no matter how severe their problems and how much sin was still in their lives.

As I counseled people and understood why they did the things they did, I learned compassion for even the worst offenders. I could relate to the struggles of each one—even if they were sexually addicted, crack addicts, angry domestic violence perpetrators, schizophrenics, or pedophiles. The truth is, I still saw some people as having it "more together than others." This was true in our church where it seemed that though we had some individuals who seemed successful, we also had people who just "did not have it together." It seemed that many worldly people who were not saved were more effective, had fewer problems, and were more competent. Our church, like many, sometimes was more like the "Motly Crew," "Hogan's Heroes," or "Mash." It also seemed that quite a few of those who regularly attended evening services and prayer meetings were those with many obvious problems, at least from a worldly point of view.

One night in evening service, God gently spoke to me and said, "Do you see these people? They are just my projects under construction." This brought to mind the verses in 1st Corinthians Chapter 1:

> 1 Co 1:26 For ye see your calling, brethren, how that not many wise men after the flesh, not many mighty, not many noble, are called:

> 27 But God hath chosen the foolish things of the world to confound the wise; and God hath chosen the weak things of the world to confound the things which are mighty;

> 28 And base things of the world, and things which are despised, hath God chosen, yea, and things which are not, to bring to nought things that are:

> 29 That no flesh should glory in his presence.

God wanted me to realize that just as He accepted me as I am without works, He accepted all of them, and loves them dearly—problems and all. And just as I have not arrived and have my own set of problems,

I am to value and esteem each of them—even the most addicted and dysfunctional—as better than myself. Everything that I have, God has given me. If I have made any progress, it is because of what God has done. And just as I have been set free to become all that God has called me to be—so have they. God does not see things as men do. He looks at the heart and the desire to serve Him, and values that more than many wonderful talents or accomplishments.

> Php 2:1 If there be therefore any consolation in Christ, if any comfort of love, if any fellowship of the Spirit, if any bowels and mercies,
>
> 2 Fulfil ye my joy, that ye be likeminded, having the same love, being of one accord, of one mind.
>
> 3 Let nothing be done through strife or vainglory; but in lowliness of mind let each esteem other better than themselves.

At another time, I was standing, waiting in line and as part of our discussion to pass the time, I was telling my new acquaintance about some of my son's recent accomplishments. Somehow, in my spirit it just did not seem right. Later God reminded me that in the conversation I was "bragging" about what he did from a purely human standpoint. Why was I "bragging" about my son's worldly accomplishments, when I stated that I believed the Bible, which views each of us as equals with different callings and which values the intents of the heart far above worldly accomplishments which pass away? I realized that I needed, once again, to correct my way of viewing other people and what I saw as truly important in life. I could not use the world's system to evaluate others primarily for their worldly accomplishments and declare myself worthwhile solely due to the love of God.

It is still true that I can relate better to some people than others in the church, but we all have a common goal—furthering the Kingdom of God. As we work together toward that goal, we develop friendships and get to know each other at a deeper level. This is not unusual. In families, certain children relate better to one another than they do to others, but all are still of equal value. We have to receive and act on the revelation that God accepts each of us unconditionally without works, that He is fond of and favors each of His children, and that each one is a unique and special treasure in the Kingdom of God.

Chapter 20

Learning Compassion
(Barnabas)

The key task in reaching a level of brotherly love or fondness is learning to have compassion on others, which leads us to want to console and help them. Compassion is "pity for the suffering with the desire to help." Consolation is "the act of consoling or comforting in grief or sorrow." (The New International Webster's Dictionary of the English Language, 1997, edited by Sidney Landau) We develop compassion for others when we see them as hurting and needy as we have been in our own lives. Those who have suffered themselves are usually the most compassionate toward others, while those who trust in themselves and are prideful usually lack compassion. Compassion leads to brotherly love, since brothers have experienced life's hardships together and know how it feels. Barnabas (son of consolation) was one of the most compassionate men in the early church.

1. <u>Because Jesus walked among us and suffered with us, He has given us an example of how we should be compassionate in all of our dealings with people.</u> He was to be the "firstborn of many brethren." (Romans 8:29) Since compassion is based on relationship and is learned by common experiences, He learned compassion as He walked with His disciples and lived among them. As we struggle together in furthering the Kingdom of God, we learn compassion, and are called to console, and help one another in brotherly love just as He did.

   2 Co 1:5 For as the sufferings of Christ abound in us, so our consolation also aboundeth by Christ.
   6 And whether we be afflicted, it is for your consolation and salvation, which is effectual in the enduring of the same sufferings which we also suffer: or whether we be comforted, it is for your consolation and salvation.

2. <u>Because God has been very compassionate to us, He expects us to have compassion on and console others.</u> We are to accept others as He has accepted us.

   Ps 78:38 But he, being full of compassion, forgave their iniquity, and destroyed them not: yea, many a time turned he his anger away, and did not stir up all his wrath.
   145:8 The LORD is gracious, and full of compassion; slow to anger, and of great mercy.
   Isa 49:15 Can a woman forget her sucking child, that she should not have compassion on the son of her womb? yea, they may forget, yet will I not forget thee.

3. <u>Jesus was constantly moved by compassion for hurting people.</u> When we realize that our brethren in Christ are just like us, we can learn to love them even with all of their peculiarities, faults, and mistakes. We can learn to love the hurting little boys and girls inside of them, in spite of their irritating actions and inadequacies.

Mt 9:36 But when he saw the multitudes, he was moved with compassion on them, because they fainted, and were scattered abroad, as sheep having no shepherd.

18:33 Shouldest not thou also have had compassion on thy fellowservant, even as I had pity on thee?

Heb 5:2 Who can have compassion on the ignorant, and on them that are out of the way; for that he himself also is compassed with infirmity.

1 Pe 3:8 Finally, be ye all of one mind, having compassion one of another, love as brethren, be pitiful, be courteous:

4. <u>We learn compassion and a desire to console others because we have been helped, supported, or consoled ourselves.</u> Barnabas' actual name, Joses, means, "helped or exalted." He was a Levite, the tribe charged with taking care of the temple of God, and he came from Cyprus, which means "love and fairness." All this suggests that Joses (also called Barnabas) came from a good family that loved and cared for others and that he had been helped by others himself. The fact that he was renamed Barnabas clearly indicates that consolation must have been one of the prime characteristics of his personality.

    Ac 4:36 And Joses, who by the apostles was surnamed Barnabas, (which is, being interpreted, The son of consolation,) a Levite, and of the country of Cyprus.

5. <u>One of the signs of brotherly love is when we will give up our own resources for the good of others.</u> Out of his compassion for others, he sold some of his land and gave it to the apostles to help the poor. It appears he may have been the first to begin this trend of selling land and giving all of the proceeds to the apostles, since these verses lead directly to the confrontation with Ananias and Sapphira. They died because they lied to the Holy Spirit trying to look like they really cared and wanted to help others.

    Ac 4:37 Having land, sold it, and brought the money, and laid it at the apostles' feet.

6. <u>Consolation is an automatic outgrowth of brotherly love, since if we are fond of our brethren we will want them to be consoled and be at peace with one another.</u> Barnabas intervened to validate Saul's ministry to the disciples in Jerusalem.

    Ac 9:26 And when Saul was come to Jerusalem, he assayed to join himself to the disciples: but they were all afraid of him, and believed not that he was a disciple.

    27 But Barnabas took him (Saul later called Paul), and brought him to the apostles, and declared unto them how he had seen the Lord in the way, and that he had spoken to him, and how he had preached boldly at Damascus in the name of Jesus.

7. <u>Men of love and compassion are many times chosen for the difficult tasks of reconciliation.</u> Since Barnabas looked out more for others than himself, he could and was trusted with the most difficult tasks of diplomacy and reconciliation. The whole idea of preaching to the Gentiles and actively accepting them into the church was still very controversial at this time. He was the right man for this delicate job and could be trusted to handle it with love.

    Ac 11:20 And some of them were men of Cyprus and Cyrene, which, when they were come to Antioch, spake unto the Grecians, preaching the Lord Jesus.

21 And the hand of the Lord was with them: and a great number believed, and turned unto the Lord.

22 Then tidings of these things came unto the ears of the church which was in Jerusalem: and they sent forth Barnabas, that he should go as far as Antioch.

8. <u>Really caring and having compassion comes out of a good heart, full of faith that God will always meet our needs. It is motivated by a life led by the Holy Spirit.</u> Consequently, Barnabas was free to focus on the needs of others and always had the best interests of his brethren in mind.

Ac 11:23 Who, when he came, and had seen the grace of God, was glad, and exhorted them all, that with purpose of heart they would cleave unto the Lord.

24 For he was a good man, and full of the Holy Ghost and of faith: and much people was added unto the Lord.

9. <u>Those who truly love as brethren constantly see and try to promote the potential in others.</u> Barnabas was constantly looking to include those who had failed or were outcasts in order to restore them. After Barnabas had sponsored and reconciled Saul (later called Paul) to the disciples at Jerusalem, Saul had caused such a commotion by his preaching that plots were made against his life, and he was sent back to his home of Tarsus. When he was finally sent away, the church had rest and grew, possibly suggesting that Saul was actually hindering rather than helping at Jerusalem. However, when the revival broke out at Antioch, Barnabas remembered him and was willing to give him another chance at the ministry.

Ac 11:25 Then departed Barnabas to Tarsus, for to seek Saul:

26 And when he had found him, he brought him unto Antioch. And it came to pass, that a whole year they assembled themselves with the church, and taught much people. And the disciples were called Christians first in Antioch.

10. <u>Brotherly love requires that we do everything we can to help a brother in need.</u> When it was prophesied that famine was to come to Judea, money was gathered and sent by the hands of Barnabas and Saul.

Ac 11:30 Which also they did, and sent it to the elders by the hands of Barnabas and Saul.

11. <u>God Himself greatly honors those who have learned to love and cooperate with their brothers for the good of the Kingdom of God, and will call them to greater things.</u> Note, that at this time even to God, Barnabas had the preeminence. His name is listed first in all of these verses.

Ac 12:25 And Barnabas and Saul returned from Jerusalem, when they had fulfilled their ministry, and took with them John, whose surname was Mark.

13:1 Now there were in the church that was at Antioch certain prophets and teachers; as Barnabas, and Simeon that was called Niger, and Lucius of Cyrene, and Manaen, which had been brought up with Herod the tetrarch, and Saul.

2 As they ministered to the Lord, and fasted, the Holy Ghost said, Separate me Barnabas and Saul for the work whereunto I have called them.

12. <u>One of the qualities of brotherly love is that position and acclaim are not valued as important.</u> Although God had called Barnabas and Saul, soon Barnabas allowed Saul to take the prime leadership role in

the expedition. When we truly love our brother and have no vested interest in being most important, we can rejoice in the promotion of others even if it means we are demoted to a lower position. Note that verse 13 reads "Paul and his company," indicating that he had now made himself leader of this missionary expedition and in verses 9 and 16 that he now became the chief speaker. John Mark, possibly offended that Saul (who now called himself Paul) had supplanted his cousin, left the missionary expedition and returned home. (See the model of John Mark for healing hurts, wounds, and scars in *Transformation!*)

Ac 13:9 Then Saul, (who also is called Paul,) filled with the Holy Ghost, set his eyes on him,

10 And said, O full of all subtilty and all mischief, thou child of the devil, thou enemy of all righteousness, wilt thou not cease to pervert the right ways of the Lord?

11 And now, behold, the hand of the Lord is upon thee, and thou shalt be blind, not seeing the sun for a season. And immediately there fell on him a mist and a darkness; and he went about seeking some to lead him by the hand.

13 Now when <u>Paul and his company</u> loosed from Paphos, they came to Perga in Pamphylia: and John departing from them returned to Jerusalem.

14 But when they departed from Perga, they came to Antioch in Pisidia, and went into the synagogue on the sabbath day, and sat down.

16 Then Paul stood up, and beckoning with his hand said, Men of Israel, and ye that fear God, give audience.

13. <u>Those who are truly focused on the good of the Kingdom of God and have achieved brotherly love do not wish or seek to be elevated.</u> In these verses, the people honored Barnabas above Paul, and Barnabas took the lead in trying to stop the people from saying that they were gods and sacrificing to them.

Ac 14:12 And they called Barnabas, Jupiter (or Zeus because he commanded a stately presence); and Paul, Mercurius (God of eloquence who attended Jupiter), because he was the chief speaker.

14 Which when the apostles, <u>Barnabas and Paul</u>, heard of, they rent their clothes, and ran in among the people, crying out,

15 And saying, Sirs, why do ye these things? We also are men of like passions with you, and preach unto you that ye should turn from these vanities unto the living God, which made heaven, and earth, and the sea, and all things that are therein:

14. <u>Accepting a supporting role and being a true team player has its advantages.</u> Paul, not Barnabas was stoned. It is possible the Jews saw Paul as the greater threat.

Ac 14:19 And there came thither certain Jews from Antioch and Iconium, who persuaded the people, and, having stoned Paul, drew him out of the city, supposing he had been dead.

20 Howbeit, as the disciples stood round about him, he rose up, and came into the city: and the next day he departed with Barnabas to Derbe.

15. <u>Brotherly love requires that nothing be done to make it harder on a brother to succeed.</u> Here, Paul and Barnabas so strongly defended the Gentile brothers that the issue had to be referred to the counsel at Jerusalem, who then agreed that nothing should be done that would hinder the Gentile believers.

Ac 15:1 And certain men which came down from Judaea taught the brethren, and said, Except ye be circumcised after the manner of Moses, ye cannot be saved.

2 When therefore Paul and Barnabas had no small dissension and disputation with them, they determined that Paul and Barnabas, and certain other of them, should go up to Jerusalem unto the apostles and elders about this question.

16. <u>Men of consolation, who love the brethren, are honored by the brethren.</u> In Jerusalem, it appears that Barnabas was more respected than Paul and given the preeminence.

Ac 15:12 Then all the multitude kept silence, and gave audience to Barnabas and Paul, declaring what miracles and wonders God had wrought among the Gentiles by them.

17. <u>True brotherly love is contagious.</u> In these verses, additional men were recruited to assist in consoling the Gentile brethren concerning this matter. God uses all types of people to help and console others.

Ac 15:22 Then pleased it the apostles and elders, with the whole church, to send chosen men of their own company to Antioch with Paul and Barnabas; namely, Judas (he shall be praised) surnamed Barsabas, (son of desire or to be pleased) and Silas (woody), chief men among the brethren:

25 It seemed good unto us, being assembled with one accord, to send chosen men unto you with our beloved Barnabas and Paul,

18. <u>For those who truly love their brethren, loving relationships and forgiveness are more important than previous offenses.</u> They are willing to give their brothers another chance even if they have failed before. John Mark had left the previous missionary expedition. Barnabas wanted to give him another chance; Paul refused. To Barnabas, people were more important than accomplishments. Barnabas took John Mark and left for Cyprus (which means "love".)

Ac 15:36 And some days after Paul said unto Barnabas, Let us go again and visit our brethren in every city where we have preached the word of the Lord, and see how they do.

37 And Barnabas determined to take with them John, whose surname was Mark.

39 And the contention was so sharp between them, that they departed asunder one from the other: and so Barnabas took Mark, and sailed unto Cyprus;

19. <u>To compassionate people, meeting their own needs and being paid for what they do is of secondary importance.</u> Barnabas and Paul were possibly the only two in the early church who continued to work a secular job to support their missionary work.

1 Co 9:6 Or I only and Barnabas, have not we power to forbear working?

20. <u>One of the dangers to be avoided, when loving the brethren, is caring too much about pleasing them and trying too hard to avoid offense.</u> When some brothers came from Jerusalem, Peter and Barnabas went along with the Jewish tradition of not eating with the Gentiles. Paul had to confront them.

Ga 2:11 But when Peter was come to Antioch, I withstood him to the face, because he was to be blamed.

12 For before that certain came from James, he did eat with the Gentiles: but when they were come, he withdrew and separated himself, fearing them which were of the circumcision.

13 And the other Jews dissembled likewise with him; insomuch that Barnabas also was carried away with their dissimulation.

21. <u>The ministry of consolation will eventually win out.</u> We find that later in the ministry of Paul, John Mark had again become a valued brother. Most likely this can be attributed to the efforts of Barnabas. Even with the conflict between Paul and Barnabas about the priority of brotherly love, Barnabas continued in a supporting role to the man he had helped find his place in ministry. Brotherly love will eventually overcome all obstacles.

2 Ti 4:11 Only Luke is with me. Take Mark, and bring him with thee: for he is profitable to me for the ministry.

Col 4:10 Aristarchus my fellowprisoner saluteth you, and Marcus, sister's son to Barnabas, (touching whom ye received commandments: if he come unto you, receive him;)

Ga 2:1 Then fourteen years after I went up again to Jerusalem with Barnabas, and took Titus with me also.

Developing Brotherly Love

1. Brotherly love is having the best interests of our Christian brothers in mind, in spite of offenses and inadequacies. It is typified by compassion and consolation. We need to accept them as God accepts us: with unlimited mercy and unmerited favor.

2. Compassion is learned by the things that we suffer. When we know what it feels like to struggle in life or be rejected and hurt, we do not want that to happen to others. Jesus was filled with compassion for us because He lived and experienced life among us.

3. Consolation is the desire to soothe the suffering and pain in others. When we have true compassion, we want to make things better for others. When we have been helped, we want to help.

4. In order to truly love our brethren, we must value who they are, above what they can currently do for us. We should also learn to look past their actions, offenses, and peculiarities, as well as value the potential of the scared little boy or girl inside.

5. True brotherly love requires forgiving what they may have done, valuing them as an asset in the Kingdom of God, and doing what is in their best interest for developing their potential.

6. It requires preferring our brother before ourselves, becoming a team player, and promoting others above ourselves if this is in the best interest of the Kingdom of God. We must seek to give all credit to God.

7. We must be willing to sacrifice anything that we have for our brothers, if they have need of it, trusting God always to meet all of our needs.

PART IX

Agape Love—Knowing That God Is Love

Chapter 21

True Benevolence
God Is Love

2 Pe 1:7 And to godliness, brotherly kindness; and to brotherly kindness charity.

The ultimate, in Christianity, is to be conformed to the very image of God, who is love. We should live, act, sacrifice and be motivated as He is. In verse 7, the word translated as charity is *agapao*, which means "to welcome, to entertain, to be fond of, to love dearly; to be well pleased, to be contented at or with a thing." "This concept of love implies a duty or obligation to care about the other person, whether you want to care or not, and whether the love is deserved or not. Agape is 'gift love,' without ulterior motives and with no strings attached. It is completely altruistic and deeply compassionate. The truly agapic lover gives the kind of loving that the beloved needs, regardless of the benefits or difficulties involved for the lover. The greatest gift of such a lover may be to step out of the beloved's life altogether and allow them to love and be loved by someone else." (John Lee in *"The Colours of Love"*)

Agape love

1. Love, as a way of life, transcends everything else.

   1 Co 12:31...And now I will point out to you a way of life which transcends all others. (WEY)

2. Whatever we do, that is not motivated by true love, counts for nothing.

   1 Co 13:1 If I can speak with the tongues of men and of angels, but am destitute of Love, I have but become a loud-sounding trumpet or a clanging cymbal.

   2 If I possess the gift of prophecy and am versed in all mysteries and all knowledge, and have such absolute faith that I can remove mountains, but am destitute of Love, I am nothing.

   3 And if I distribute all my possessions to the poor, and give up my body to be burned, but am destitute of Love, it profits me nothing. (WEY)

3. Agape, God's type of love, is benevolence toward everyone.

   1 Co 13:4 Love is patient and kind. Love knows neither envy nor jealousy. Love is not forward and self-assertive, nor boastful and conceited.

   5 She does not behave unbecomingly, nor seek to aggrandize herself, nor blaze out in passionate anger, nor brood over wrongs.

   6 She finds no pleasure in injustice done to others, but joyfully sides with the truth.

   7 She knows how to be silent. She is full of trust, full of hope, full of patient endurance.

   8 Love never fails....(WEY)

4. <u>All the other things we think are important will eventually pass away and are imperfect.</u>

    1 Co 13:8 …But if there are prophecies, they will be done away with; if there are languages, they will cease; if there is knowledge, it will be brought to an end. For our knowledge is imperfect, and so is our prophesying; (WEY)

5. <u>The perfect state of the future is love-based, so we should put away the childish ways of this world.</u>

    1 Co 13:10 but when the perfect state of things is come, all that is imperfect will be brought to an end.

    11 When I was a child, I talked like a child, felt like a child, reasoned like a child: when I became a man, I put from me childish ways. (WEY)

6. <u>Current things will be replaced by true intimacy and love for God and others.</u>

    1 Co 13:12 For the present we see things as if in a mirror, and are puzzled; but then we shall see them face to face. For the present the knowledge I gain is imperfect; but then I shall know fully, even as I am fully known. (WEY)

7. <u>Love is the most important of eternal things.</u>

    1 Co 13:13 And so there remain Faith, Hope, Love—these three; and of these the greatest is Love. (WEY)

8. <u>The amount of love we have for God is determined by what we perceive He has done for us.</u>

    Lu 7:41 There was a certain creditor which had two debtors: the one owed five hundred pence, and the other fifty.

    42 And when they had nothing to pay, he frankly forgave them both. Tell me therefore, which of them will love him most?

    43 Simon answered and said, I suppose that [he], to whom he forgave most. And he said unto him, Thou hast rightly judged.

    47 Wherefore I say unto thee, Her sins, which are many, are forgiven; for she loved much: but to whom little is forgiven, the same loveth little. (AV)

9. <u>The very essence of God is love.</u>

    1 Jo 4:7 Beloved, let us love one another: for love is of God; and every one that loveth is born of God, and knoweth God.

    8 He that loveth not knoweth not God; for God is love.

10. <u>God's love is not based on the desirability or performance of the object.</u>

    Ro 5:8 But God commendeth his love toward us, in that, while we were yet sinners, Christ died for us.

11. <u>Loving God leads to a desire to please and obey Him.</u>

Jo 14:23 Jesus answered and said unto him, If a man love me, he will keep my words: and my Father will love him, and we will come unto him, and make our abode with him.

24 He that loveth me not keepeth not my sayings: and the word which ye hear is not mine, but the Father's which sent me.

12. <u>Obedience perfects love, because it leads to greater manifestation of God, and the more we really know God, the more we love and appreciate Him.</u>

1 Jo 2:5 But whoso keepeth his word, in him verily is the love of God perfected: hereby know we that we are in him.

13. <u>Christians are to be known for loving one another in the same way that God loves us.</u>

Jo 13:34 A new commandment I give unto you, That ye love one another; as I have loved you, that ye also love one another.

35 By this shall all [men] know that ye are my disciples, if ye have love one to another.

14. <u>We are to love everyone, even our enemies, unconditionally, just as God loves all of His creation.</u>

Mt 5:44 But I say unto you, Love your enemies, bless them that curse you, do good to them that hate you, and pray for them which despitefully use you, and persecute you;

46 For if ye love them which love you, what reward have ye? do not even the publicans the same?

47 And if ye salute your brethren only, what do ye more [than others]? do not even the publicans so?

48 Be ye therefore perfect, even as your Father which is in heaven is perfect.

15. <u>The Holy Spirit within us fills our hearts with the love of God.</u>

Ro 5:5 And hope maketh not ashamed; because the love of God is shed abroad in our hearts by the Holy Ghost which is given unto us.

16. <u>Love provides the ultimate motivation to work for God's kingdom.</u>

2 Co 5:14 For the love of Christ constraineth us; because we thus judge, that if one died for all, then were all dead:

12:15 And I will very gladly spend and be spent for you; though the more abundantly I love you, the less I be loved.

17. <u>Our faith is manifested through our love.</u>

Ga 5:6 For in Jesus Christ neither circumcision availeth any thing, nor uncircumcision; but faith which worketh by love.

18. <u>Fear and love are opposites and work to displace each other.</u>

    1 Jo 4:18 There is no fear in love; but perfect love casteth out fear: because fear hath torment. He that feareth is not made perfect in love.

19. <u>Love is manifested in sacrificial action.</u>

    1 Jo 3:16 Hereby perceive we the love [of God], because he laid down his life for us: and we ought to lay down [our] lives for the brethren.

    17 But whoso hath this world's good, and seeth his brother have need, and shutteth up his bowels [of compassion] from him, how dwelleth the love of God in him?

    18 My little children, let us not love in word, neither in tongue; but in deed and in truth.

20. <u>Nothing can ever separate us from the love of God.</u>

    Ro 8:35 Who shall separate us from the love of Christ? [shall] tribulation, or distress, or persecution, or famine, or nakedness, or peril, or sword?

    37 Nay, in all these things we are more than conquerors through him that loved us.

    38 For I am persuaded, that neither death, nor life, nor angels, nor principalities, nor powers, nor things present, nor things to come, .

    39 Nor height, nor depth, nor any other creature, shall be able to separate us from the love of God, which is in Christ Jesus our Lord.

21. <u>Love has always been the ultimate purpose of God.</u>

    Eph 1:4 According as he hath chosen us in him before the foundation of the world, that we should be holy and without blame before him in love:

22. <u>Love leads us to accept others as they are and put up with what they do.</u>

    Eph 4:2 With all lowliness and meekness, with longsuffering, forbearing one another in love;

23. <u>We are transformed into Christ's image and the fullness of God through the exercise of love.</u>

    Eph 3:19 And to know the love of Christ, which passeth knowledge, that ye might be filled with all the fulness of God.

    4:15 But speaking the truth in love, may grow up into him in all things, which is the head, even Christ:

24. <u>Love is what knits or holds the Body of Christ together.</u>

    Eph 4:16 From whom the whole body fitly joined together and compacted by that which every joint supplieth, according to the effectual working in the measure of every part, maketh increase of the body unto the edifying of itself in love.

    Col 2:2 That their hearts might be comforted, being knit together in love, and unto all riches of the full assurance of understanding, to the acknowledgement of the mystery of God, and of the Father, and of Christ;

25. <u>True love began when God demonstrated His love for us, by sending His son.</u>

    1 Jo 4:10 Herein is love, not that we loved God, but that he loved us, and sent his Son to be the propitiation for our sins.

26. <u>Love begins when we experience love, just as a child must first be loved in order to become a loving person.</u> Those who do not experience love do not learn to love. However, this does not excuse us from God's command to love others; because He has demonstrated His love to us, even in cases where our parents neglected to do so.

    1 Jo 4:19 We love him, because he first loved us.

27. <u>The measure of love is what we are willing to sacrifice for others.</u>

    Jo 3:16 For God so loved the world, that he gave his only begotten Son, that whosoever believeth in him should not perish, but have everlasting life.
    15:13 Greater love hath no man than this, that a man lay down his life for his friends.

The entire process of spiritual and psychological development has one goal—other-centeredness, which is love. We, as Christians, begin life completely self-centered and progress step-by-step through the process of salvation, until we have the best interest of others as our primary focus, just as God does. Finally, the ultimate expression of love is a willingness to sacrifice ourselves as Jesus did, for the benefit of others—even for the most despicable of people. Jesus died for us while we were yet sinners. (Romans 5:8)

We also see how this is to be achieved. It begins when we experience the unconditional love of God. Without experiencing love, we cannot give it, just as the child who never received love from its parents and thus never bonded with them, usually suffers from Reaction Attachment Disorder and is completely self-focused, without feelings of remorse for hurting others. When we accept Christ into our hearts, we accept the Holy Spirit who "sheds abroad love" into our hearts, drawing us to want to love others. As we grow in our relationship with God, we learn that He will meet all our needs, so that we do not have to pursue the needs of the self (selfishness) in order to meet them. The more that this becomes a reality in our lives, the more we are set free to love others and not compete with them. As we overcome our rebellion (wanting to be our own God) and become more obedient to the will of God, God is able to more fully manifest Himself to us. As we get to know and trust Him more, we want to be more like Him. As we focus more on the things of God and walk according to His Spirit, God's Spirit helps us displace our flesh and our self-bias, thus setting us free to allow God to be manifested through us. As we become more conformed to His image, we manifest more of His Spirit, which is love—first to our brothers in Christ and then to all men.

When we have the full revelation of God's love, so that we absolutely know that God has and will always meet all our needs for love, security, worth, and significance, we realize that we have a problem. We no longer have the selfishness that motivates the entire world. Since we no longer have to do anything to meet our needs, we should go to God and ask if He has anything He would like us to do—like rename the animals (as Adam did), or something? Of course, God would reply that He does have something that is more important than anything else we have ever done before: "Go and love everyone else with no strings attached, just because you value and love them as I do." After coming to this revelation, I had one client, who was an aircraft engineer, say, "Then why would I go to work?" Of course, the answer is that we are to do everything out of love and do everything, even our work, for the glory of God. (1 Corintians 10:31)

My Experience

During my assignment as Chief of Air Traffic Control Operation at a base in the Southwestern part of the United States, I was teaching Bible studies at the church that I attended. The Lord spoke to me suggesting that for the next topic I should study the subject of love. As I began studying the Word of God and a number of books on this subject, I learned what I have just presented in this book on the subject of unconditional love.

At the time I was dating a young lady named Nancy from Denver, Colorado who I had been introduced to, when I had visited my grandmother who lived there. Our relationship had become somewhat serious and based on my study of the subject of love, I made an unconditional love commitment to her. This did not necessarily mean that we would get married, but that I would always have her best interests in mind no matter how things turned out. We were writing to each other every day. However, one day I did not receive a letter from her. I wrote anyway. Again the next day—no letter. I wrote yet again and on the third day—no letter. I was considering calling to see if I had been "dumped," when the Lord spoke to me, "What kind of commitment did you make to her?" "Was it unconditional?" I had to admit that it was and that I had agreed that no matter what she did—even if she did not write—I would always have her best interests in mind so I wrote anyway. The next day I received four letters! Somehow, they had been held up in the mail. This was my first introduction to the subject of true unconditional love.

One day, as I was thinking of what nice thing I could do next for Nancy, it was as if God tapped me on the shoulder and said, "That is what I am like. I am just sitting up here in heaven thinking of nice things to do for you!" Sometimes we have a hard time grasping that that is what God is like—pure unconditional love.

Just before I was reassigned to Colorado Springs to help in the development of computer software for the Space Computation Center (it keeps track of all space objects), I was married to my dear wife, Nancy. To shorten a long story, after my retirement, we were sent out into the ministry, first as pastors, and later I became director of the Word of Life Counseling Center and the Word of Life Institute, where we train Christian counselors.

As this new phase of my life was beginning, it was God's plan to fill me more with His unconditional love for everyone as I struggled with my clients to help them find complete wholeness in Christ. In the beginning of my life, He first showed me love through my parents, then He brought me into a closer relationship with Him, and filled me with His Holy Spirit. He set me free from the law, so that I could serve Him out of appreciation rather than obligation, and He accepted me just as I was. But it was when I acted according to my faith to reach out to others in love, especially the struggling and hurting people of this world, that I turned a corner from being driven to accomplish things, to really caring about people.

It is when we start looking beyond the stories of emotional pain and tragedy in the lives of people and learn to love the scared little boys and girls inside that we begin to love people in the way God loves. It is when we can look past—but not condone—the sin and see the heart of the struggling person who has trusted in the flesh and is trying to be their own god, that we can learn to love them anyway just as they are. Love of course, leads us to have their best interests in mind, which sometimes requires confronting the sin, showing them that what they are doing will not work, and leading them to a saving knowledge of Jesus Christ. Love then leads us to sacrifice to do whatever is required to really help them in the long run even if they do not want to hear what we have to tell them right now. Without this kind of love, after a number of years, a counselor can become hard and uncaring, and eventually burn out. It is only through God, Who can so fill us by His Holy Spirit with compassion for all men that we can steadfastly carry out this kind of ministry for a lifetime. Does this mean that I have arrived? Absolutely not, but God is giving me more and more of His revelation of what it really means not to just love others, but to be so consumed with His love that we become the personification of love itself. I still have a long way to go.

Chapter 22

Learning to Love as Jesus Loved
(John, the Disciple Whom Jesus Loved)

When we realize that the Apostle John began his discipleship nicknamed by Jesus as one of the "sons of thunder," it is intriguing how he was transformed into the "Apostle of Love." This is especially true when his brother James, the other "son of thunder," died as a martyr. But this is exactly what God wants to do with each of us—change us from selfish sinners into the image of Jesus Himself—pure love. Because of his dramatic transformation and the emphasis in his writing on love, I believe that the Apostle John provides us with the best biblical model concerning the achievement of agape love.

1. <u>Jesus was the ultimate demonstration of God's love and grace.</u> Grace or undeserved favor is the very essence of love.

   Jo 1:14 And the Word was made flesh, and dwelt among us, (and we beheld his glory, the glory as of the only begotten of the Father,) full of grace and truth.

   16 And of his fulness have all we received, and grace for grace.

   17 For the law was given by Moses, but grace and truth came by Jesus Christ.

2. <u>The first step in developing true love is to choose to become a loving person.</u> Jesus called John and his friends and they forsook all and followed Him. John means "Jehovah is a gracious giver." Nothing could be a better description of love. His father's name, Zebedee, means "my gift." Leaving one's profession, boat, and father indicates that John was making a major commitment to follow Jesus.

   Mt 4:21 And going on from thence, he saw other two brethren, James the son of Zebedee, and John his brother, in a ship with Zebedee their father, mending their nets; and he called them.

   22 And they immediately left the ship and their father, and followed him.

3. <u>Although all of us are called to develop true agape love, few actually experience it.</u> When we think of the disciples, each struggled to grow in God and learn to love one another. Judas betrayed Him, Peter denied Jesus three times, and all the rest of the disciples fled when He was arrested.

   Jo 13:35 By this shall all men know that ye are my disciples, if ye have love one to another.

4. <u>We all begin our journey toward the development of love, from different places, based on our character and experiences.</u> John was definitely not a prime candidate because he and his brother James struggled with anger and a drive for prominence. These negative attributes were clearly demonstrated during their discipleship.

Mr 3:17 And James the son of Zebedee, and John the brother of James; and he surnamed them Boanerges, which is, The sons of thunder:

Lu 9:53 And they did not receive him, because his face was as though he would go to Jerusalem.

54 And when his disciples James and John saw this, they said, Lord, wilt thou that we command fire to come down from heaven, and consume them, even as Elias did?

55 But he turned, and rebuked them, and said, Ye know not what manner of spirit ye are of.

Mr 10:35 And James and John, the sons of Zebedee, come unto him, saying, Master, we would that thou shouldest do for us whatsoever we shall desire.

36 And he said unto them, What would ye that I should do for you?

37 They said unto him, Grant unto us that we may sit, one on thy right hand, and the other on thy left hand, in thy glory.

5. <u>Jesus demonstrated His love by reaching out to even those most despised by men.</u> God wants all of us, no matter what our background or problems, to experience His love and become loving people.

Jo 4:6 Now Jacob's well was there. Jesus therefore, being wearied with his journey, sat thus on the well: and it was about the sixth hour.

7 There cometh a woman of Samaria to draw water: Jesus saith unto her, Give me to drink.

9 Then saith the woman of Samaria unto him, How is it that thou, being a Jew, askest drink of me, which am a woman of Samaria? for the Jews have no dealings with the Samaritans.

6. <u>We must have a revelation of Who Jesus truly is—the expression of God's love.</u> John was among the disciples on the Mount of Transfiguration.

Mt 17:1 And after six days Jesus taketh Peter, James, and John his brother, and bringeth them up into an high mountain apart,

2 And was transfigured before them: and his face did shine as the sun, and his raiment was white as the light.

3 And, behold, there appeared unto them Moses and Elias talking with him.

5 While he yet spake, behold, a bright cloud overshadowed them: and behold a voice out of the cloud, which said, This is my beloved Son, in whom I am well pleased; hear ye him.

7. <u>We must spend as much time with Jesus as possible, in order to learn from Him how to truly love others.</u> John had the privilege of being one of Jesus' inner circle of the disciples that accompanied Him most of the time, even when He raised the dead.

Mr 5:37 And he suffered no man to follow him, save Peter, and James, and John the brother of James.

41 And he took the damsel by the hand, and said unto her, Talitha cumi; which is, being interpreted, Damsel, I say unto thee, arise.

42 And straightway the damsel arose, and walked; for she was of the age of twelve years. And they were astonished with a great astonishment.

8. <u>God wants us to know what He is really like.</u> John was one of the few disciples that Jesus confided in, even when He was struggling in the Garden of Gethsemane. Unfortunately, John and the rest failed Jesus time and time again.

> Mr 14:33 And he taketh with him Peter and James and John, and began to be sore amazed, and to be very heavy;
>
> 34 And saith unto them, My soul is exceeding sorrowful unto death: tarry ye here, and watch.
>
> 35 And he went forward a little, and fell on the ground, and prayed that, if it were possible, the hour might pass from him.
>
> 37 And he cometh, and findeth them sleeping, and saith unto Peter, Simon, sleepest thou? couldest not thou watch one hour?
>
> 39 And again he went away, and prayed, and spake the same words.
>
> 40 And when he returned, he found them asleep again, (for their eyes were heavy,) neither wist they what to answer him.
>
> 41 And he cometh the third time, and saith unto them, Sleep on now, and take your rest: it is enough, the hour is come; behold, the Son of man is betrayed into the hands of sinners.

9. <u>We must do everything we can to have a very close, intimate relationship with Jesus.</u> It is clear that at the last supper John was so close to Jesus that he describes it as lying on Jesus' breast. Because of this close relationship, Jesus revealed to him who it was that would betray Him. John describes himself as "the disciple whom Jesus loved."

> Jo 13:23 Now there was leaning on Jesus' bosom one of his disciples, whom Jesus loved.
>
> 24 Simon Peter therefore beckoned to him, that he should ask who it should be of whom he spake.
>
> 25 He then lying on Jesus' breast saith unto him, Lord, who is it?
>
> 26 Jesus answered, He it is, to whom I shall give a sop, when I have dipped it. And when he had dipped the sop, he gave it to Judas Iscariot, the son of Simon.

10. <u>When we get to know Jesus, we also get to know the character of the Father.</u>

> Jo 14:8 Philip saith unto him, Lord, shew us the Father, and it sufficeth us.
>
> 9 Jesus saith unto him, Have I been so long time with you, and yet hast thou not known me, Philip? he that hath seen me hath seen the Father; and how sayest thou then, Shew us the Father?
>
> 10 Believest thou not that I am in the Father, and the Father in me? the words that I speak unto you I speak not of myself: but the Father that dwelleth in me, he doeth the works.

11. <u>We get to know God better as we work for Him and He provides for us.</u>

> Jo 14:11 Believe me that I am in the Father, and the Father in me: or else believe me for the very works' sake.
>
> 12 Verily, verily, I say unto you, He that believeth on me, the works that I do shall he do also; and greater works than these shall he do; because I go unto my Father.
>
> 13 And whatsoever ye shall ask in my name, that will I do, that the Father may be glorified in the Son.
>
> 14 If ye shall ask any thing in my name, I will do it.

12. <u>If we keep God's commandments, He will send the Holy Spirit to comfort us so that we can experience His love, and He will manifest Himself to us.</u> It is the Holy Spirit Who manifests God's love within us.

    Jo 14:15 If ye love me, keep my commandments.

    16 And I will pray the Father, and he shall give you another Comforter, that he may abide with you for ever;

    17 Even the Spirit of truth; whom the world cannot receive, because it seeth him not, neither knoweth him: but ye know him; for he dwelleth with you, and shall be in you.

13. <u>One aspect of the manifestation of God's love within us is His peace which overcomes our fear.</u>

    Jo 14:27 Peace I leave with you, my peace I give unto you: not as the world giveth, give I unto you. Let not your heart be troubled, neither let it be afraid.

14. <u>A deep, abiding relationship with God is required if we want to be fruitful in expressing His love</u>. He purges us, cleanses us through His Word, and produces His life in us through this close relationship.

    Jo 15:1 I am the true vine, and my Father is the husbandman.

    2 Every branch in me that beareth not fruit he taketh away: and every branch that beareth fruit, he purgeth it, that it may bring forth more fruit.

    4 Abide in me, and I in you. As the branch cannot bear fruit of itself, except it abide in the vine; no more can ye, except ye abide in me.

    5 I am the vine, ye are the branches: He that abideth in me, and I in him, the same bringeth forth much fruit: for without me ye can do nothing.

15. <u>As we become more in unity with the Godhead, we are filled with the same love that is between the Father and the Son.</u>

    Jo 17:20 Neither pray I for these alone, but for them also which shall believe on me through their word;

    21 That they all may be one; as thou, Father, art in me, and I in thee, that they also may be one in us: that the world may believe that thou hast sent me.

    22 And the glory which thou gavest me I have given them; that they may be one, even as we are one:

    23 I in them, and thou in me, that they may be made perfect in one; and that the world may know that thou hast sent me, and hast loved them, as thou hast loved me.

16. <u>The closer the spiritual relationship we have, the more we will be influenced and changed into the image of God, which is love.</u> The more we are in tune with the very heart of God (which is love), the more He will be able to share with us and ask us to do for Him. John was so close to Jesus that he was chosen to take care of Mary, Jesus' mother, at the crucifixion; and he was the first to recognize Jesus when He stood at the seaside when they were fishing. The closer we are to someone; the more we are influenced by them, and the more we become like them.

Jo 19:26 When Jesus therefore saw his mother, and the disciple standing by, whom he loved, he saith unto his mother, Woman, behold thy son!

21:7 Therefore that disciple whom Jesus loved saith unto Peter, It is the Lord. Now when Simon Peter heard that it was the Lord, he girt his fisher's coat unto him, (for he was naked,) and did cast himself into the sea.

17. <u>Our love will be perfected as we know Him better and keep His commandment to love one another.</u> We are to act like He acted and do the things He did.

1 Jo 2:3 And hereby we do know that we know him, if we keep his commandments.

4 He that saith, I know him, and keepeth not his commandments, is a liar, and the truth is not in him.

5 But whoso keepeth his word, in him verily is the love of God perfected: hereby know we that we are in him.

6 He that saith he abideth in him ought himself also so to walk, even as he walked.

18. <u>In order to become like God (Who is love), we must purify ourselves from sin, because He is pure.</u> Jesus came to take away sin, so if we continue to sin, we show that we do not truly love Him.

1 Jo 3:2 Beloved, now are we the sons of God, and it doth not yet appear what we shall be: but we know that, when he shall appear, we shall be like him; for we shall see him as he is.

3 And every man that hath this hope in him purifieth himself, even as he is pure.

4 Whosoever committeth sin transgresseth also the law: for sin is the transgression of the law.

5 And ye know that he was manifested to take away our sins; and in him is no sin.

6 Whosoever abideth in him sinneth not: whosoever sinneth hath not seen him, neither known him.

19. <u>True love is laying down our lives in order to truly help others.</u>

1 Jo 3:16 Hereby perceive we the love of God, because he laid down his life for us: and we ought to lay down our lives for the brethren.

20. <u>We must understand that God is love. We become like Him and know Him as we love others.</u>

1 Jo 4:7 Beloved, let us love one another: for love is of God; and every one that loveth is born of God, and knoweth God.

17 Herein is our love made perfect, that we may have boldness in the day of judgment: because as he is, so are we in this world.

On the following page, I have diagrammed the process of the development of agape love so that we can more clearly understand it. It all begins when we first experience the love of God and trust Him to meet our needs. As He provides for us and we get to know Him better, we grow in our appreciation of what He has done for us. Because we believe He has our best interest in mind (that He loves us), we trust Him enough to obey Him and His commandments. When we truly know that He will always meet all of our needs, we are willing to purify our lives from the lusts of the flesh so that we might have closer fellowship with Him. When we obey His commandments, God more fully reveals and manifests Himself to us and gives us a greater revelation of Who He really is—love. Because we love Him, we are willing to obey His commandment to love others unconditionally. Because we feel loved by Him, we overcome our fear that our needs will not be met if we focus on the needs of others and are, therefore, more able to love our brothers. As our loving relationship with God grows, we want to please Him more and are willing to sacrifice for Him. Finally, the more we actually love others and our love is perfected, the more we become like Him because He is love.

Before going on to the application of these steps and principles for counseling for spiritual growth, let us again review the promises that God has given us, if we diligently apply these steps to our lives.

> 2 Pe 1:8 For if these things be in you, and abound, they make you that ye shall neither be barren nor unfruitful in the knowledge of our Lord Jesus Christ.
>
> 9 But he that lacketh these things is blind, and cannot see afar off, and hath forgotten that he was purged from his old sins.
>
> 10 Wherefore the rather, brethren, give diligence to make your calling and election sure: for if ye do these things, ye shall never fall:
>
> 11 For so an entrance shall be ministered unto you abundantly into the everlasting kingdom of our Lord and Saviour Jesus Christ.

These verses promise us tremendous victory in our life in a number of areas. Let us review how these victories are accomplished through these steps.

1. Fruitfulness. According to John Chapter 15, our fruitfulness or accomplishments for Christ must come from His power within us. It states that we are the branches, Christ is the vine, and that we cannot do anything that will last without being connected to Him. From the previous chapters, it is clear that the basis of all spiritual development is our personal relationship with God. Through this process, we have a greater revelation of Who God really is. With a good spiritual foundation (root system), the tree (Christian) does not have to work at producing fruit, it is just a natural outgrowth of being a fruit tree.

2. Victory over sin. The defeat of the old man within us was accomplished for us by Christ on the cross. Now we have the ability to choose to do what is right, but most Christians are still under the law. Consequently, they are still struggling as Paul did trying to do what is right out of obligation in their own strength. Complete success can only come when we have a revelation of the grace of God and develop self-discipline.

3. Never falling. This implies that we never fall again into sin or fall from our faith in God. This can only happen when we realize who we are in Christ and that we have been adopted into the family of God with all of its blessing and obligations. We can only have consistent victory over sin, when our actions are dictated by who we are—not by our efforts to become victorious over sin.

4. Achieving our calling. When the Bible states that "many are called but few are chosen" (Matthew 22:14), it implies that although all of us have a specific call, many never end up fulfilling what they are called to do. Many who have begun a ministry have just not seen it blossom as they had hoped. Others who have entered into a powerfully anointed ministry have fallen into sin. Without the foundation of these later steps, we are all vulnerable to the attacks of Satan without the stability to defeat him at every turn. Ministry will be challenged both before and after it has begun. The stronger the spiritual basis of the ministry, the greater the chance it will be productive and successful in the Kingdom of God.

5. Ensuring our election. Some suggest that once we accept Christ, we can never choose to turn back to our old life and forfeit our election. If this is true, then these verses would be meaningless. Many times, they will cite John 10:28-29, which states "neither shall any man pluck them out of my (God's) hand." In the Greek, these verses use the third person (he, she, or it), not the first person (I). It is

clear that I am the only one that can lose faith and choose to forfeit my election to be part of the Kingdom of God. Although we can be eternally secure when we choose to follow Christ and never change our minds, without these steps we are vulnerable to the attacks of Satan and his lies to try to get us to turn back on our faith which is the basis of our salvation. (Hebrews 10:38-39) The solution is simple: as we diligently apply ourselves to our own spiritual development and to these steps, we will make our election sure.

6. <u>An abundant entrance into heaven.</u> Even though we are saved through what Jesus has done for us and will eventually make heaven our home, that does not guarantee that we will be welcomed into heaven as victorious and receive the crowns that are available to the saints. These are reserved for the overcomers and for those with fruitful lives who have significantly contributed to the Kingdom of God. Yes, God loves all of us, but some will receive a more "abundant welcome." Again, our diligence in our spiritual development will determine our fruitfulness and our victory over sin. These, in turn, will determine the level of our victorious welcome into heaven.

If we are to sum this up, we can go back to the initial promises that precede these verses. God has provided, through these steps, all we need for "life and godliness." (2 Peter 1:3) In other words, we have here, all we need to live the Christian life, but it is up to us to seek diligently these revelations in the knowledge of God, that will set us free and bring these great blessings to our lives.

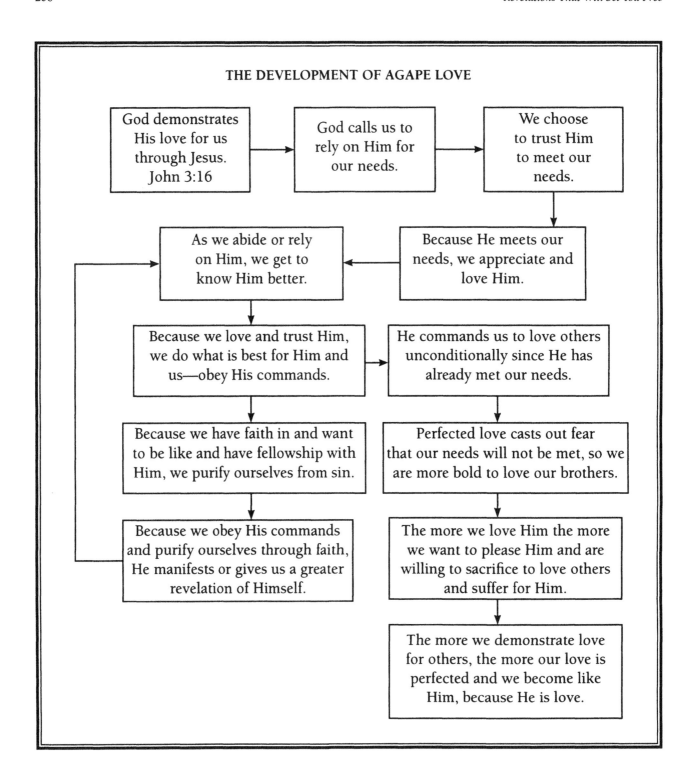

THE DEVELOPMENT OF AGAPE LOVE

God demonstrates His love for us through Jesus. John 3:16

God calls us to rely on Him for our needs.

We choose to trust Him to meet our needs.

As we abide or rely on Him, we get to know Him better.

Because He meets our needs, we appreciate and love Him.

Because we love and trust Him, we do what is best for Him and us—obey His commands.

He commands us to love others unconditionally since He has already met our needs.

Because we have faith in and want to be like and have fellowship with Him, we purify ourselves from sin.

Perfected love casts out fear that our needs will not be met, so we are more bold to love our brothers.

Because we obey His commands and purify ourselves through faith, He manifests or gives us a greater revelation of Himself.

The more we love Him the more we want to please Him and are willing to sacrifice to love others and suffer for Him.

The more we demonstrate love for others, the more our love is perfected and we become like Him, because He is love.

Developing Agape Love

1. Agape love is having the best interests of everyone else in mind to such a degree that we would lay down our lives for them.

2. Agape love is primarily learned through a close intimate relationship with God. We must abide in Him in order to produce the fruit of love.

3. When we receive the Holy Spirit into our lives, He begins to fill us with a desire to love others just as Jesus did.

4. In order to manifest God's love like He did, we must purify ourselves from sin and be willing to obey His commandments. The more we obey His commandments, the more God will manifest Himself to us and reveal His love in our lives.

5. God's love is perfected in us, as we love others as He does, with no strings attached, and when we are willing to give our lives, so that their needs can be met.

6. We know that God's love is perfected in our lives when we no longer fear that our needs will not be met and are able to focus completely on the needs of others. This is true unconditional love.

7. Since God is Love, the more we manifest love in our lives toward God and toward others, the more God will dwell in our lives. If we truly love God, we will walk and act as Jesus did, loving others so much that we will lay down our lives for them (as Jesus did on the cross for us).

PART X

Application

Chapter 23

The Cyclical Path to Spiritual Maturity

It is my hope that the steps to spiritual and psychological growth presented so far in this book have made the path to maturity clear and easy to follow. However, what I have described so far still lacks some of the specific details as to exactly how each step is to be achieved in a counseling situation. Is it possible that each step follows a specific pattern or cycle as it progresses? After studying this subject for some time, I have reached the conclusion that each step does follow a specific pattern. Studying this pattern will give us a better understanding of the mechanism that God uses in the process as each step is achieved.

I want to make it clear that God is working in our lives at numerous places and at different steps at the same time, but the attainment of each step is dependent on each new revelation about God. In the same way, each part of this cycle may be in progress at some specific time, but all of the cycle is required in order for a particular step to become a reality in our lives.

As I outline this cycle as it applies to the last step of agape love (which we have just discussed), I suggest that the reader glance at the chart at the end of this section to see how this cycle applies to each of the preceding steps. To follow the chart, start at the top line of each box for the first step and remain on that line until that cycle is finished. Then move to the second line for the second step, etc. Each follows the same sequence demonstrated below:

1. <u>The Holy Spirit draws us.</u> Without the drawing of the Holy Spirit, we cannot even be saved in the first place. At each step, the Holy Spirit draws us to want to grow as Christians and begins to bring us into a fuller knowledge of God. Spirits work by pulling at our will. Our will must yield to this spiritual influence in order for us to begin to move on to the next step. In order to draw us to want to be loving, God sent His Son to demonstrate His agape love to us. As we receive His love, He strengthens our inner man through His Spirit, and sheds abroad His love in our hearts. This love within us makes us want to love others as He does.

   Jo 3:16 For God so loved the world, that he gave his only begotten Son, that whosoever believeth in him should not perish, but have everlasting life.

   Ro 5:5 And hope maketh not ashamed; because the love of God is shed abroad in our hearts by the Holy Ghost which is given unto us.

2. <u>We are taught what is right and wrong</u>. Without the knowledge of what is right and wrong, we would be left to decide for ourselves what is right. When we are saved, we naturally want to do what is right because the Holy Spirit draws us to be holy (to do what is right). The Scriptures are extremely clear that God, Who is love, wants us to love Him and others with His kind of unconditional agape love. In fact, the Scriptures suggest that agape love is the very basis of the commandments themselves.

Mr 12:30 And thou shalt love the Lord thy God with all thy heart, and with all thy soul, and with all thy mind, and with all thy strength: this is the first commandment.

31 And the second is like, namely this, Thou shalt love thy neighbour as thyself. There is none other commandment greater than these.

3. <u>We realize that we cannot do it by our own effort.</u> As soon as we realize what is right and want to do it, we naturally try to do it, at least to some degree, in our own strength. It is amazing to me why it seems we often have to relearn this again at each step. I am not sure about everyone, but I have found that at least I tend to do this. Unfortunately, this learning usually has to be experiential; we have to try and fail over and over before we <u>know</u> we cannot do it. When we realize that God's standard of love is that we be willing to die for even the worst person we know, we understand how far short we come from the type of love God desires for us to have. In addition to absolute selflessness and total sacrifice, He wants us to love as He does. Do we love others so much that we would ask our own son to suffer and die on a cross for some absolute apostate stranger?

    1 Jo 3:16 Hereby perceive we the love of God, because he laid down his life for us: and we ought to lay down our lives for the brethren.

    4:11 Beloved, if God so loved us, we ought also to love one another.

4. <u>We receive a revelation of what God wants to teach us.</u> Somehow, through direct revelation, experience, meditation on the Word, preaching or some other means; we must come into a revelation about God that will make the truth that we must learn real to us and part of our spirit or subconscious mind. Maybe someone sacrifices for us, or maybe it is the Spirit of God moving on our heart to see people as He sees them. Something takes place to help us learn and experience the kind of love that God is. It is not enough to know that God loves us, but we must understand that He is love.

    1 Jo 4:7 Beloved, let us love one another: for love is of God; and every one that loveth is born of God, and knoweth God.

    8 He that loveth not knoweth not God; for God is love.

5. <u>We believe and trust God to do it for us.</u> "According to your faith be it unto you." (Matthew 9:29) This is what Jesus said to the blind man. Until God opens our spiritual eyes according to our faith, we will remain blind and not see. We may not even know how He does it, but, somehow, as we trust Him and not ourselves, the new revelation about God becomes clear. Without it, we can go no further in our spiritual development in this step. In this step, we must be "rooted and grounded in love" before it can be manifested in our lives.

    Eph 3:17 That Christ may dwell in your hearts by faith; that ye, being rooted and grounded in love,

6. <u>We are set free by it.</u> Once we have a particular revelation about God, it sets us free. When we learned that we could not direct our lives and turned them over to God, we found a new freedom from stress and the rat race. When we learned about grace, we found freedom from the curse of the law. When we learn about the unconditional love of God, we find the freedom to love everyone just as they are. I have heard it stated, and I believe it, that love and freedom are the opposite sides of the same coin, because love always sets us free. If God loves others no matter what they have done, then we can believe that He still loves us no matter how bad we fail, and we can love others even if they fail. If God loves me and wants me to be like Him, then I can trust Him to fill me with His love.

Mt 5:45 That ye may be the children of your Father which is in heaven: for he maketh his sun to rise on the evil and on the good, and sendeth rain on the just and on the unjust.

46 For if ye love them which love you, what reward have ye? do not even the publicans the same?

7. <u>Out of our experience of freedom, we die to ourselves.</u> It is interesting to me that freedom should lead to the death of self. We would normally think that if we were set free then we would use the freedom as an occasion for the flesh to meet the needs of the flesh. This would be true if our freedom was based on our own self-effort. In this case, our freedom is a gift from God and through it we are able to accept ourselves as we are. This reduces our need to make ourselves into something different. Since our need is reduced, so is our selfishness. Consequently, my striving to be someone different in my own strength is reduced; and I am no longer so self-centered. This is very clear in the case of agape love. When I realize how God loves me, it frees me to accept myself; and when I can accept myself, I am free to accept others as they are. Because we are not critical of ourselves, we have no need to be critical of or judge others (so that we can bring them down to our level). Because our needs are met, we are more willing to sacrifice (or die to self) for others.

Jo 15:13 Greater love hath no man than this, that a man lay down his life for his friends.

8. <u>We are now actually able to obey what God has called us to do through His power.</u> Each new revelation about God sets us free and leads to less selfishness on our part. Therefore, we are better able to trust and obey God in what He has called us to do. What is amazing to me is that, at this point, we are now able to carry out the very commandments that were a curse and stumbling block to us. Nevertheless, it is in God's power, and not in any effort of our own. True transformation is effortless on our part. As we choose to obey God, relying on His strength, we experience a fuller manifestation of God Himself and a deepening relationship with Him that increases our trust and faith. Consequently, we are able to obey Him more completely the next time, which leads to a fuller manifestation. As we are set free to love each other, we experience more of God's love, and love is further perfected in us.

Jo 14:23 Jesus answered and said unto him, If a man love me, he will keep my words: and my Father will love him, and we will come unto him, and make our abode with him.

1 Jo 4:12 No man hath seen God at any time. If we love one another, God dwelleth in us, and his love is perfected in us.

9. <u>We have now achieved the next step in the roadmap to spiritual maturity.</u> When we find ourselves automatically carrying out the goal of a particular step and it becomes a part of our character, we can conclude that we have progressed to that level. God judges us by our actions, not by our intentions. Although the heart must be changed, it is not until the change of the heart has been manifested in our behavior, that we can declare victory. Through these steps, God is able to do abundantly more in transforming our lives than we could ever imagine. Our job is to apply ourselves diligently to seek all He has for us.

Mt 25:31 When the Son of man shall come in his glory, and all the holy angels with him, then shall he sit upon the throne of his glory:

32 And before him shall be gathered all nations: and he shall separate them one from another, as a shepherd divideth his sheep from the goats:

33 And he shall set the sheep on his right hand, but the goats on the left.

34 Then shall the King say unto them on his right hand, Come, ye blessed of my Father, inherit the kingdom prepared for you from the foundation of the world:

35 For I was an hungred, and ye gave me meat: I was thirsty, and ye gave me drink: I was a stranger, and ye took me in:

36 Naked, and ye clothed me: I was sick, and ye visited me: I was in prison, and ye came unto me.

37 Then shall the righteous answer him, saying, Lord, when saw we thee an hungred, and fed thee? or thirsty, and gave thee drink?

38 When saw we thee a stranger, and took thee in? or naked, and clothed thee?

39 Or when saw we thee sick, or in prison, and came unto thee?

40 And the King shall answer and say unto them, Verily I say unto you, Inasmuch as ye have done it unto one of the least of these my brethren, ye have done it unto me.

THE CYCLICAL PROCESS OF SPIRITUAL GROWTH

Holy Spirit drawing:
1. To accept Christ
2. To follow Christ
3. To want to do right
4. To do right
5. To build the kingdom
6. To be holy
7. To love brothers
8. To love all

Achieving
1. Faith
2. Virtue
3. Knowledge
4. Self-control
5. Perseverance
6. Godliness
7. Brotherly Love
8. Agape Love

Knowing right and wrong
1. Being my own God
2. Running my life
3. The law
4. Actions
5. Who I am
6. Self-reliance
7. Feelings
8. Motivation

Actually **obeying** God
1. God's invitation
2. Direction for life
3. Trying to do right
4. Law of liberty
5. Responsibly
6. Law of Spirit life
7. Brotherly affection
8. Law of love

Realizing I can't do it
1. Earn eternal life
2. Direct my life
3. Obey the law
4. Control myself
5. Be responsible
6. Be holy
7. Have compassion
8. Love as I should

Dying (**Yielding**)
1. To being my God
2. To directing my life
3. To the law
4. To disobedience
5. To my old identity
6. To self-life and flesh
7. To preferring myself
8. For others

Experience or Revelation
1. As Savior
2. As Lord
3. Fear of God
4. Grace of God
5. Adoption of sons
6. Walking in Spirit
7. Affection
8. Unconditional love

Freedom
1. From death
2. To yield to God
3. From the law
4. To obey
5. From sin
6. To live in the Spirit
7. To care for brothers
8. To love everyone

Trusting God (faith)
1. For heaven
2. For direction
3. In God's Word
4. For unmerited favor
5. For who I am in Him
6. To live through me
7. To care for me
8. To never fail me

Chapter 24

Assessing Spiritual Growth

Analysis of Growth

In order to assist the client through this process of spiritual growth, we must assess where he is in these steps and lead him through the cycle of development to the next step. Each new step requires a new revelation in our knowledge of God.

Christian maturity can be assessed through asking a series of revealing questions. Depending on the answer to these questions, additional questions may be required as verification. It is important to make it clear that this assessment will only be valid if each question is answered as honestly and as thoughtfully as possible according to how they think God sees them. Below are the initial questions that will help to determine each level of maturity:

Faith:

1. Have you accepted Christ as your Savior and are you convinced that if you died right now you would go to heaven?
2. If God asked you why He should take you to heaven, what would you say?
3. Do you tend to see God as someone who is there to meet your needs and make life good?
4. Do you really want to do what God asks you to do?
5. Are you able to clearly hear from God to direct your life, or do you decide yourself what you feel is best for you?

Virtue:

1. Who is really in charge of and directing your life—you or God?"
2. Do you have a personal relationship with God?
3. Have you ever specifically heard the voice of God speaking to you?
4. Have you ever felt the manifested presence of God?
5. Do you tend to give priority to the things of God or to doing what you want first?

Knowledge:

1. Does it sometimes seem that God's commandments are designed to ruin your fun?
2. Do you have an in-depth knowledge of the Bible and what it says about what is right and wrong?
3. Do the Old Testament laws of God apply to us today?
4. Do you try to obey the law of God out of obligation, to avoid consequences, out of fear of punishment, or so that He will not be disappointed with you?
5. Have you been able to control your fleshly desires through your own will-power?

Temperance:

1. What does it mean to you that Christ has set you free?
2. Are you free to do anything you want without endangering God's favor for you?
3. Do you feel condemned when you sin?
4. Do you tend to use your liberty as an occasion for the flesh?
5. Do you follow what God tells you to do because you want to or only to avoid the consequences of your actions and possible discipline from God?

Patience:

1. Do you see yourself as a servant or child of God?
2. Have you had a revelation of what it means to be adopted into the family of God?
3. Are there certain things that you do not do because it would bring reproach on Christ?
4. Do you sometimes hide the fact that you are a Christian?
5. Have you achieved consistent self-control over all aspects of you life?

Godliness:

1. Do you have a very intimate and personal relationship with God, walking in His Spirit throughout your entire day?
2. Would you rather spend time with God than do anything else?
3. Do you find yourself exhibiting the fruit of the Spirit without any significant effort on your part?
4. Are you still trying to do what you want in your own strength or have you achieved victory over the selfish desires in your life?
5. Have you successfully purified your life from sin or do you still have certain lusts and strongholds that you have not yet overcome in your life? Are you able to consistently maintain the peace of God in your spirit?

Brotherly Kindness:

1. Do you feel completely accepted and loved by God even when you fail?
2. Do you tend to be critical and irritated with other Christians when they are incompetent or fail?
3. Do you love to be with and fellowship with other Christians?
4. Are you deeply concerned and fondly care about the welfare and the best interest of even the most dysfunctional of your Christian brothers?
5. Are you able to work together with other Christians that have significant differences in doctrine?

Charity:

1. Are you able to have care and concern for even the most despised and hated persons like Saddam Hussein, Mosavick, and Ben Laden?
2. Are you deeply concerned for the salvation of everyone you meet, especially those who you view as the most dysfunctional and immoral?
3. When someone mistreats you do you have a difficult time forgiving them?
4. Do you tend to care more for your friends who love you and treat you right than for those who do not seem to have your best interests in mind?
5. Do you usually succeed at valuing and treating everyone equally?

If the client cannot correctly answer one of the questions under each step, additional clarification may be required. If the client has not reached an experiential understanding of any question, this indicates that this step requires additional work. Once the specific step has been determined, we next need to assess where the client is in the development cycle for that next step.

Determining Progress in the Developmental Cycle

Once the step has been determined, additional questions similar to those below can be asked to determine where the client is in the developmental cycle for that step.

1. The Holy Spirit draws us.
   a. Do you feel drawn or motivated to grow in _____?
   b. Has God confronted you or brought the need to your attention for _____?

2. We are taught what is right and wrong.
   a. What does the Bible say concerning _____?
   b. In your spirit, what do you believe is right concerning _____?

3. We realize that we cannot do it by our own effort.
   a. Have you attempted and failed to _____?
   b. Are you now convinced that no matter how hard you try you can never_____?

4. Through our experience we receive a revelation of what God wants to teach us.
   a. Have you received a revelation concerning _____? If so, what is it?
   b. Is this revelation in your mind, have you experienced it, or do you know it in your spirit?

5. We trust God for it.
   a. Do you actually believe (know in your spirit) that you have _____?
   b. Are you acting as if you have _____?

6. We are set free by it.
   a. Do you feel freed by your revelation and experience of _____?
   b. In what way are you free?

7. Out of our experience of freedom, we die to ourselves.
   a. Have you noticed a change in your level of anxiety in _____?
   b. Do you seem to care less about the importance of _____?

8. We are now actually able to obey what God has called us to do through His power.
   a. Are you consistently obeying what you believe is right in _____?
   b. Do you find that you want to do what is right or do you have to make yourself do it?

9. We finally achieve the next step in the roadmap to spiritual maturity.
   a. Do you feel peace that you have fully reached the level of _____?
   b. In your spirit are you ready to go on to the next step?

Acquiring the Next Revelation in the Knowledge of God

The most essential part in this process is acquiring a new revelation concerning the knowledge of God. This is not easy since it involves not only obtaining the necessary information, but moving it from our mind to our spirit so that the knowledge becomes revelation.

We have already discussed some of these basic methods such as Bible study, biblical meditation, prayer, preaching, and acting according to the Word of God. The method for counseling for spiritual growth will be discussed in the next chapter.

Chapter 25

How to Counsel for Spiritual Growth

We now have the specific building blocks necessary for putting together a complete counseling methodology to counsel others for spiritual growth. It is interesting to realize that the developmental cycle that we have recognized as a pattern of spiritual growth at each step correlates closely with the "Biblical Plan for Christian Counseling" that I developed using the types and shadows interpretation of the story of the children of Israel in my book, *Transformation!* Because of these similarities between the cyclical process of spiritual growth and the plan for Christian counseling, we can directly apply these concepts to that plan. I will discuss each part of the cyclical process as they directly apply to each of the steps from "A Biblical Plan for Christian Counseling."

1. <u>Determine the problem.</u> The very fact that clients come to us requesting counseling suggests that the Holy Spirit has been drawing them. This drawing of the Holy Spirit is, of course, the first step in the cycle of spiritual development previously discussed. In this and the next two steps, the counselor should continue to assist in this process of motivation. It is good to ask the client what motivated them to come for counseling. Various factors motivate clients to come, including sermons by their pastor, some friend suggesting that they need help, or possibly negative consequences they have received from their actions. Nonetheless, in most cases clients come due to a crisis in their lives.

   After determining the psychological problem, the next issue is to decide if an emphasis on spiritual growth is appropriate for this client at this time. As a general rule, clients who are not saved, clients with problems concerning evil spirits, clients struggling with issues that relate directly to a specific step (as listed below), and those who have so many problems that it is difficult to determine where to start, are prime candidates for spiritual growth therapy. Below is a list of each step and the psychological problems that are addressed by each. Of course, prior steps will have to be addressed as building blocks before reaching and addressing the actual issue.

   1. Faith—salvation, grief, fear of death, fear of hell, fear of the future
   2. Virtue—anxiety, drivenness, failure, competitiveness, stress, or feeling overwhelmed
   3. Knowledge—lack of biblical knowledge, worldly ways, influenced by friends
   4. Self-control—problems with lust, anger, addictions, affairs, or conduct
   5. Perseverance—problems with security, love, self-worth, or significance
   6. Godliness—domination by the flesh or selfishness
   7. Brotherly love—being critical, judgmental, church conflicts, or divisions
   8. Agape love—prejudice, struggles to forgive, and problems loving others

   Using the questions developed in the previous chapter or a basic counseling interview approach, the counselor needs to determine where the client currently is in his spiritual development. It is then the counselor's job to lead the client from this step through each of the following steps until the required level of Christian maturity is achieved. Although fully experiencing each step and having a complete revelation of God at each level would be ideal, significant progress can still be made in the client's life through simply teaching each of these steps. This is important since fully achieving some of these steps could take a lifetime for many of us. Of course, as counselors or pastors, we cannot effectively lead clients in the steps beyond the level that we have already achieved in our own lives. We must experientially understand what we are teaching in order to lead someone else on the same path. Since most pastors or counselors are reasonably mature Christians, this should not be a problem except possibly for some of the more advanced steps.

2. <u>Demonstrate that what the client is doing will not meet his needs and build hope that his problems can be overcome through Christ.</u> In the development cycle, this is the step called "Knowing." In this step, the counselor needs to help clients learn what is right or wrong and what will work and not work in their life from a biblical point of view. Sin should be confronted as dysfunctional and working against God and the good of everyone. Is this truly what they and God want for their lives? They also need to learn that God is not out to punish them or make their lives miserable, but only to do them good. If they wish, they can continue as they are, or they can decide to change and do it God's way. They need to understand that salvation leads to complete wholeness; and that no matter how difficult their problem, Jesus is the answer. He never fails if we will yield to His will and really trust Him.

3. <u>Use the biblical principles and models to help the client perceive and understand the problem from a biblical perspective.</u> This is also a part of the development cycle that I have called "Knowing," but it relates to increasing our knowledge about God instead of our situation. Here the counselor needs to teach clients what they need to know about God to achieve the next step. The models presented after each step are very useful for this purpose. By analyzing what the client believes and asking appropriate questions, (some of which were provided in the previous chapter) the counselor can help the client "discover" what he needs to learn about God. Teaching the client more about God usually takes the form of a block of information concerning a specific set of biblical principles. In order to use the names of God that we have discussed earlier in this book in this process, I have provided a chart at the end of Chapter 3, which correlates each of the names of God with each of Peter's steps. Additional biblical principles and "proof texts" for each of the spiritual growth steps have already been presented for study in the previous chapters. Understanding what the Bible teaches about God is clearly foundational to later achieving the revelation about God required for each level of spiritual growth.

4. <u>Determine where the client is in the process of salvation and, if appropriate, lead him to accept Christ, be baptized, yield the control of his life to God, and help him get established in a church.</u> This is the part of the developmental cycle that I have called, "Realizing I can't do it." As long as our clients believe that they can be their own god, direct their own lives or even do what God requires of them, they forfeit the power of God to change their lives. They need not only God, but also the people of God—His church.

The first part of this counseling step is to assess where our clients actually are in their spiritual walk rather than what they know about the Bible and believe mentally. Here the counselor needs to examine the actual level that clients have achieved based on how they act and what they know in their hearts. Actions are the key. It is not unusual to meet baby Christians that have excellent Bible knowledge that is little more than mental ascent. Of course, the goal here is to get clients to actually act on what they believe, whether that means accepting Jesus as their Savior, being baptized, making Jesus Lord, joining a church, overcoming the shame of the law, obeying God, dying to self in their actions, or actually loving others with no strings attached. In order to help in this assessment process, I have already provided at the end of Chapter 3, a "Correlation of Spiritual Growth Models

Chart" which correlates the more familiar terms used in the other biblical models discussed early in this book with Peter's steps.

The more our clients try in their own strength to live the Christian life, the more they will eventually realize that they cannot do it. This is the key to the entire developmental cycle, since until we know in our heart that we cannot do it, we will not really fully rely on God to transform our lives. God will allow us to try to do it ourselves until we realize that we cannot live the Christian life without totally relying on Him. It is the counselor's job to help the client come to this realization by comparing what he has hoped to achieve with his level of actual success in carrying it out. I have also provided at the end of this chapter an "Outline of Peter's Steps" which correlates each step with the specific realization of what we cannot do without Christ and the experience we have at each step (which will be discussed next).

5. <u>Help the client take responsibility for his own actions, not blame others or react to what they do, and do everything as unto God.</u> This is the part of the developmental cycle I have called "Experiencing." It involves having and acting upon a revelation until we actually experience the reality of it. This part of the process is when the counselor helps his clients move their knowledge of God from head to heart. As already discussed, this is done by helping clients apply the spiritual disciplines in their lives on these specific truths and encouraging them to act upon what they say they believe until this mental knowledge becomes revelation knowledge. Using the "If it is true…," method discussed earlier in this book is especially helpful.

6. <u>Help the client grow in his personal relationship with Christ and build faith that, with God's help, he can overcome the problem.</u> Just because someone believes something, acts upon it, and even achieves some level in experiencing it, this does not necessarily mean that it will have its full effect on transforming his life. This is the part of the developmental cycle that I have called "Trusting." It is only as we fully trust and rely on God, integrate what we have learned into our personal relationship with Him, and truly believe that He will accomplish in us what He said He would, that we experience major changes. As we do this, the second aspect, "Freedom," becomes a reality for us. For example, when we fully understand that God loves us and accepts us just as we are without works, we feel a new freedom to be ourselves in our relationship with God and others; and this in turn deepens our appreciation for what God has done for us.

7. <u>Assist the client in receiving the empowerment of the baptism of the Holy Spirit if he chooses to do so.</u> The baptism of the Holy Spirit also falls into the category of "Trusting." It is received by faith in the same way we first accepted Christ by faith. For most of us, this can be a major catalyst in moving forward in our spiritual development. As we trust God enough to yield fully our spirit to the control of His Spirit, our desire to serve Him, our spiritual sensitivity and our spiritual anointing significantly increases. This again provides us new freedom in our spiritual walk and in our ability to operate in the gifts of the Spirit.

8. <u>Help the client apply the biblical principles or model to overcome the identified psychological problem.</u> In the developmental cycle, this includes two very interrelated issues, "Dying to self," and "Obeying." This is because until we have successfully overcome the dominance of the self-life and the flesh in our lives, we will always have difficulty in obeying what God directs us to do. As we have already discussed, these steps are accomplished as we learn to walk more fully in our lives according to and in the power of the Holy Spirit. As we quit relying on our flesh and obey God, we are also more able to carry out the biblical principles or complex Bible models that apply to the specific psychological problem that we are addressing. In this counseling step, the counselor needs to relate directly the accomplishment of the increased spiritual level to the fulfillment of the psychological goal. As an example, if we have given the direction of our lives fully to Jesus as Lord, the anxiety of the rat race

of life will be reduced; and we will be more able to trust God to meet all of our needs. The specific models presented in this book were designed for use in this step.

9. <u>Determine the root cause of the difficulty and assist the client in developing and applying faith to overcome this root problem.</u> In the developmental cycle, I have called this "Achieving." Only when the revelation of God affects our innermost needs has a full transformation occurred. It is interesting to note that Peter's steps of spiritual development correlate directly to our basic psychological needs. Faith and virtue address our need for security. Knowledge and self-control address our need for self-worth. Perseverance and godliness address our need for significance. Clearly, brotherly kindness and agape love address our need for love.

10. <u>Release the client again to the care of the Holy Spirit to continue orchestrating this growth process of salvation in his life.</u> When the achievement of the next spiritual level successfully overcomes the psychological presenting problem, the counseling process is complete. If multiple psychological problems or a number of spiritual steps need to be achieved, the process of achieving the next step begins again at counseling step three.

There are a large number of tools that can be integrated with the process just described. These include using a Christian 12 Step program, the Workbook *Experiencing God* by Blackaby, The *Freedom from Addictions* Program by Anderson and Quartes, the model of the Tabernacle to assist getting closer to God, and the other biblical spiritual growth analogies that I briefly described earlier in this book. Other excellent books that are useful in spiritual growth are the *Pursuit of God* by Toser, *God Chasers* and *God Catchers* both by Tenney, and *Knowing God* by Packer. Biographies of famous Christians also provide excellent motivation for spiritual growth. Of course, the counseling models in *Transformation!* and the other books in *The Just Shall Live by Faith Series of Books* are also highly recommended.

OUTLINE OF PETER'S STEPS

Peter's step	God's Provision	Realizing that without Christ, I cannot do it	My experience
UNSAVED (Unmet needs)	Election of all	Make life work for me	Selfish living meeting needs without God Not enough information to direct my life Everything is corrupted by fleshly lust All eventually lose in the rat race of life
FAITH (Security need)	Justification	I cannot earn eternal life	Accepting Jesus as Savior Repentance and forgiveness of sins Holy Spirit motivating me to do right Accepting Eternal Life
VIRTUE (Security need)	Regeneration	I cannot direct my life	Making Jesus Lord Yielding to the Spirit for direction Experiencing His voice and presence Having a personal relationship with God
KNOWLEDGE (Self-worth need)	The Law	I cannot obey the law	The fear of God Knowing the law External motivation by the fear of God Learning I cannot obey the law in my strength
SELF-CONTROL (Self-worth need)	Grace	I cannot control myself	A Revelation of God's grace Knowing God will always do me good All things are lawful unto me Freedom to choose to do right
PERSEVERANCE (Significance need)	Adoption	I cannot be responsible	Revelation of our adoption as sons Knowing who I am in Christ Doing right consistently Knowing all my needs are met
GODLINESS (Significance need)	Redemption	I cannot be holy	Walking in the Spirit Dying to the flesh Dying to the self-life Purifying the heart
BROTHERLY LOVE (Love need)	Acceptance	Have real compassion	Affection for Christians Accepting myself as I am Learning compassion Accepting other Christians as they are
AGAPE LOVE (Love need)	Imparted Sanctification	Love as I should	Demonstrating unconditional love to all Understanding that God is Love Being fully and only motivated by love Conformed to the image of Jesus

Conclusion

As I look around in the church of Jesus Christ, observe the spiritual level of most clients that I counsel, and examine my own life; I am struck by the spiritual poverty of our present day and age. I am able to identify few in the church who have achieved any real level of godliness and true love. Most of us seem content to use the Christian life simply to benefit our families and ourselves, and to make life more palatable. This is not really what God intended for us. His deepest desire is that we be conformed to the image of His Son Jesus and actually love others so much that we are willing to lay down our lives for even a total stranger.

In this book, we have learned that God has provided all that we need for life and godliness through His promises and the knowledge of God. Living the authentic Christian life is not hard; it is impossible if we try to rely on ourselves and do not apply "all diligence" to our spiritual walk. God has promised us fruitfulness, victory over sin and selfishness to the degree that we will never fall, success in our calling, and an exceedingly abundant entrance into heaven itself if we will simply heed the roadmap to spiritual and psychological maturity that He has provided in 2nd Peter Chapter 1.

As we have investigated each of these steps, we have discovered a developmental cycle that leads to their achievement. The key issue is that achieving each of these steps requires a new revelation in our knowledge of God. It is not good enough to believe it in our mind. We must know it in our heart and spirit.

This roadmap to spiritual and psychological maturity provides a foundation for counseling many of the more difficult problems that a Christian counselor might face. Because spiritual and psychological problems are so intermeshed, assisting in one area greatly affects the other. It is especially applicable when treating Christians with solid biblical backgrounds, who are still dominated by the flesh, besetting sins, and addictions. No other type of therapy can ever claim that if they reach a certain level in their spiritual maturity, they will never fall. I am not making this claim; the Holy Spirit is through the writings of the Apostle Peter!

This book was originally written in an attempt to integrate the many different concepts of spiritual growth for a class in Christian counseling, but it has application far beyond its originally intended audience. Every Christian needs a clear roadmap to follow in order to reach spiritual maturity. Without it, he may become lost in the many concepts and biblical truths that relate to spiritual growth. This book complements and in no way negates anything that has been written before by any of the great spiritual giants of past ages. I realize that the concepts described in this book do not provide the in-depth analysis of the subjects addressed in many of these books. It simply provides a framework concerning where, when, and how to apply each of these spiritual concepts or insights.

Although I believe that I have been clearly led and inspired by the Holy Spirit in the writing of this book, I take full responsibility for any lack of clarity or mistakes that may still remain in this text. If you, the reader, should disagree on any specific point, I request that you search the Scripture thoroughly to determine for yourself "if these things be so." (Acts 17:11)

As I have applied these steps for spiritual growth in my counseling, many of my clients have experienced dramatic results. The experience of others has not been as dramatic but, as a minimum, they have made progress in their lives and have received the Word of God (which does not return void, Isaiah 55:1) as clearly as I currently understand it. With each new client, God continues to reveal more and more about how to most effectively implement His roadmap for achieving spiritual and psychological maturity in His people.

It is my deepest desire to move on in the things of God, and it is my prayer that each of us will diligently apply what we have read in the Scriptures and in this book to our lives, so that we might make our calling and election sure, that we would never fall, and that each of us would have an exceedingly abundant welcome into God's heavenly kingdom.

References

Anderson, Neil T., and Quarles, Mike and Julia (1996). <u>Freedom From Addiction.</u> Regal Books, Ventura, California.

Blackaby, Henry T., and King, Claude V. (1990). <u>Experiencing God: Knowing and Doing the Will of God</u>. Lifeway Press, Nashville, Tennessee.

Carothers, Merlin (1970). <u>Prison to Praise.</u> Foundations of Praise, Escondido, California.

Filmore, Duncan (2002). Sermons on Grace. Christian Life International, Camarillo, California.

Hagin, Kenneth E. (1976). <u>Growing Up Spiritually.</u> Rhema Bible Church, Tulsa, Oklahoma.

Landau, Sidney I (1997). <u>The New International Webster's Concise Dictionary of the English Language.</u> Trident Press International, Naples, Florida.

Lee, John (1973). <u>The Colours of Love.</u> New Press. (Out of Print).

Mumford, Bob (1971). <u>Take Another Look At Guidance.</u> Logos International, Plainfield, New Jersey.

Nee, Watchman (1968). <u>The Spiritual Man.</u>Vol. 1-3. Christian Fellowship Publishers, Inc., New York.

Nee Watchman (1957). <u>Sit, Walk, Stand.</u> Richard Clay (The Chaucer Press), Ltd, Bungay, Suffolk, Great Britain.

Nee, Watchman (1957). <u>The Normal Christian Life.</u> Christian Literature Crusade, Fort Washington, Pennsylvania.

Nee, Watchman (1965). <u>The Release of the Spirit.</u> Sure Foundation, Cloverdale, Indiana.

<u>One Year Bible</u> (1991). Tyndale House Publishers, Inc., Wheaton, Illinois.

Packer, J. I. (1973). <u>Knowing God.</u> InterVarsity Press, Downers Grove, Illinois.

Pierce, Larry (2000). <u>The Online Bible Millennium Edition.</u> Timnathserah, Inc., Ontario, Canada.

Reiner, Troy D. (2005). <u>Faith Therapy: The Ultimate Program for Salvation-based Counseling in the Church</u>. Pleasant Word Publishing, Enumclaw, Washington.

Reiner, Troy D. (2005). <u>Principles of life: Using Biblical Principles to Bring Dynamic Psychological Healing</u>. Pleasant Word Publishing, Enumclaw, Washington.

Reiner, Troy D. (2005). <u>Transformation! How Simple Bible Stories Provide In-depth answers to Life's Most Difficult Problems.</u> Pleasant Word Publishing, Enumclaw, Washington.

Slemming, C. W. (1974). <u>Made According to Pattern.</u> Christian Literature Crusade, Fort Washington, Pennsylvania.

Smith, Ed M. (1996). <u>Beyond Tolerable Recovery.</u> Family Care Ministers, Campbellsville, Kentucky.

Smith, William (1970). <u>Smith's Bible Dictionary.</u> Fleming H. Revell Company, Old Tappan, New Jersey.

Stone, Nathan (1944). <u>Names of God.</u> Moody Press, Chicago, Illinois.

Sumrall, Lester (1982). <u>The Names of God.</u> LeSEA Publishing Company, Inc., South Bend, Indiana.

Tan, Paul Lee (1988). <u>Encyclopedia of 7700 Illustrations.</u> Assurance Publishers, Rockville, Maryland.

Taylor, Dr. and Mrs. Howard (1939). <u>Hudson Taylor's Spiritual Secret.</u> Moody Press, Chicago, Illinois.

Tenny, Tommy (2000). <u>God Catchers.</u> Thomas Nelson Publishers, Nashville, Tennessee.

Tenny, Tommy (1998). <u>God Chasers.</u> Destiny Image Publishers, Shippensburg, Pennsylvania.

Towns, Elmer L. (1991). <u>My Father's Names.</u> Regal Books, Ventura, California.

Tozer, A. W. (1993). <u>The Pursuit of God.</u> Christian Publications, Camp Hill, Pennsylvania.

Wilkerson, David (1963). <u>The Cross and the Switchblade.</u> Fleming H. Revell Company, Old Tappan, New Jersey.

Wilson, Lewis (1957). <u>Wilson's Dictionary of Bible Types.</u> Wm. B. Eerdmans Publishing Co., Grand Rapids, Michigan.

To order additional copies of books by Dr. Reiner:

Faith Therapy
A Biblical Program for Salvation-based Counseling in the Church

Understand:

- How Salvation Works from a Psychological Viewpoint
- A New Modality of Salvation-based Counseling
- How to Win the Trial of Faith
- How to Assess and Grow Faith
- How Faith Overcomes Problems with Worth, Significance, Security and Love

Transformation!
How Simple Bible Stories Provide In-depth Answers for Life's Most Difficult Problems

Learn:

- A New Bible-based Comprehensive Method for Counseling
- In-depth Psychological Insights Based on Bible Stories
- A New Biblical Categorization of Psychological Problems
- A Biblical Understanding of Six Types of Codependency
- In-depth Counseling Models for 20 of Life's Most Difficult Problems

Revelations That Will Set You Free
The Biblical Roadmap for Spiritual and Psychological Growth

Perceive:

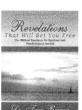

- The Biblical Roadmap for Spiritual and Psychological Growth
- How the Steps in 2nd Peter Chapter 1 Lead to Spiritual Maturity
- Assess the Process of Spiritual Growth
- The Revelation Necessary to Move On to the Next Level
- How to Counsel Other People to Assist Them in Their Spiritual Growth

Principles for Life
Using Biblical Principles to Bring Dynamic Psychological Healing

Know:

- The 13 Classical Methods of Biblical Change
- 44 Biblical Principles and Methods Leading to Wholeness
- An In-depth 9 Component Model of the Human Heart
- The "Train of Psychological Wholeness" Based on Proverbs Chapter 3
- An In-depth Method for Developing Counseling Plans from Biblical Principles

To order these books please call: 1-316-729-7997
or visit our website at www.reinerpublishing.com.
Also available at: www.amazon.com and www.barnesandnoble.com

For DVD courses based on these books, certification as a Faith Therapist
or a BA or MA degree in Christian Counseling from LOGOS University,
contact Word of Life Institute at 316-838-9200
or visit our website at www.freechristiancounselingtraining.com
E-mail Dr. Reiner at treiner@wolm.org
or write to us at: 3811 N. Meridian Ave., Wichita, KS 67204

CPSIA information can be obtained
at www.ICGtesting.com
Printed in the USA
LVOW05s0021010617

536528LV00006B/500/P